chicago

the companion guidebook to the
wildly popular television show

WILL CLINGER, MINDY BELL, AND HARVEY MOSHMAN

The
Globe
Pequot
Press

GUILFORD, CONNECTICUT

Text design: M.A. Dubé
Maps created by Rusty Nelson © The Globe Pequot Press

Library of Congress Cataloging-in-Publication Data is available.

ISBN 0-7627-0816-6

Manufactured in the United States of America
First Edition/First Printing

CONTENTS

Acknowledgments   v

Introduction   vii

ADVENTURES   1
Over, under, and around the Windy City

SPORTS & CONTESTS   13
Thrilling and Outrageous Competitions

INSTRUCTION & SELF–IMPROVEMENT   43
Classes and Clubs for an Out-of-the-Ordinary Education

MAGNIFICENT OBSESSIONS   57
Quirky Hobbies and Offbeat Social Groups

THAT'S ENTERTAINMENT!   81
Odd Music and Rare Theatrics

ARTISTS   103
The Gifted among Us

MUSEUMS, COLLECTIONS & TOURS   119
Curators of the Curious

OLD & ALMOST FORGOTTEN CHICAGO   141
A Long, Strange Trip Down Memory Lane

MADE IN CHICAGO   155
Wild Wares from the Windy City

FOOD & DRINK   167
Lift Your Glass, Fill Your Plate

SHOPPING 183
An Eclectic Selection for the Selective Consumer

SERVICES 217
How Can We Help You?

ANIMAL STORIES 243
A Cacophony of Critters

DAY TRIPPIN' 257
Expeditions to the Wilds Beyond

MAPS 271
   Downtown 272
   Chicago North 274
   Chicago West 276
   Chicago South 278
   Suburban North 280
   Suburban West 282
   Suburban South 284
   Multistate 286

Index 289
About the Authors 295

ACKNOWLEDGMENTS

It's not easy launching a new TV show. In 1988, against considerable odds, John Davies and Ben Hollis created a television series with its own slightly skewed take on the Windy City. From those humble beginnings the show went on to become Chicago's longest running magazine program, and on a local PBS station no less! And while Ben and John have long since moved on, their influence remains.

Television is the ultimate collaborative art, and the collaborators need to be recognized. Harvey Moshman has worked on *Wild Chicago* since its inception. Initially he sat in the editor's chair, and since 1992 he's been the series producer. Will Clinger became the affable host and weekly tour guide to Chicago's urban jungle in 1992. Over the years, he has been joined on-camera by several capable "wild correspondents." The current cast includes Mindy Bell, Tava Smiley, Denise LaGrassa, Sarah Vetter, Choky Lim, and Richard Knight Jr.

The efficient running of the program and the comprehensive fact checking of this manuscript are due to the tireless efforts of associate producer Lisa Marshfield. Our sincere thanks go to her and our intern Nick Bon, whose meticulous attention to detail insures the accuracy of this guidebook. Ignacio Lopez, Joy Fischer, Cheryl Romanoski, and Sarah Moshman capably handled additional research and typing chores.

Clearly our program would not continue to attract an audience and annually win Emmy awards if not for the creative input from our crews. In the field, the principal cameramen who have kept the show fresh with their innovative style are Emmett Wilson, Roy Alan, Tom Siegel, Tim Boyd, Chuck Haynie, Charles Evans, Dave Moyer, and Mike Davis. The engineers in the edit rooms who have yet to tire of working on this show are Tim Jackson, Al Williams, Paul Thornton, Mark Anderson, Ricky Wells, Jerry Binder, Barbara Allen, Jim Mancini, and Don DeMartini. The aural excitement of our show is due to the efforts of one person, Roger Adler, who created our theme song and provides us brilliant music to use each week. And Margalit Neusner designed our very cool logo.

We can't forget to mention (nor would it be advisable to overlook) our bosses at WTTW, Fawn Ring and V. J. McAleer, who, thankfully, give us a very long leash.

Will would like to thank Wendi Weber for her love and suggestions, and his parents for reading to him as a child. Mindy is on her knees in gratitude to Lorraine Bell for rescuing her from many literary potholes and making every word she wrote better and to Roberta Bell for her ferocious support and enthusiasm. And Harvey thanks his wife, Diane, whose patience and encouragement know no bounds.

INTRODUCTION

omplaints. We really don't get that many. For a show that has such a high potential to offend, that's surprising. Still, when we do hear criticism, it's of the "Why so many damn reruns?" variety.

Unfortunately, our reruns garner the same ratings as our new shows, so it's hard to make the economic argument to the bean counters upstairs that we have to produce more original programs to keep viewers. So for better or worse, we're fortunate to have a very loyal audience.

We also hear, "Why don't you guys put all of this useful information contained in your programs into a guidebook?" Well, after a decade and a half on the air and more than one thousand stories on everything from the Ancient Astronaut Society to Zoe the Barbie Doll Collector, you hold in your hands the first edition of the *Wild Chicago* guidebook.

This is not meant to be a comprehensive collection of every place we've ever been. No, that would be too onerous of a task. Besides, the mortality rate for our subjects is alarmingly high. Instead, we've selected three hundred of our favorite unconventional people and places to profile and another one hundred or so "honorable mentions," all of which have been seen on *Wild Chicago*.

Where do we find all of these stories? Research, tedious and exhaustive research. We're fortunate to have the best research staff that money can't buy— our audience. We get thousands of suggestions by phone, fax, e-mail, and wet cocktail napkins.

Sometimes, finding a suitable story for the show is a snap. A viewer writes, "Dear Wild Chicago: My father taxidermies the heads of turkeys and dresses them up in doll clothes. He calls them 'Poultry Personalities.' Would you be interested in that?" Yes, Virginia, we'll be right over. Other letters are more like, "Hey, me and my brother refinish furniture. Come shoot us! We're wild guys." No, they weren't.

So for those of you who have seen *Wild Chicago* and have always wanted a hard-copy guide to the abundance of offbeat, unusual places in our beloved Chicagoland, this book is for you. And for those adventurous visitors to the Windy City who would rather shop Maxwell Street than Michigan Avenue or rather see sock-puppet theater than Shakespeare, please, buy this book. And stop complaining.

Harvey Moshman
Wild Chicago producer

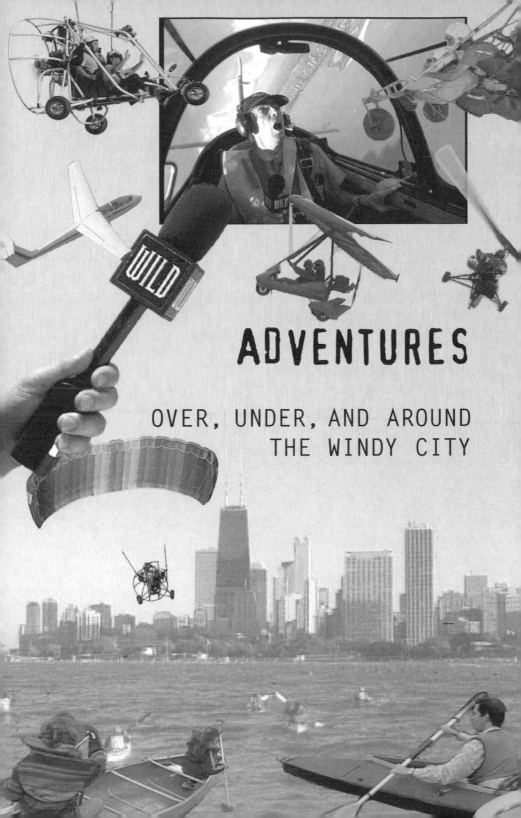

ADVENTURES

OVER, UNDER, AND AROUND
THE WINDY CITY

A&M AIRSPORTS

Cushing Field
Newark, IL 60541
(630) 879-6568
www.airsportscr.com
Map: Suburban West

Nothing, and we mean nothing, can prepare you for the sheer exhilaration of flying a Trike. With three wheels, a hang glider wing, and a big propeller on the back, it might seem like you're just one step above ol' Wilbur and Orville Wright. Until, that is, you take off after just 200 feet of runway and go 85 miles per hour, reaching heights of up to 35,000 feet in the air. With its speed and excellent maneuverability, the Trike is the closest thing to flying like a bird that you'll ever experience. Maybe that's why it was once used to guide a fledgling gaggle of geese south for the winter, as portrayed in the 1996 motion picture *Fly Away Home.*

Trikes were developed in Europe in the early '80s and have gained considerable popularity here in the States. They are a lot cheaper than planes and helicopters, and unlike those modes of flight, they can go very low to the ground without fear of engine failure. Why? Because you can land these things just about anywhere, and if worst comes to worst there's a ballistic parachute built into the back that can deploy as low as 30 feet off the ground.

If you want to learn how to fly a Trike, drive out to Cushing Field in Newark, Illinois for some lessons. Pretty soon you'll be flying solo and probably pretending you're a hawk or an eagle—or maybe a Wilbur or an Orville.

ADVENTURERS' CLUB

555 North Franklin Street
Chicago, Il 60610
(312) 822-0991
www.theadventurersclub.org
Map: Chicago North

If you think travel should involve risking life and limb, have we got the club for you! It's called the Adventurers' Club, and it's been around since 1912. To join, you supposedly must have a death-defying adventure on your résumé, though some of the older members grumble that the requirements have gone soft lately. Nevertheless, we met one recent inductee who had skydived onto the North Pole and another who had just gotten back from swimming with the great white sharks of Australia. We'd say that's enough to make former members Teddy Roosevelt and Sir Edmund Hillary stand up and take notice!

The club is primarily an eating and drinking establishment, though occasionally a member will give a presentation on an amazing journey he or she has just completed. The walls are lined with stuffed animals that were hunted by the

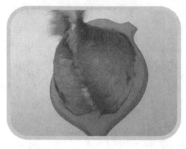

adventurers themselves, and we're not talking deer here—think rhinos, tigers, and bears. A display case is filled with items brought back from exotic lands (the array of shrunken heads caught our attention), and you can't miss the 9-foot long sperm whale's penis mounted above the bar. From the ceiling hang dozens of small flags commemorating trips taken by members over the last ninety years, and a brief perusal leaves little doubt that there must be plenty of one-upsmanship at the lunch table: "Don't suppose you've crossed the Sahara on foot, old chum?" "Sorry, too busy capturing beluga whales in the Arctic, old bean!"

As for the food served at the club, it's pretty good, though we wouldn't risk our lives for the yak burger.

CHICAGOLAND CANOE BASE

4019 N. Narragansett
Chicago, IL 60634
(773) 777-1489
www.chicagolandcanoebase.com,
www.caska.org
Map: Chicago West

For Ralph Frese, canoeing is a religion, and he looks at every visitor to his Chicagoland Canoe Base as a potential convert. Indeed, the store is a mecca for practitioners of the paddling arts, with everything you could possibly need for your next canoe trip, including the canoes themselves. You can either rent or buy, and you'll receive ample advice on care and maintenance from the irascible Ralph. The base also restores damaged canoes and has quite a collection of rare old ones that they'll gladly show off to the curious.

Oh, and if kayaking is your preferred paddle sport, the Canoe Base has that covered, too. Talk to Vic Hurtowy, Ralph's right-hand man and an avid kayak specialist. He'll introduce you to the latest models and tell you about a little organization called CASKA—the Chicago Area Sea Kayaking Association. The group has been kayaking on Lake Michigan every Wednesday and every other Friday since 1986. They usually embark at Diversey Harbor (check the CASKA Web site) at about 6:00 P.M. and are always looking for new members.

Now back to canoes and rivers: Ralph and his staff can direct you to myriad waterways within the city limits, places where you'd swear you were gliding through a vast wilderness when in fact you're only a stone's throw from a major intersection. You'll see the occasional deer on the riverbank, maybe a great blue heron above your head. And if your route takes you through the occasional storm sewer outfall, do like Ralph does—just hold your nose and pretend it's the Tunnel of Love.

POPULAR ROTORCRAFT ASSOCIATION
Lansing Airport
Lansing, IL 60438
pra18.8m.com
Map: Suburban South

The Nazis used the insectlike rotorcraft to sting the Allies during World War II. Now this club is swarming in the air for fun. The members of Chapter 18 of the Popular Rotorcraft Association meet to fly what appears to be a lawn chair with wheels. Actually, it looks more like a kid's science project . . . a kid who's not getting an "A." This lightweight craft consists of a seat, a joystick that controls the rotor head, a 23-foot blade, and some skeletal framing.

Unlike fixed-wing aircraft, the rotorcraft (also called a gyrocopter, or gyro for short) can fly in any direction and needs much less space for takeoff and landing. One member calls them "the Harley Davidsons of the skies." Whether he meant that they were an exhilarating, just-you-and-the-elements kind of ride or that they're loud and you don't want your unmar-

ried sister hanging with them was unclear. These bad boys up in the blue can take their steel steeds up to 40 or 50 mph. And many of them they built themselves. Kits start at around $16,000 (minus the engine) and allow for some inventive customization. If you think you might enjoy not just sitting on patio furniture but flying around in it, then check out the club's Web site. They have current news—like upcoming fly-ins and cookouts—gyros for sale, and info on training (have your reading glasses on, it's deeply detailed). Then put on your flying finery and join these cowboys of the clouds. May your rotor always rotate.

POWERED PARACHUTE FLYING CLUB

Bill and Bonnie Hunt
29262 South Will Center Road
Peotone, IL 60468
(708) 258-0055
www.powerchuters.com
Map: Suburban South

Wheeeee! Ahem, sorry, just the residual exhilaration from flying in a powered parachute. This aircraft consists of a parachute with an open-framed, two-seater, 65-horsepower-water-cooled-oil-injected motor underneath. Now, *that'll* straighten your wind sock. A powered parachute flies like a plane with a chute in place of a wing. How does it work? Oh, by winning the ageless battle between thrust and drag, lift and gravity—but who cares? All you need to know is that the canopy retards free fall and once you're up, it's just you and the ozone, baby. The Powered Parachute Flying Club in Peotone boasts the Midwest's largest flyport. The club offers classes in aviation education and safety, instructional flights, and gift certificates. Got to p.p. all the time? Then buy your Dream

Machine or PC2000 here, new or used. Remember, on used planes you're looking for low hours, not low mileage. But, at a cost of around $15,000, you're probably capable of remembering lots of things . . . like where you put your disposable income. The club also offers a fellowship of flying fun with cross-country trips, guest speakers, and even a food drive. So, this is your captain speaking: Go *hit the silk!*

RAVEN SKY HANG-GLIDING

Twin Oaks Airport
N463 County Road N
Whitewater, WI 53190
(262) 473-8800 or (312) 360-0700
www.hanggliding.com
Map: Multistate

Feel like you're in the doldrums, like your life needs a jolt of pure adrenaline? Maybe you need to go up 2,500 feet in the air with nothing but a glorified kite keeping you from a premature return to mother earth. In that case, you'd want to head to Raven Sky, the only full-time hang-gliding park in the Midwest and a mere two hours from Chicago. Forget about those hang gliders you've seen launching off cliffs in movies and TV; the flat terrain of our area necessitates that Raven Sky tow its gliders up into the air with an ultralight airplane. It's still a pretty good rush to ascend 300 feet per minute,

then release the towrope and realize that it's just you, a nylon wing, a few pipes, and some wire. No wonder they make you initial that waiver in ten places!

Raven Sky offers a training curriculum that can have you solo gliding in less than a week. It involves tandem flying with an instructor in a two-tiered glider that casts him as Superman and you as Lois Lane (or Jimmy Olson for you guys). Basically, you're looking over his shoulder as he teaches you to ride the thermals (pockets of warm, rising air) upward and shift your weight to steer. Take it from us, there's nothing quite like soaring through the sky with just the sound of the wind in your ears and a view that's to die for. Wait, maybe that's the wrong wording . . .

SCUBA DIVING

Discovery Dive Charters
Burnham Harbor, Chicago
(815) 786-1337
www.discoverydivecharters.com

Elmer's Watersports
1310 Oakton Street
Evanston, IL 60202
(847) 475-SWIM
www.elmerswatersports.com
Map: Suburban North

You'll find more than smelt and zebra mussels below the surface of Lake Michigan—lurking down there are actually quite a few sunken ships. In fact, in addition to being called the City of Big Shoulders, Chicago probably deserves the nickname Shipwreck Capital of the Great Lakes. It's estimated that more than three hundred vessels dating back to the early 1800s lie off our city's coast, and of those, only about thirty-five have been discovered. Oh, and let's not forget the nearly two hundred World War II fighter planes (pilots from Glenview Training Station used to practice takeoffs and landings on carriers near Navy Pier), three 1920s automobiles (they went down with a ferry) and a World War I submarine (long story) that are also out there. Dive boats such as the *Discovery* out of Burnham Harbor are willing and able to take you out to explore these victims of the deep as long as you're a certified scuba diver. If you aren't, there are plenty of dive shops that

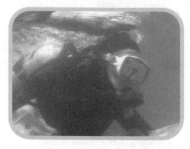

can teach you the basics, like Elmer's Watersports in Evanston.

There's one wreck that you don't need a boat or even scuba gear to see. It's the *George Morley,* and it lies just off Dempster Beach in Evanston (you'll find its propeller lying in a field just across the road). The *Morley* caught fire in 1897 and sank about 220 feet offshore in 17 feet of water; the bow and stern are just 7 feet from the surface, quite visible to snorkelers willing to swim out that far. Just watch out for incoming golf balls, since a number of area golfers use the *Morley* for driving practice. And if you do get conked, track down the golfer and throw a zebra mussel at him. It seems only fair.

SKYDIVE CHICAGO

3215 East 1969th Road
Ottawa, IL 61350
(815) 433-0000 or (800) SKY-DIVE
www.skydivechicago.com
Map: Multistate

Some would say that jumping out of a perfectly functioning airplane displays the intellectual capacity of a turnip, but at Skydive Chicago they've been flouting common sense since 1993. If you've been considering taking up skydiving as a sport or simply want to do it once so you can say you did, this is a great place to take the plunge. The staff of instructors have a combined total of a quarter million jumps to their credit. And they haven't lost a student yet—although frankly we were worried when the two guys who welcomed us were named Roger and Rabbit.

After signing the release form that says you don't blame Skydive Chicago if you go *splat,* it's off to the classroom for an orientation film and one hour of instruction. Then it's time to don your colorful jumpsuit and other necessary skydiving accoutrements. Your first jump will almost always be tandem, which means that instead of a para-

chute attached to your back, you'll have an instructor (don't worry: *he's* wearing one). Some people wear impressive-looking helmets, but let's face it, if your chute doesn't open, that helmet won't really be much use; maybe that's why they call it a "brain bucket."

SKY SOARING GLIDERS
I-90 at Route 20
Hampshire, IL 60140
(847) 683-SOAR
www.skysoaring.com
Map: Suburban North

It might be hard to comprehend at first, but there is a sizable section of the pilot population that prefers planes without an engine. A glider is their aircraft of choice, and they relish it for the purity of the flying experience it provides. The members of Sky Soaring, Inc. in Hampshire, Illinois, would love the chance to give you that experience for a reasonable fee (it's just $50 to go up as a passenger). Their airport is the only one in this area devoted solely to gliders, though calling it an airport is a stretch; it's really just a strip of grass and a hangar. Sky Soaring employs several planes with engines to tow the gliders up to 2,000 feet,

at which point the pilot pulls a yellow handle that releases the towrope. Then it's just a matter of manipulating two pedals and a stick and riding the thermals (pockets of warm, rising air) higher and higher. On a good day it's possible to stay aloft for hours at a time— which you may try to do when you find out there is only *one wheel* for landing.

If the peace and quiet and healthy risk involved in this sport appeal to you, you may choose to get your gliding license and join Sky Soaring. Full membership gets you unlimited flying (with your glider or one of theirs), a subscription to a gliding magazine, and a beer at the end of the day. And just think of all the money you'll save on gas!

WILL-U-CANOE
501 East Romeo Road
Romeoville, IL 60446
(708) 839-2311
Map: Suburban South

Only fifteen minutes from the concrete canyons of Chicago is a waterway just waiting for your paddling pleasure. Let these ferrymasters drift you down a river filled with ducks, dense foliage, and deer rutting . . . now *that's* a sight the kids won't forget.

The canoe-conveying company of Will-U-Canoe (yes, we will, so don't ask us again) will set you up and set you off on the Des Plaines River in a 17-foot canoe and turn

you from landlubber to river rat in no time. If you've never been in one before, the canoe will quickly become a gondola you're fondola. Once you synchronize the paddling part with your partner, you'll fall into an easy rhythm and under the spell of a continuous parade of wildlife and a symphony of sounds. You'll discover plenty of migrating and resident birds (blue herons, egrets), fish (bass, catfish) and the assorted forest creatures one associates with a Disney film. At the end of your trip, you'll disembark at the only island left on the river, Isle a la Cache. A museum there contains the artifacts from the isle's origins as an eighteenth-century trading post. Tours are lead by period-costumed guides who affect the French accents of the isle's early inhabitants: "Ze beaver pelt was ze most valuable sing to ze trapper." Learn what a typical day was like at the post back then. For men: catching, killing and skinning "ze" beaver. For women: washing, washing, and washing, interrupted by some cooking. Will-U-Canoe (Yes, now cut it out!) offers several packages. If you're looking for an unusual, beaver-dam good time, you won't egret booking these canoeists for your next corporate outing or class field trip. Will-U-Canoe? Well, as James Joyce said when asked that very same question, "yes I said yes I will Yes."

WINDY CITY BALLOON PORT

100 Ski Hill Road
Fox River Grove, IL 60021
(847) 639-0550
Map: Suburban North

There are plenty of ways to get up into the wild blue yonder above Chicagoland, but few can match the quiet and serenity of a balloon. The people at Windy City Balloon Port would love to prove this by taking you for a ride; they're even willing to teach you how to fly one of their colorful crafts. Once high in the air, the trick is to steer the darn thing, which is accomplished by finding wind currents at various altitudes. If the wind direction is taking you the wrong way, then you climb or descend to find a more favorable current, either by adding heat with a blast from a flamethrower-like contraption attached to the top of the basket or by releasing the heated air with a rope attached to the balloon. A clever balloonist will often spit over the side to check what the wind's doing below, hopefully missing any people or plates of food at ground level.

Ballooning is a fairly safe sport, since if anything goes wrong, the balloon serves as a parachute floating the passengers back down to terra firma (landing in water, however, can be problematic). You'll notice that there's a bottle of champagne in the basket. Don't be alarmed; it doesn't mean your pilot is going to get blotto in midflight. The tradition started when early French balloonists were mistaken for space aliens by a populace that had never witnessed a bag of gas come out of the sky. The champagne was a peace offering and proof that the balloonist came from earth. Now it's used to smooth things over with a landowner whose property gets landed upon or a hapless soul whose head has been inadvertently spat upon.

MORE ADVENTURES

LASALLE BANK CHICAGO MARATHON
www.chicagomarathon.com
Annual international 26.2-mile race on Chicago's streets.

SKYDIVE ILLINOIS
9980 Route 47
Morris, IL 60450
(815) 941–1149 or (800) FREEFALL
www.skydive-illinois.com
Map: Suburban South
More skydiving.

URBAN ADVENTURE RACE
www.urbanadventureracing.com
Navigating around Chicago using kayaks, in-line skates, and bicycles.

WILMOT MOUNTAIN
Box 177
Wilmot, WI 53192
(262) 862–2301
Map: Multistate
Mountain biking, skiing, snow-boarding, and snowmobiling.

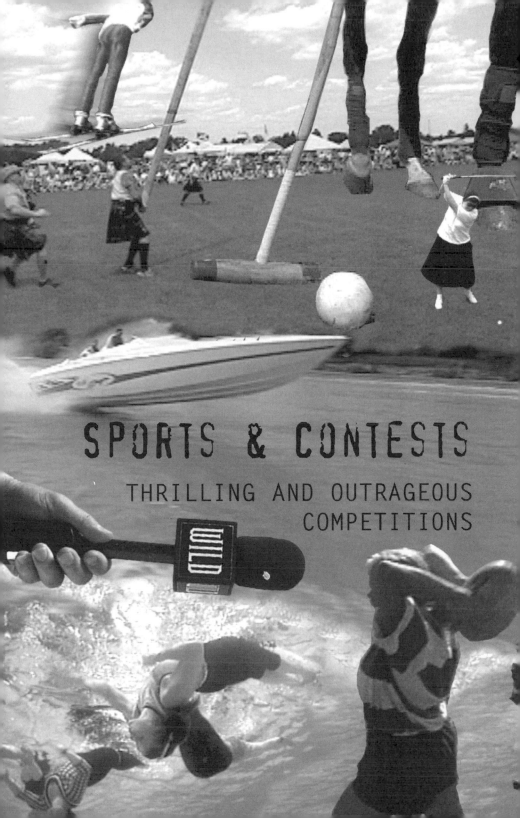

SPORTS & CONTESTS

THRILLING AND OUTRAGEOUS COMPETITIONS

WILD

AQUATIC ART TEAM

North Suburban YMCA
2705 Techny Road
Northbrook, IL 60062
(847) 272-7250
www.nsymca.org
Map: Suburban North

Whether you call it "synchronized swimming" or "aquatic art," these suburban water nymphs have turned a YMCA pool into their own little Atlantis. Dressed in matching swimsuits and executing their tightly synched maneuvers, these gals are obviously serious about their sport. They'd have to be, since some of them have been at it for more than twenty-five years. The team is under the gentle but firm guidance of coach Fran Sweeney, who chooses their music and does the choreography. The main prerequisites for being an aquatic artist seem to be strong swimming skills, good balance, agility, and a willingness to go for a long time without breathing. Oh, and freedom from chlorine allergies is a good thing, too.

If you think you meet these criteria (and you're female), you might consider joining the team, but be aware that while synchronized swimming may look delicate and graceful from a seat in the stands, it's hard work and squirming limbs underwater. All that effort pays off, though, when the North Suburban YMCA Aquatic Arts (NSYAA) team does well in one of the aquatic arts competitions they occasionally enter. You think maybe coach Fran would give her swimmers the week off when they win a blue ribbon? Don't hold your breath.

BALL HAWKS

Outside Wrigley Field at Waveland
Avenue and Kenmore Avenue
Chicago, IL 60613
Map: Chicago North

You'll see them gathering near Waveland and Kenmore for every Cubs home game, a baseball glove on their hand and a hopeful look in their eye. They're the Wrigley Field Ball Hawks, and they've been a Chicago tradition since anyone can remember. They all have one thing on their mind, and that's to grab the next home run that comes over the fence. Currently about eight or nine regulars have earned the right to call themselves Ball Hawks, but many more have come and gone over the years. During Sammy Sosa's record-breaking home-run tear, the number of wanna-bes ballooned to three thousand. Remarkably, it was the King of the Ball Hawks, Moe Mullins, who managed to chase down Sosa's sixty-

second, only to have it wrestled away by a voracious newcomer. He would eventually sue to have the ball given to Sammy himself.

At last count Moe was closing in on 3,900 balls over the forty-some years he's been hawking. He takes into account factors such as wind direction, the starting pitcher and whether the batter is lefty or righty when positioning himself on Waveland. Like his fellow Hawks, he knows that if you get directly under the ball, you'll get stampeded; far better to arrive just as the ball does, catch it, and then keep running.

If you choose to try your hand at Moe's specialty, keep in mind that passing traffic can make it a dangerous pastime. We pointed out to one Ball Hawk that a big catch wouldn't mean much if he got hit by a bus. He answered, "Well, if you hang on to the ball . . ."

BEAT THE NUN

Cog Hill Golf & Country Club
12294 Archer Avenue
Lemont, IL 60439
(312) 787-2852
Map: Suburban South

In the annals of charity golf events, there are few that can claim a more intriguing name or potentially offensive premise than the one we discovered going on at the Cog Hill Golf Club. It's called Beat the Nun, but rest assured that there is no sister battery involved. You've heard of the Flying Nun and the Singing Nun, now meet the Golfing Nun! Sister Mary Anne, a devout Franciscan and life-long golfer, stands on the seventeenth tee in full habit once a year and basically takes on all comers. As a foursome approaches, they're asked if they'd like to try their chances against the nun, and those who say yes then hand over five bucks. If they can drive the ball closer to the pin than Sister Mary Anne can, they get a T-shirt that says, "I Beat the Nun." If they fail, hey, at least they know their money is going to the church.

You'd be surprised at how few golfers end up with a T-shirt. Not only does the sister have a sweet swing, but a lot of her would-be rivals seem a little intimidated by the idea of competing with a nun. Maybe they're afraid she's going to brandish a ruler in the middle of their swing or make them say their catechism if they get their golf ball closer to the hole than she does. Whatever the reason, we witnessed a lot of slices and hooks, and of the forty-six golfers we watched, only four managed to beat Sister Mary Anne. Perhaps God was working in not-so-mysterious ways.

BICYCLE RACING

Velodrome at Meadowhill Park
1479 Maple Avenue
Northbrook, IL 60062
(847) 291-2974, ext. 7
www.northbrookvelodrome.com
Map: Suburban North

Bicycle track racing is marked by blazing bursts of speed, intricate strategy, and ever-present physical danger. All good reasons to venture out to the Northbrook Velodrome to watch the Thursday night Racing! Racing! Racing! It's been going on every spring and summer since 1959, part of Chicago's rich biking tradition. The Northbrook Velodrome plays host to amateurs and pros alike, all of whom ride single-gear bikes that do not allow for coasting or braking—stop pedaling, and you'll flip right over the handlebars. Considering that the quarter-mile track is concrete and their shoes are attached to the bikes, it's no wonder that the riders shave their legs to reduce the severity of a possible scrape.

Big-time bikers Greg Lemond and Erik Heiden have raced here, but most of the participants are pushing pedals as a sideline, especially since the prize money is nothing to write home about. The races at times seem to be a test of who can go the *slowest*; contestants can save energy by "drafting" off the rider in front, so early on nobody wants to take the lead. Then suddenly somebody makes a break for it and  everybody turns it on, reaching speeds of up to 40 miles per hour as they sprint for the finish.

As exciting as it is to watch, it's more exciting to do, and on Friday nights anyone age six or older with a working bike is welcome to hit the Velodrome track and race. Shaving your legs is optional.

BLARNEY ISLAND BOAT RACES

Shuttle runs from Port of Blarney
27843 West Grasslake Road
Antioch, IL 60002
(847) 395-4122
www.blarneyisland.com
Map: Suburban North

Blarney Island is a massive bar complex that sits atop a bunch of pilings in the middle of Grass Lake. It's the ideal summer escape for those who like a place where the beer flows freely and the flesh is bared frequently. Outside of Mardi Gras, we've never seen so many women flash their breasts and men hang moons as at Blarney's. And you can't help but notice the bras, panties, and boxers (all signed) that hang from the ceilings, a tradition that's existed since before owner Jack Haley can remember.

As it turns out, the place has an awfully colorful history: starting as a rod and gun club in the 1800s, it later served as a gangster hangout during Prohibition and was eventually the prize in a high-stakes poker game. Seems Shorty Shobin lost his island to some card shark named Jack O'Connor, then promptly went in the back room and shot himself.

You won't find much gambling out there these days unless it's on the Thursday night powerboat races that take place during the summer. About thirty boats compete for prize money on an 800-foot-long "drag strip" just off the island, reaching speeds of up to 150 miles per hour—and decibel levels that are off the charts. If you don't like loud noise or crowds (the races routinely attract three thousand spectators), come on another night. And don't forget to wear clean underwear, since it might wind up on the ceiling.

CAL-SAG POKER RUN

Riverside Marina and Lounge
13601 South Calhoun Avenue
Chicago, IL 60633
(773) 646-9867
members.aol.com/riverside136
Map: Chicago South

It's still possible to find pleasure boaters on the Little Calumet River, but a lot of the pleasure involves reveling in how polluted and thoroughly unscenic this river really is. If the slagheaps and glow-in-the-dark fish aren't your cup of tea, there are other diversions on this stretch of water, like the Cal-Sag Poker Run. In this semiannual event, card playing, fast boats, and alcohol form a somewhat hair-raising alliance. It works like this: a flotilla of participants coagulates at one of the many watering holes that flank the Little Calumet and then proceeds down the river to five waterside bars, picking up a playing card (and usually a couple of

drinks) at each one. At the end of the day, the boats with the best and worst poker hands split the pot, which has been known to reach up to $4,000.

The adventure aspect of the Poker Run takes place between stops, where it is not unusual to see sleek "cigarette" boats racing each other to the next bar or jumping each other's wakes. This can sometimes lead to traffic that's as scary as the Edens on a Saturday night, so the Poker Run is not recommended to the faint of heart or, when the water's rough, the weak of stomach.

CHICAGO CURLING CLUB

555 Dundee Road
Northbrook, IL 60062
(847) 564-9877
www.curlingchicago.org
Map: Suburban North

Curling—it's not just for hair anymore! It's also an Olympic sport that began in Scotland back in the 1500s. In case you've never seen it played, the game involves ice, brooms, and round, smooth rocks of granite. The object is to glide your rocks across the ice toward the center of a target area on the other side. Like shuffleboard, you can bump your rocks into position or knock the opposition's rocks out of position. Unlike shuffleboard, or any other known sport, curling calls for two team members to frantically flail at the ice with brooms as the rock proceeds toward its target. They do this to control the rock's speed and direction; no rock ever goes in a straight line but instead curls in the direction of the spin put on it by the curler.

As it turns out, curling is a very popular pastime for women. We attended a Ladies' *bonspiel* (curling tournament) at the Exmore Curling Club in Highland Park. The competition was often intense, but when a team was between matches it would invariably cheer on its rivals. Actually, the camaraderie among these female curlers was refreshing to witness, especially considering not everyone was partaking in the hot chocolate laced with whiskey. We did, though . . . hey, its cold on that ice!

CHICAGO HASH HOUSE HARRIERS

(312) 409-BEER
www.chicagohash.com

"This is not a race, there are no winners, no losers, only survivors." And beer drinkers. And rowdy runners. The Hash House Harriers meet weekly to stage a cross-country version of "hounds and hare." The leader, or hare, is given a head start to mark a trail through city streets and parks for the other runners, or hounds, to follow. The "wiley wabbit" leaves his or her scent along the way by marking the course with chalk, flour, or pieces of paper. At the heel of the hunt, the hounds gather for food and drink and bay over the achievements of the good dogs and behavior of the bad dogs. This "paper chase" was originated in Malaysia in the 1930s by a group of British civil servants who were bored with solo running and looking for a cure to the weekend hangover. (Makes you wonder why they lost their empire.) Today, you don't need to be a tipsy, tea-loving attaché to partake in this sporting and social event. All drinkers and nondrinkers, all occupations, all ages, all harriers and harriettes (Irenes, Lorraines, and Lanas, too) are welcome. You will need to be able to run a physically challenging route and, judging by the club's roster, have a racy name: Ann Slanders, Tequila Cocking Bird, and Soar Balls. "Sore" you might be, as the course length varies between 3 and 7 miles, depending on the day and season. "Balls" you will have, as the Harriers schedule several parties and theme-based runs. To quote what the runners bark on the course, "On, On!"

CHICAGO RUSH

Allstate Arena
6920 Mannheim Road
Rosemont, IL 60018
(773) 243-3434 for info
(877) RUSH-TIX for tickets
www.chicagorush.com
Map: Suburban North

If the NFL season ends and you still haven't had quite enough of the old pigskin, you might want to give arena football a try. In Chicago that means the Rush, who play, appropriately, at the Allstate Arena in Rosemont. At first glance this brand of football might seem a little kooky—it's played indoors during the summer months on a field that's half the size of the NFL variety; there's no out of bounds, but instead the field is rimmed by padded boards into which players are often slammed, like in hockey; and there are big nets on either side of the goalposts that serve to keep the ball in play on kickoffs and missed field goals.

Each team has eight players on the field (most of whom play on both offense and defense), and the scoring is fast and furious—final tallies of 65 to 62 are not uncommon. But all the strange rules and crazy action still don't fully explain how arena football could be in existence for over fifteen years while the XFL went one year and out. After all, it's the same NFL castoffs playing the game, and the XFL cheerleaders were just as scantily clad. Maybe it's all the other entertaining distractions provided by the arena folks that have nothing to do with football, like the pregame

fireworks (indoors?!) or the Goodyear Pass-for-Cash promotion at halftime. The evening we attended it was Bahamas Night, with a reggae band playing in the parking lot and a free trip to the Bahamas for the best island costume. It adds up to a fun time for all, except, maybe, for the authors of this book—after that "NFL castoffs" crack, we wouldn't come within 100 yards of those arena football players!

CHICAGO SWANS

Warren Park
6601 North Western
Chicago, IL 60645
www.chicagoswans.com

It's a sport that combines elements of American football, rugby, basketball, and soccer, brought to you by the people who created the boomerang and share their country with kangaroos. Australian Rules football often leaves the uninitiated spectator quite clueless trying to make sense of all the kicking, dribbling, and tackling. One thing seems clear: you get six points for a goal (putting the ball between two tall posts) and one for a "behind" (doing the same through two shorter, wider posts). The action is chaotic and continuous, with no time-outs except for grievous injury—and considering the violence of the sport along with the lack of any protective equipment ("Real men bring their own equipment!" bragged one player), such injuries are not all that uncommon.

At the game we watched, the Chicago Swans vs. the Milwaukee Bombers, there was a refreshingly casual feel to the festivities. The players recruited a passerby to work the scoreboard, and the flags being waved to signify goals and behinds were, upon closer inspection, men's underwear tacked to sticks. The two teams were made up of both Aussies and Yanks, and they all seemed to be having a sweaty good time. By game's end, only one player had been taken to the hospital to have his upper lip sewn back on. No worries, mate!

FIREMAN'S MUSTER

5-11 Club, Inc.
P.O. Box 8511
Chicago, IL 60680
(773) 777-4511
Map: Downtown

Every year, right near the spot where Mrs. O'Leary's cow supposedly kicked over the lamp, a hardy group of fire-fighting buffs gathers to show off their vintage trucks and compete for fun and prizes. It's called a Fireman's Muster, and it's organized by the proud members of the 5-11 Club. The muster, held at the Chicago Fire Academy at 558 West De Koven Street, is open to the public and features an impressive array of shiny red antique fire engines. The machines are all lovingly preserved and still mobile—even if they occasionally need a little push.

Then there's the pumping events, which test competitors in some of the skills demanded of the average firefighter. It should be noted that not all of the 5-11 Club members and muster participants are actual firefighters; many are just enthusiasts who grew up wanting to be one. It doesn't seem to make a difference once the pumping competition starts. In one typical event, teams are required to run a hose up to a fire truck, attach it and turn on the water, and then aim at three beer kegs, knocking them over in succession. The team that accomplishes this task in the fastest time wins. At the end of the day, the victors are greeted with a chorus of sirens, and the spectators depart secure in the knowledge that if those kegs had been fires, the Musterites were clearly their master.

GLISSON ARCHERY

22900 East Main Street
Plainfield, IL 60544
(815) 436-5803
Map: Suburban West

The bow and arrow has come a long way since the days of Robin Hood, and at Glisson's they have the latest technology in the archery arts. Remember the old wooden bows they had at summer camp? Well, Walter "Sonny" Glisson can show you some fiberglass dual-cam designs with the three-string cabling system that can provide surprising accuracy at 300 feet per second; those poor deer don't stand a chance! Sonny's shop carries all the equipment and accessories you need to take up this ancient sport, including forearm protectors that prevent the arrow from slicing your flesh—best not to leave a blood trail, or the animals might come after you!

For those archers who want to test-drive a new purchase or simply practice their technique, Glisson's has not one but two shooting ranges on the premises. The indoor version has the requisite paper targets on the far wall as well as several "McKenzie" (artificial) animals that pop up from the floor. Out back is the 3-D range, where thirty-eight McKenzies stand at various distances in a wooded area to test not just accuracy but depth perception. It's almost like miniature golf for archers, with bears, wolves, and wild boar staring back and daring you to hit them.

Some final advice: *Do not* retrieve your arrows from the targets until you're sure no one else is still shooting, and avoid at all costs placing an apple on your head. That's just common sense.

GREAT CARDBOARD BOAT REGATTA

Lake Ellyn Boathouse
645 Lenox Road
Glen Ellyn, IL 60137
(630) 858-2462
www.gcbr.com
Map: Suburban West

It's not often that you get a chance to see a boat sink and rarer still that you get an opportunity to witness a bevy of boats go down. What's most remarkable—and uniquely American—is that one of the boats from this flooded fleet will be rewarded for its unworthiness with the *Titanic* award for the most spectacular sinking. These maritime disasters are all part of the fun when you spectate or participate in Glen Ellyn's version of cardboard boat racing. On regatta day, the Glen Ellyn Park District allows anyone with a life jacket to take to the water in a vessel constructed entirely of corrugated cardboard. The goal is to navigate your construction-grade clipper around a 200-yard course on the village lake. If you take a second to remember the basic physics equation of "water + cardboard = foundering failure," then you'll understand why the park district's Matt Karth predicts, "There's a lot of people who will go down in cardboard today." The designs range from simple kayaks to replicas of Sherman tanks, pink Cadillacs, and Eskimo bars. Even if you sink, you can still win an award, and the racing is open to all, ages eight and up. If you don't have a spare five or six hundred hours to spend constructing your pulp pontoon, there's also a special "instant" boat category where you build your boat the same day as the races. Voyage on-line to learn the details. Then, come to the regatta ready to sail to victory or to gargle some lake water. Of the approximately one hundred boats that enter the water, Matt says, "hopefully, half of them will come back."

GREAT LAKES DRAGAWAY

18411 First Street
Union Grove, WI 53182
(262) 878-3783
www.greatlakesdragaway.com
Map: Multistate

You're idling at the stoplight, listening to Yanni, and you glance over at the driver next to you. You look at him in his Honda Civic and think, *I can take him.* The need to out speed someone else is the third basic human want, right up there after food and shelter. Why be content to be a suburban speedster when you can drag your chassis for real at Wisconsin's Union Grove? The Great Lakes Dragaway has open racing challenges on its quarter-mile track. Pay a nominal entrance fee, bring your car and driver's license, and get ready for eight seconds of unfettered, asphalt-eatin' drag racing. Now, hold your horsepower there, Wilbur, eliminations are done through the bracket system. If you drag your feet (or your Ford does), you're knocked out of the competition. Continue to win and you can claim the purse—and purses are particularly attractive to drag queens. The challenges are

open to all cars, so you can do the *Fast and Furious* in a Fiesta or feel like James Dean in a Dodge Dart. Hey, that's not so far-fetched—at one race someone placed driving an Astro minivan. The GLD Web site can answer many of your questions, plus it has info on the junior dragster and high school programs. Get your kids involved legally and then you won't have those tearful reunions at the police station. Stick around at the track and catch the pros' cars: modified Malibus, Chargers, Rancheros, Impalas, and El Caminos. It's just like a rerun of *Starsky and Hutch.*

HIGHLAND GAMES

Oak Brook Polo Club
700 Oak Brook Road
Oak Brook, IL 60523
(708) 447-5092
Illinois St. Andrews Society
www.chicago-scots.org
Map: Suburban West

During the Middle Ages in Scotland, large men in skirts would test their physical prowess by throwing heavy objects in the air, and the clan chieftains would watch in hopes of finding the strongest men to be their warriors. Thus was born the Highland Games, which are still celebrated annually wherever there are Scotsmen. The Chicago version takes place in Oak Brook and has all the trappings of a village fair. Yes, they still throw the caber (a 104-pound, 20-foot-long treelike thing), but you'll also be treated to dance competitions, scotch whiskey tastings, and a border collie demonstration in which a dog runs circles around some very scared sheep.

Another Highland highlight is the parade, where the Scottish-born get to march around the grounds to the blaring of bagpipes. All the families in attendance (the McDonalds, the MacDougals, the McTavashes, etc.) march in groups wearing their "clan colors," which are basically the different plaid designs on their kilts. By the way, non-Scots are heartily welcome at the festivities, and they won't

even make you throw something heavy. Just refrain from asking the McAnyones who wears the pants in the family—nobody does!

ILLINOIS ARM WRESTLING

www.geocities.com/SouthBeach/
Tidepool/6124

There's a group that's promoting arm wrestling in Illinois by holding a series of tournaments across the state and in Chicago. Led by director Greg Wilson, they're hoping to eventually make it an Olympic sport, but for now they'd settle for it being considered something for people other than lumberjacks and drunks. Their events welcome both men and women to try their strength. Contestants are separated into weight classes,

then the refs/announcers give a brief demonstration to get things under way. Soon the participants are approaching the regulation table in pairs and commencing to grunt and grimace. The champion in each class is rewarded with a trophy and some admiring glances at his or her bulging biceps.

The prevailing wisdom is that arm wrestling is 90 percent technique and 10 percent brute strength; though there are frequent attempts to intimidate the competition with a steely glance or a flexing muscle, inevitably it's the brain and the brawn that win the day. Oh, and lumberjacks and drunks seem to do pretty well, too.

INTERNATIONAL CHERRY PIT SPITTING COMPETITION

Tree-Mendus Fruit Farm and
U-Pick Cherry Orchard
9351 East Eureka Road
Eau Claire, MI 49111
(616) 782-7101
www.treemendus-fruit.com
Map: Multistate

It's the pits, in a good way. The Tree-Mendus Fruit Farm's annual festival celebrates the fleshy fruit with the heart of stone with everything from jubilees to juice to the international pit-spitting contest. Participation in this rural Olympics of the orchard is free and open to all ages. They supply the pits, you supply the spit. To compete, choose your cherry, chew all the soluble solids, and spit that pit—all in under one minute. Judging is decidedly low-tech. The asphalt field is marked off in 1-inch increments, and they use a wooden ruler to determine the precise landing spot of the sputtered stones. The record distance is over 72 feet. Don't

think you have enough pucker power to play? Then sit in the bleachers with a piece of pie and cheer the sinewy gladiators on. Just don't place yourself too close to the contestants; there's some serious phlegm-flinging going on. Men are traditionally the spitter's spitters, but you'll marvel at the contortions and body English used by all as they try to pop that pebble. You just know they're going to need a heating pad when they get home. This cheery cherry celebration happens the first Saturday in July and it's only a stone's throw from Chicago. Like they say on the farm, cherry pit spitting is like a good sneeze . . . they're both therapeutic. Ohhh, that's pithy!

KANE COUNTY COUGARS
Philip B. Elfstrom Stadium
34W002 Cherry Lane
Geneva, IL 60134
(630) 232-8811
www.kccougars.com
Map: Suburban West

For fans fed up with the high prices of Major League Baseball (and the selfish, standoffish attitudes of its high-priced players), a minor-league game may be just the antidote. For us Chicagoans, there are several to choose from, but our favorite would have to be the Kane County Cougars, who play down the road in Geneva. Not only are the prices good and the players eager to please, but the Cougars organization will try just about anything to put on a good show for the crowd: skydivers landing in the outfield, cockroach races, a hot tub in the bleachers, après-game fireworks—you name it, you'll probably see it at a Cougars game.

Nobody seems too concerned about the quality of play on the field, or even who's winning; there's way too much else happening to care. You will almost always find a goofy promotion going on. The night we went it was Bald with Glasses Night, where everybody who fit that description got in free. Check out the giant ceramic glove in deep center: if a player manages to hit it with a home run, some lucky ticket holder wins a million dollars. And keep an eye out for Mr. Tidy, the hapless hunk in the tuxedo who's in charge of picking up trash. As for our intrepid host, he's waiting for Skinny Guy with Camera Crew Night.

MIDWEST CRICKET CONFERENCE
Washington Park
Fifty-fifth Street and
Martin Luther King Drive
Chicago, IL
www.midwestcricket.org
Map: Chicago South

The South Side of Chicago is an odd place to find a cricket match, but then again cricket is an odd sport. From May through September, you can find it being played in Washington Park between neighboring games of softball and soccer. The day we spectated, the players seemed to be of mostly Indian and Pakistani origin, and they coexisted quite peaceably—not one nuclear threat the whole afternoon! Maybe it helps that everyone was dressed in white; "shirts and skins" simply isn't done in this gentlemen's game.

The object of cricket seems to be for the "bowler" of one team to pitch a hard wooden ball at the "wicket" (two wooden pieces resting horizontally across three wooden stakes) in an attempt to knock it over. Meanwhile, the batter from the other team wants to prevent this and hit the ball into the field in the hopes of scoring some runs. A number of fielders are situated behind the bowler in order to stop any hits from getting through, and one of these position players is actually called the "silly mid-on." We're not sure why.

Make no mistake, cricket is not a fast-paced sport. If you think baseball moves slowly, you'll be interested to hear that international cricket matches normally take *five days* to complete. Yet there can be occasional bursts of activity: it's not unusual to have 200 runs scored in an inning. Cricket also seems to have a delightful element of uncertainty built into it. When we asked the official scorekeeper for the score, he replied, "Right now, I can't tell," and at one point the umpire's ruling on a controversial play was "Yes and No." Oh, and there don't seem to be any boundaries, so be careful where you put your lawn chair, or you may have an encounter with a hard wooden ball that would not be silly in the least.

MINNOW EATING

Aquarium Bar and Grill
139 Arthur Avenue
Fox Lake, IL 60020
(847) 587-4544
Map: Suburban North

If you're out at Grass Lake for the Blarney Island Speedboat Races, there's an après-race activity nearby that you might want to sample. At the Aquarium Bar and Grill they have a fifty-year tradition of ingesting minnows, straight up or with a beer chaser. Legend has it that one night some ice fishermen stumbled into the bar after a bad day on the lake, and without a catch to their credit, they angrily swallowed their bait, which happened to be minnows. Thus was born a fad that's lasted a half-century and is still going strong.

The bar now provides the minnows in question, and patrons quaff up to twenty at a time! When last we checked, the record holder was a hearty soul who downed 280 in one hour (the only rule is that they can't come back up). Rest assured that if you choose to partake in a small, squirming fishlet, you'll get a memento to remember it by—a membership card in the Minnow Swallowers Club, dated and signed by a

server. And for the really brave, there's the Minnow Munchers Club. Either way, you might want to bring breath mints: those minnows have a nasty aftertaste.

MISS CONTINENTAL USA COMPETITION

Baton Show Lounge
436 North Clark Street
Chicago, IL 60614
(312) 644-5269
www.thebatonshowlounge.com
Map: Chicago North

All beauty pageants offer a flotilla of pretty women. But the Miss Continental USA pageant is . . . different. The women competing here are beyond pretty; they're exotic, maybe even extravagant. There's a bit more lip gloss, a tad more décolletage, a few more sequins. It's much more theatrical, more dramatic, like, maybe in a movie, like, maybe *The Crying Game*, like, maybe 'cause they're all men. The Baton nightclub has long been famous for presenting the best in female impersonators, but did you know it also hosts this national competition? Every September, winners from other states' competitions converge in Chicago to compete for the Miss Con crown. Unlike the Miss America pageant—where women play women—the contestants here are not disqualified for augmenting their assets with plastic surgery, hormones, or implants, anything to help with the illusion. Backstage, though, it's pretty much the same. They, too, use Vaseline on their teeth to keep their smiles unglued, use double-stick tape to tame a traveling bathing suit bottom, use duct tape for . . . what's the duct tape for? One backstage dresser said, "Oh, no, you don't want to know." But we did. One very helpful contestant finally told us that they use the tape when "you're hung like a horse." Y'know, maybe backstage is not so similar to other pageants after all.

About the contest, one hopeful said, "Anyone can be a woman, but it takes a real man to be a lady." All are welcome to watch the competition. Men, come to see the best you can be. Women, gee, come for tips.

MUD BUG CLUB

901 West Weed Street
Chicago, IL 60622
(312) 787-9600
www.arlingtonpark.com
Map: Chicago North

If you think off-track betting involves stale cigar smoke, fluorescent lighting and the stink of desperation, you haven't been to the Mud Bug Club. Located in the very cool Weed Street neighborhood, the Mud Bug lets you blow your disposable income in a delightfully comfortable setting, complete with a well-stocked bar and ninety-nine TV screens! You can place your bet with one of the helpful cashiers, then settle in to watch the races in one of the several well-appointed rooms; one could be called the Christian Science Betting Room, with reading stalls for studious bettors to peruse their racing sheets.

We grant you, it's not quite the same as hearing the pounding hooves on the track as you cheer for your horse from the stands. So for a real day at the races go to Arlington or Hawthorne, but if you want to save money on gas or play hooky from work for an hour or so, the Mud Bug Club might be just the ticket. Just don't make too many bad bets or you might be having mud for dinner.

NIGHT GOLF

Raymond Heights Golf Center
1331 South Twenty-seventh Street
Caledonia, WI 53108
(262) 835-2020
Map: Multistate

A short trip into Wisconsin will take you to Raymond Heights Golf Center, where Friday night is Golf Night in June, July, and August. And they mean Golf *Night!* It seems that there are some who think the game of golf isn't hard enough to play as it is, so they've got to add the handicap of *pitch blackness.* But while the course may be dark, it turns out the people playing are pretty well lit! See, they all congregate in the center's bar for some rounds before their round, and everyone seems to have a good foundation buzz before a swing has been swung. Included in their greens fees are a glow-in-the-dark golf ball and a handful of "chem lights" to put on themselves and their clubs so that other golfers will avoid hitting at them. The flag sticks also glow to provide contestants with a suitable target, and once on the green there's a chem light in the cup to facilitate putting.

Besides the obvious danger of combining heavy drinking, golf and darkness, there are other slight drawbacks to this nocturnal pastime. It's sometimes hard to keep track of whose glowing ball is whose (though by the end of the evening nobody seems to care), and there have been some inebriates who have stumbled into the occasional irrigation pit. If you can overcome these minimal hazards, however, night golf can be a peaceful and almost otherworldly experience; the sounds of nighttime are only sporadically punctuated by shouts of "Fore! Fore!", and the chem-light outerwear makes everybody look like Martians invading Racine.

By the way, if night golf still isn't challenging enough, we've got one word for you: blindfolds.

NORGE SKI CLUB

100 Ski Hill Road
Fox River Grove, IL 60021
(847) 639-9718
www.norgeskiclub.com
Map: Suburban North

Do you remember that ski jumper's breathtaking crash that played during the intro to ABC's *Wide World of Sports*? If you thought that was cool and not cruel, then this Fox River Grove club is for you, my masochistic friend. While Northern Illinois is not exactly known as Nordic heaven (Algonquin in the Alps?), the club has solved that need for speed by constructing a warm-weather jump. Importing a plastic material from Finland (it resembles huge, interlocking toothbrush bristles) and lubricating it with water, the track surface simulates snow. And it's slick. Now, don't worry, the club won't leave you adrift at the top—they offer year-round training for ages four and up. Then, it's all downhill from there. You can snowball down the jump at over 70 mph while the weather screams for ice cream.

Norge has been around since 1905 and is the oldest continuous ski club in the United States. Plus, it has the Midwest's most popular practice run. You'll have a chance to bump skis with Olympic hopefuls and world-class athletes. If you prefer to be a snow*flake* and not a snow*ball*, then join the thousands who picnic on the adjoining hills during the

club's fall tournament. You'll see plenty of those "thrill of victory" jumps and maybe spot one of those spectacular schussing smashups that'll remind you of the "agony of defeat."

NORTH SHORE RUGBY CLUB

(773) 296-9877
www.northshorerugby.com

If you think rugby is too rough a sport for women, you'd better not say it to the members of the North Shore or Chicago Women's Rugby Clubs, or they're liable to hurt you very badly. Sure, the game goes against everything women are socialized into believing, but as the North Shore coach puts it, "Can women play a physical sport? Yes. Can they hit people and get sweaty? Yes, they can. And are they proud of their bumps and bruises afterwards? Yes, they are!" Sometimes it's more than a bump or a bruise; at the game we attended in Dan Ryan Woods, the sidelines were littered with players who had sustained injuries during the course of the season. It's not all that surprising, considering that even with all the physical contact the sport entails, mouthguards are the

only protection worn by these ladies.

Before each game both teams canvas the playing field looking for broken glass, bottle caps, or other sharp objects. Then the referee checks the players themselves for sharp objects—long fingernails are strictly forbidden. Once the game starts, the rules are simple: the ball can be moved forward by either running it or kicking it, and all passes must be laterals. Otherwise it's a lot like football without pads, except for those crazy "scrums" and that "drop-kicking on the run" thing. Oh, and each position has a corresponding jersey number, so if you're replaced in the lineup you have to give your shirt to your sub. That's why you'll see a lot of women in sports bras standing on the sidelines—and a lot of attentive men sitting in the stands!

POLO

700 Oak Brook Road
Oak Brook, IL 60523
(630) 990-2394
www.chicagopolo.com
Map: Suburban West

The sport of polo is five hundred years old, but they've only been playing it in Oak Brook since 1922. To the uninitiated observer it may look like eight guys on horseback whacking at a hard white ball with wooden mallets, but to those in the know—actually, that's pretty much what's going on.

There are four horsemen per side with a goal at either end of a large playing field (but no goalies). A game has six periods of play, which are called *chukkas*, and two referees, who are called *referees*. The players ride a different horse for each chukka, which means they need to have a minimum of six horses. But though the cost makes it a tad elitist as far as its participants are concerned, you don't have to be wealthy to watch. It's actually a pretty

exciting spectator sport, especially when the action takes the horses over the sidelines and practically into your lap (as we were lucky enough to experience). Between chukkas the spectators are invited onto the field to help stamp down the divots. But be careful: the ones that are smelly and steaming are not divots at all. Those are called *horse manure*.

RACEWORLD SLOT CAR RACEWAY

4312 West Elm Street
McHenry, IL 60050
(815) 759-9300
www.raceworldslotcar.com
Map: Suburban North

If you always dreamed of being a NASCAR Driver or an Indy 500 champ, but the dangerous risk of life and limb makes you nervous, maybe Raceworld Raceway in McHenry is more your speed. Here they haven't had even one fatality since they opened for business in 1980. That's because Raceworld is for slot cars, miniature models that fly around an electrified track at speeds controlled by a trigger mechanism. For a small fee, entrants race in eight heats of two minutes each, vying for bragging rights and some obligatory prize money (the most you can win is about $10). There are three tracks of varying difficulty on the premises, and the secret seems to be (as in real racing) to speed up on the straightaways and decelerate on the turns, otherwise your car will tend to flip over or spin out.

Tuesday through Friday evenings it's adult racing, while Saturday afternoons are for the kids. The grown-ups take their slot car racing pretty seriously, often bringing their own customized cars to the track; it's not uncommon to see models with painted-on sponsor decals, vinyl seats, and a little plastic driver behind the wheel who bears a definite resemblance to the owner. When you overhear comments about gear ratios and torque, you realize that these are the guys who probably excelled in high school shop class. But don't be intimidated by their fancy automobile talk if you decide to try your hand at slot cars. You don't need to know the vocabulary, you don't even need your own car (Raceworld will rent you one). What you do need is the heart of a champion and a trigger finger that's not too itchy.

RIVERBEND BENDERS WATERCROSS

County Lakes Resort
900 West Belvidere Road
Round Lake, IL 60073
(847) 289-RBSC
www.riverbendbenders.com
Map: Suburban North

There are those who would say that racing snowmobiles on a lake in the middle of summer is just plain stupid, but here at *Wild Chicago* we say, "Bravo!" The sport is called watercross, and it all started when several intrepid snowmobilers discovered while crossing a frozen lake that they could go right over the occasional patch of thin ice if they just sped up a little. It was only a matter of time before the challenge of taking their machines across an *unfrozen* lake proved too tempting to resist. Thus was born the International Watercross

Association ("international" meaning the United States and Canada). The organization's world championships are held on Fox Lake in Illinois, a series of four-man heats that take off from land and circle a series of buoys before returning to terra firma—theoretically. Take a turn too sharply or dip below 20 miles per hour and your snowmobile will do what it's supposed to do in H$_2$O: sink like a stone.

Should this happen, there's a pontoon boat with a hoist on it to lift the snowmobile off the bottom of the lake and ferry it to dry land, at which point the owner simply tips it on its side, cleans the water out of the engine and dries the carburetor, then starts it up for the next heat. Sinkings are not rare in watercross. At the 1997 world championship, the three finalists *all* sank in midrace; the winner was the one who stayed above water the longest.

Most serious watercrossers no longer even use their snowmobiles in the winter, since they've got so much invested in racing during the summer. *Wild Chicago* thinks there can only be one response to this lunacy: let's see what those Jet Skis can do on snow!

ROLLE BOLLE

Ray's Evergreen Tavern
1400 West Main Street
St. Charles, IL 60174
(630) 584-3535
Map: Suburban West

There's a tavern in St. Charles where they've been playing something called rolle bolle for more than one hundred years. Ray's Evergreen Tap claims to be the Home of Rolle Bolle, but the sport was actually created in Belgium back in 1300. The bolle is a solid eight-and-a-half-pound rubber disk, and it resembles a spare tire for a very small car. The object of the game is to roll your bolle across a flat dirt surface toward a wooden stake, with any luck placing it closer to the stake than your opponent's bolle. Much like shuffleboard or lawn bowling, if a competitor has a commanding position near the stake, it's perfectly legal to knock 'em out of there with a good hard throw. Otherwise the sport demands a gentle touch to curve your bolle at slow speed toward a favorable resting place.

Most of the participants at Ray's have been given colorful nicknames, which they engrave on the sides of their bolles. There's Boomer (played football), the Coyote (hunts coyotes), and V-Man (short for "Victorious, Voluptuous and Very @#$%# good!"). Then there is June Bug, who got her nickname by enthusiastically carrying on an Evergreen Tap tradition. It seems that one summer night one of the bowlers found that the June bugs cluttering the playing surface were affecting the speed of his bolles. Out of frustration, and perhaps a desire to intimidate his opponents, he promptly picked several of the pesky insects off the ground and *ate*

them. Thus began a pastime that's only grown over the years. Whether it's the sport of rolle bolle that brings out this strange behavior or the copious amount of beer that is consumed before, during, and after a typical game, we're really not sure. But trust us when we tell you that those June bugs go down a lot easier with a large swig of your favorite brew.

"SHORTEST BUTT, BIGGEST ASH" CONTEST

Up Down Tobacco Shop
1550 North Wells Street
Chicago, IL 60610
(312) 337-8025
www.updowntobacco.com
Map: Chicago North

Walk south on Wells from Second City and you can't miss it—a bigger-than-life-size wooden Indian that marks the entrance to the Up Down Tobacco Shop. Also prominently displayed in large letters right next to the door are the words SMOKING PERMITTED. If that opportunity appeals to you, you'll have myriad tobacco options to choose from here, what with the 450 different types of cigars for sale, not to mention the pipe paraphernalia and exotic cigarettes also available. The Up Down is a smoker's paradise, and the reigning goddess is Diana, owner and occasional operator. When in residence, she can often be found smoking her "Diana" brand cigars and dispensing advice to customers; we watched her talk a couple out of buying a pack of Egyptian cigarettes: "They've got saltpeter in 'em, kills the sex drive."

Every November this brassy broad hosts a "Shortest Butt, Biggest Ash" contest down the street at O'Brien's Restaurant (contact Up Down Tobacco Shop for details). Contestants are given the same size Diana cigar, which they then carefully smoke in an effort to keep their ash from falling off. When it does, their butt is measured, and the shortest one wins. The secret seems to be to smoke your stogie while pointing it straight up in the air, all the while making no sudden moves. Last year's winner was a woman, one Carmen Lackquitz, who got her butt down to a mere 9 millimeters. Bravo!

Even if you aren't victorious, you'll get to rub elbows with Chicago's cigar connoisseurs, who all seem to share a deep affection for the taste and relaxing qualities of a good smoke. One of them, though, put that fondness in perspective when he told us while sniffing an unlit Cuban, "I try to get to know my cigars intimately before I snip their heads off and murder them."

SLED HOCKEY AND BEEP BASEBALL

Chicago Park District
Therapeutic Recreation
Department
Jim Mullaghy
(312) 742-4985

Do you have a mobility or vision impairment? Only those who do can take advantage of two sports offered through the Chicago Park District. The Therapeutic Recreation Department of the CPD has sled hockey for those with physical disabilities and beep baseball for the blind. Sled hockey has the same rink, rules, and stratagems used for those who play standing ice hockey. The downside is there's still a penalty box, so no charging, high-sticking, or slashing. The upside is the teams are coed. You'll race around

the rink on regulation ice hockey skate blades mounted to a tubular frame. To propel the puck and your sled, there are two dual-purpose sticks. One end has the blade— she shoots, she scores!—and the other is tipped with metal teeth. You'll be clawing through the ice like a polar bear on the tundra.

If you run from cold to hot, then beep

baseball's your baby. A regulation 16-inch softball is implanted with an audible signal so the sightless batter can "hear" the pitch. The batter then advances to a padded base, which emits a buzz. It beeps, it buzzes, it's a blast. The bad news is there's no "home"; batters run only to first or third base to score. The good news is . . . the teams are coed.

If you're thinking cost will be your only impairment to playing either sport, don't, they're free. The CPD supplies everything: the protective equipment, sleds, sticks, ice time, bats, and balls. When you play on one of these teams, you'll get fellowship, fitness, and self-esteem, plus a chance to let off some steam.

TEST AND TUNE

Route 66 Speedway
500 Speedway Boulevard
Joliet, IL 60433
(815) 727-RACE
www.route66raceway.com
Map: Suburban South

Tuesday nights at Route 66 Raceway in Joliet is an auto racing free-for-all called Test and Tune, where anybody with a car can try their luck on the quarter-mile drag strip. You basically "run what ya brung," though you've got to pass a tech inspection before you can hit the track. Participants range from a husband and wife with the family Suburban to professional drag racers who use Tuesday night to fine-tune their engines. The cars form two lines that sometimes snake several hundred yards outside the stadium; whoever happens to be in the neighboring lane when you reach the starting line is your competition, and it's not unusual to see a minivan go up against a Corvette.

This fun evening of burning rubber is not without risk: you could blow out your engine and not have a way to get to work the next morning. But there's nothing like puttin' that pedal to the metal and lettin' her roar, and hey, if a Jag cleans your clock in one heat, maybe you'll face a pickup truck in the next. Eventually somebody's bound to eat your dust!

TOUR DE DONUT

Boeing Employees Bicycle Club
of St. Louis
(314) 232-4614
www.bebikeclub.com

If you're an avid cyclist with a knack for eating glazed donuts, you can combine those skills at the venerable Tour de Donut in downstate Staunton, Illinois. The event happens every summer at around the same time as the Tour de France, only instead of taking weeks, it's a one-day, 30-mile race. Here's the catch: You have to eat to compete. You see, there are two stopping points along the course at which you have ten minutes to cram as many donuts down your gullet as you can. Why? Because you get five minutes off your finishing

time for every donut consumed. The 2001 winner ate thirty donuts for a corrected time of *minus* 23 minutes and 36 seconds.

The race starts at Staunton High School, 701 Deneen Street in Staunton, and takes an average of five hundred entrants over flat country roads that pass mostly farms and gas stations. Though there are some world-class cyclists in the field, it's really a Homer Simpson with leg strength who has a better chance of winning. And if you think the more dedicated competitors are stopping to savor the pastry, think again; the normal method of consumption is to mash six donuts together, dip them in water to aid

digestion, and then wolf 'em down. Eating too many donuts can backfire, however, when for every minute you gain, you lose many more having to stop and puke in the bushes.

At the end of the race, we asked one contestant where he felt it most—the stomach, the legs, or the heart—and he answered, "My throat, as the donuts are backing up into my esophagus." 'Nuff said.

TURTLE RACES

Big Joe's
1818 West Foster Avenue
Chicago, IL 60640
(773) 784-8755
Map: Chicago North

Arlington Park racing it's not. This is a marathon for marine reptiles. Every Friday night, Big Joe's, a woodsy, neighborhood dart bar, hosts its Turtle Races. It's called the Fastest Game in Town because the actual contest only takes a few seconds, but it's the buildup to each race that makes it worth your bother. Here's how it works. You receive a numbered ticket for each drink you buy. Before a race, six numbers are drawn. If one of them's yours—and you're not too inebriated to know it—you get to pick a number that corresponds to one of six turtles. The shelled competitors are placed at the center of a large table and released. The first one to touch the outside line is the winner. First place receives a Big Joe's T-shirt, second through fifth place are loudly declared "Losers!" and sixth place wins a free cocktail. Needless to say, most of the patrons we spoke with in this boisterous bar preferred placing sixth. There's a randy racetrack announcer who calls each tortoise run and who also adds color commentary on the customers. If he sees that you're new to race night, you're labeled a "turtle virgin," if you're a regular, you're a "turtle slut." After six races—and approximately sixty rounds of drinks—a final, winner's race is held. Each of those who won T-shirts in the previous races competes to see whose name will be entered for a chance to win the top prize, a trip for two to Las Vegas. And we thought it would be a trip for two to the Galapagos.

ULTIMATE FRISBEE
Chicago Ultimate Summer League
www.ultimatechicago.org

It's no surprise that a sport born in the 1960s would be nonviolent, free-spirited, and boast some far-out terminology, man. The Chicago Ultimate Summer League contains elements of several different sports to hopefully arrive at the *ultimate* sport, a fast-moving Frisbeefest that tests the endurance and versatility of its players. The idea is to "flick" the disk down the field from teammate to teammate (or perhaps "huck" it or throw a "hammer") until it winds up in the opponent's end zone—hey, that's a little like football! When a player catches the Frisbee, he or she must come to a stop and plant the pivot foot, and when a defender comes up on that player to try to block his or her next pass, it starts to look a little like basketball. The game is played to 15 points with no time-outs, and that's just like volleyball. No wonder some of the spectators at the game we attended seemed a little confused!

Everything starts with both sides giving their team cheer, which is always loud and usually R-rated. Then instead of a coin, they flip the Frisbee to see who will huck and who will receive. Once the action starts, it's a mile a minute; even when a player stops after a catch, he or she has only ten seconds to get rid of it. There are no referees, so the players are on the honor system to admit fouls. That's typical of the generally laid-back attitude that prevails. Sure, there's competition, but there are also several male contestants who regularly wear skirts on the field (we're not sure why) and a mandatory party for all at a local bar after the game. We can definitely dig that!

UNDERWATER HOCKEY

Tom & Patty Redig
(630) 960-1771

Think ice hockey on a hot day. Your Poseidon adventure begins when you strip and flip into the pool version of this sport. Men and women team up weekly to become wet Wayne Gretzkys competing to shove a rubber disk into their opponent's goal, all the while underwater. You'll go off the deep end trying to coordinate when to surface for air or when to stay submerged and go for the hat trick. Though the action is sort of slow-motion (you *are* playing on the bottom of a pool, after all), this game is no Esther Williams aquacade. One player got pucked, requiring nine stitches. Fortunately, she later confessed, her forehead blocked the goal that that little pucker was trying to make. And, slinking along the rough floor of a pool, you'd better expect to receive a full-body "exfoliation" (men, kiss your chest hair good-bye; women, wear a one-piece). If you want to become a "bottom speeder"—or you know someone with an excessively hairy back—bring your goggles and snorkel. As for the stick, well, it looks like a windshield ice scraper. Veterans of the game also sport chin guards and gloves. Need anything else? One pool player recommends you bring "a token amount of insanity and a good set of lungs." No prior experience is necessary, and it's open to all mermaids and mermen. When you do take a dive with these toned terrapins, look forward to a little naval networking. There's some serious body contact going on beneath the sea.

VINTAGE BASE BALL ASSOCIATION

www.vbba.org

"The hurler delivers to the striker, and oh! It's a foul tick that's caught by the behind, making it three hands dead. The cranks huzzah!" If you recognize the preceding lingo, you're either impossibly old or you've attended a recent "match" put on by the Vintage Base Ball Association. For the players of the VBBA, every trip to the plate is a trip back in time; that's because they play by the original rules for "base ball" written in 1858. Back then it was a more gentlemanly pastime, with no spitting, spiking, stealing, scratching, or swearing allowed— *Sacre Bleu!* Then there's that crazy vocabulary: a "foul tick" is not an insect bearing Lyme disease, it's a foul ball; a "rover" is not Irish, he's a

shortstop; and you don't score a run, you "tally an ace." Huzzah! (Yay!)

The Vintage Base Ball folks play it all to the hilt, dressing in period uniforms, bringing homemade bats, even playing bare-handed despite the very hard ball (broken fingers were common then and now). The umpire is done up in top hat and tails and looks like the millionaire from Monopoly. If he catches a "hand" (player) doing any of the S-words, he fines them a day's wages—25 cents. It's all good fun, and if you end up becoming a "crank" (fan), feel free to shout at your team, "Hey guys, nice behind!" You're just saying they've got a good catcher.

MORE SPORTS & CONTESTS

BELT SANDER DRAG RACING
Lindner Lumber and Hardware
44 West Railroad Street
Sandwich, IL 60548
(815) 786-2117
www.beltsander-races.com
Map: Multistate
Souped-up belt sanders compete on an 85-foot track.

CHICAGO PAINTBALL FACTORY
1001 West Van Buren Street
Chicago, IL 60607
(312) 563-1777
www.onlinepaintball.com
Map: Chicago West
Amateur war games using paint for bullets inside a postapocalyptic-themed warehouse.

DISC GOLF
Adler Park
1300 North Milwaukee Avenue
Libertyville, IL 60048
www.discontinuum.org
Map: Suburban North
Organized league of Frisbee golfers.

NOVELTY GOLF AND BATTING CAGES
3650 West Devon Avenue
Lincolnwood, IL 60712
(847) 679-9434
www.noveltygolf.com
Map: Suburban North
Miniature golf among enormous chickens and other odd sculptures.

PAINTBALL BLITZ
Routes 41 and 21
Gurnee, IL 60031
(847) 545-9999
www.paintballblitz.com
Map: Suburban North
Amateur war games using paint for bullets in the northern Illinois woods.

WHEELS RALLYE
www.wheelsrallyeteam.com
A board game by car, combining elements of a scavenger hunt and a trivia contest.

INSTRUCTION & SELF-IMPROVEMENT

CLASSES
AND CLUBS
FOR AN
OUT-OF-THE-
ORDINARY
EDUCATION

ACTORS GYMNASIUM

Noyes Cultural Arts Center
927 Noyes Street
Evanston, IL 60201
(847) 328-2795
www.actorsgymnasium.com
Map: Suburban North

I f you think an actor's job is mostly learning lines and looking good in costumes, you haven't witnessed the brand of athletic theater that has taken Chicago by storm lately, and you certainly haven't heard of the Actors Gymnasium. Founded in 1995 by Tony Adler and members of the Lookingglass Theatre, it calls itself a "school for interdisciplinary theatre arts." Judging by what we saw on our visit, though, it seemed that they really specialized in *circus* arts (no surprise, since one of their main teachers is Cynthia Hernandez, who once performed with her family in the Ringling Brothers Barnum and Bailey Circus). Students are trained in tumbling, walking on stilts, sending each other aloft on a teeterboard, even swinging on the flying trapeze—not always with ease. We were talked into trying "the Web," which involves climbing a rope, placing your hand through a loop, and being swung in circles at dizzying speed. They say after a few tries you don't even feel nauseated afterwards!

What the Actors Gym is giving its students is the confidence that they can handle any type of movement or acrobatics they're called upon to do onstage. But don't assume the training regimen is meant only for thespians. Plenty of nonactors, bored with repetitive aerobics or the tedium of the StairMaster, are finding the challenge of learning these physical stunts to be an exhilarating workout. Plus, their new high-wire act is sure to be a hit at the office Christmas party.

ADVENTURES UNLIMITED PRESS

One Adventure Place
Kempton, IL 60946
(815) 253-6390
www.adventuresunlimitedpress.com
Map: Multistate

M illionaire David Hatcher Childress calls himself "a publisher, archeologist, and adventurer," and you might add "conspiracy theorist" to that job description. The books that he's written and had published deal with alien abduction, underground tunnels, mind control, and other similar topics. He owns bookstores in the Netherlands, New Zealand, and Nepal, and on Easter Island, but his headquarters (which doubles as a bookstore and cafe) is in Kempton, Illinois, about 60 miles south of Chicago. Why? According to Childress, "it's a power spot in a vortex area."

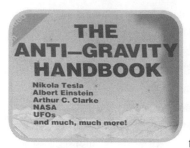

When you drive into town, you can't miss Adventures Unlimited—it's at First and Main, or One Adventure Place, and has a huge mural of pyramids on the outside wall. Once inside you'll find it to be either an oasis of open-minded thinking or a clearinghouse for wackos. Curious about time travel, antigravity, or NASA's involvement in the JFK assassination? You'll find it here, and if you like, you can pull a book off the shelf and sit down at the cafe to nosh and theorize. Definitely leave yourself time to wander around Kempton, a delightful little town with a Norman Rockwell feel to it. And if you sense a certain electricity in the air, it's probably that dang power spot.

CHICAGO LAUGHTER CLUB

(866) LUV-2LAF
www.chicagolaughterclubs.com

We found a group of people who take laughing very seriously. The stated mission of the Chicago Laughter Club is to achieve world peace through laughter, and if this sounds like a lofty goal for forty Chicagoans to take on, keep in mind that this is just one branch of an international organization. It started in India in 1995, where they initially got the hilarity rolling by telling their favorite jokes. But eventually everybody had heard each other's punch lines, so they resorted to what they call "laughter exercises," in which members force themselves to laugh together until the chortles and guffaws become real. Their theory is that simulated laughter becomes stimulated laughter, or, as one of the certified laughter leaders told us, "you've gotta fake it 'til you make it."

The result is that attending one of the club's meetings can at first feel like you've walked into a mental ward, with everyone laughing maniacally at each other for no apparent reason. But stay until the end and you'll see how relaxed and happy these people seem when they leave. The healthy benefits of a good belly laugh have been clinically proven, so maybe these folks aren't clinically insane!

The club wants to spread its philosophy far and wide, and their Certified Laughter Leaders are available for laughing sessions at schools and businesses. Who knows, maybe world peace is not such an impossible aim, although you rarely see Saddam Hussein even crack a smile.

COOKING AND HOSPITALITY INSTITUTE OF CHICAGO

361 West Chestnut Street
Chicago, IL 60610
(312) 944-0882
www.chicnet.org
Map: Chicago North

For those of you who like to wear silly hats and play with your food, the Cooking and Hospitality Institute of Chicago (CHIC) is awaiting your enrollment. Ever wondered how to make a bouillabaisse? Curious about what the heck giardiniere is? CHIC can turn you into a qualified chef in two years, and a certificate program could put you in a tall white chapeau in about seven months. While you're there, you'll delve into subjects like "sauces and chutneys" and "pastries and desserts"—just about every food group has a department, and the aromas coming from these classrooms are to die for.

Of the five hundred full- and part-time students attending CHIC, most seem to be making the culinary arts a second career, while others just want to improve their cooking skills at home. They better come here with their A game, since part of the training involves chefing in an actual restaurant kitchen with actual lunchers eating the results. The institute's dining room is open to the public for lunch seven days a week (reservations required), with a different menu each day. The prices are right, since the kitchen crew is a revolving cadre of trainees, all hoping that nothing gets sent back. While a sinking soufflé or a rancid ratatouille might not earn you an automatic F, you may be assigned to chopping parsley for the foreseeable future.

DEGERBERG MARTIAL ARTS ACADEMY

4717 North Lincoln Avenue
Chicago, IL 60625
(773) 728-5300
www.degerberg.com
Map: Chicago North

You'd be hard-pressed to find someone who looks the part of a martial arts expert more than Fred Degerberg. With a body like an oil drum, a shaved head, and Fu Manchu facial hair, it comes as no surprise that Fred once played a villain in the Steven Seagal movie *Above the Law*. His academy teaches seventeen kinds of martial arts, from Filipino stick-fighting to French savate, with students as young as three years old (that would be the "ninja turtle" class) and as famous as John Belushi. The facility is a labyrinth of rooms leading into rooms, and you'll usually find five or six classes going on at the same time. Everywhere you look there are people punching, chopping, and kicking, but if you're put off by all the violence, slip into the tai chi wing, where everything is calmness and silence.

Any martial arts discipline you choose to practice will provide a challenging and beneficial workout, and as you progress you'll have a bunch of different-colored belts to show for your effort. But whatever they offer you, *don't* volunteer for "attacker" duty in the women's self-defense class. Trust us.

DREAM HOTLINE

School of Metaphysics
1653 West Cortland Street
Chicago, IL 60622
(773) 772-0966 local
(417) 345-8411 national
www.som.org, www.dreamschool.org
Map: Chicago North

Do your dreams speak a language you don't understand? Then get them translated at this Berlitz of Bedtime when you call the Dream Hotline at the School of Metaphysics in Chicago. During the last weekend in April, the school offers you, free, the chance to have a faculty member interpret your "nocturnal emissions." With this service project, they hope to educate people about the importance of understanding dreams to improve their lives. Dreams are your subconscious mind's way of giving you feedback on how you're using your life experiences. Think of them as a nighttime news report, sort of like going to bed with Ted Koppel. But since your mind can't use plain old English to send these messages, it's got to use symbols: you were flying in your dream or you died or you were buck naked. The metaphysicians here will decode your psychic e-mail: flying means you feel free, a death means change, being naked means you are open and honest (and . . . cold). The Cortland campus has only one phone for this event, so you might want to call in with your slumber vision at an off-hour. And if you miss the call-in, SOM offers self-study on its Web site and classes and literature at the school. So tonight, when you fall into the arms of Morpheus and he gives you the gift of dreams . . . open it!

FENCING 2000

328 South Jefferson Street
Chicago, IL 60661
(312) 879-0430
www.members.aol.com/fencing2k
Map: Downtown

Listen up—no matter what you've heard, size doesn't matter. In fact, strength doesn't matter, either. In fencing, it's all about your brains. Okay, and a little coordination. This is a sport that depends on your ability to strategize to outwit your opponent. Fencers liken it to "chess on wheels." If you're more Bobby Fischer than bodybuilder, then quit sitting on the fence and start doing it. Fencing 2000 has training classes and private lessons for all, ages five and up. They supply the equipment, you supply your willingness to wear those winning white knickers. When you learn to thrust and parry with the various swords—épée, foil, and saber—you'll be in like Flynn . . . Errol, that is. Fencing offers you a pretty challenging mental workout, plus it's not too shabby for your body. (Have you ever seen a flabby fencer? Alive?) If you want something truly original, how about letting Fencing 2000 host your next corporate party? Your group will get a lesson and then do some dueling. It's a safe way to pierce the ego of a pompous boss; however, unlike the office, there's no backstabbing allowed. How about getting your kids involved in this saber-rattling sport? Think of what it'll do to your daughter's playground cred when her playmates learn she's a real swashbuckler. And why should you be stuck with the mundane moniker of Soccer Mom? Wouldn't you prefer Sword Squire?

GARRETT HYPNOSIS AND WELLNESS CENTER

3020 North Kimball
Chicago, IL 60618
(773) 395-6100
www.garrettwellnesscenter.com
Map: Chicago North

What's stopping you from being the very best you can be? Tiptop-ophobia? If your life is ruled by a destructive habit or an irrational fear (frogophobic?), then seek solace and a solution at Garrett's. Their philosophy is that "taking care of the mind as well as the body is vital," and they consider themselves a "one-stop wellness center." (Stay away if you're multitaskophobic.) They offer classes and workshops in aromatherapy, acupuncture, reflexology, nutrition, Rolfing, and hypnotherapy. Larry Garrett has been a practitioner of hypnosis for more than thirty years and he's mesmerized Carol Burnett's husband, Ann Landers's daughter and Rock Hudson. (Hmm, makes you wonder what he was trying to cure . . . Dorisdayitus?) Hypnosis has changed since Rock was around; there's no more swinging a watch in front of your face.

Now, the patient reclines in a Barcalounger, covered with a blankey while Larry's soothing incantations stream through headphones.

If you're trying to quit smoking or overcome some other body bugaboo, you might want to give hypnosis a shot. Unless, of course, you're hypnophobic. Garrett's believes they can help you feel good every day, even if you're not prone to be a happyoholic. Go to their Web site to find out more about their therapies and specialists or visit them during one of their monthly open houses. That is, unless you're agoraphobic.

JADE'S DUNGEON
(312) 460-8689
www.jadesdungeon.com

A dungeon that's on the third floor? A dominatrix who teaches R-rated S and M classes for the decidedly PG-rated Discovery Center? What's going on here?!

Mistress Jade has plenty of surprises up her latex sleeve, not the least of which is her clientele, which are predominantly white-collar professionals. Apparently, people who make a living ordering other people around want to be dominated during their off-hours. At Jade's Dungeon they'll find a bevy of dominatrices willing to do just that, with all the tools they need to do it. The rooms are chock-full of ominous-looking contraptions with plenty of chains and leather straps, and the walls are lined with all the appropriate accessories: whips, handcuffs, shackles,

and dog collars. You don't want to know what they do with the clothespins.

The "mistresses" are decked out in the finest fetish wear, and, from what we heard, are all extremely adept at providing punishment without crossing the pain threshold of their "slaves." For those customers who'd rather dish it out than take it, Jade also has a selection of submissives available. Everything is done discreetly and within legal limits, and, as we mentioned before, classes are available for the uninitiated. So if you're hankerin' for a spankin', look no further. Now say, "Thank you, *Wild Chicago*." Say it!

MCGARRY'S BOXING

10210 South Hoyne Avenue
Chicago, IL 60643
(773) 881-1406
Map: Chicago South

Need a new workout? Think of something old. Boxing's been around (ten rounds, actually) since before, well, the Boxer Rebellion. Besides being a spectacle of punching an opponent for a purse, it offers you a full-body cardio and muscle fitness routine, plus it keeps you off the streets. McGarry's gym has classes and personal training in fancy fisticuffs for both the primitive and professional pugilist. They'll teach the art of the jab, hook, and roundhouse to males and females, ages eight to eighty, pinweight to super-heavyweight. Trainer Martin McGarry is no pretender-contender. He's a former state and Golden Gloves Champion (the old "one-two") who's sparred with Messrs. Ali, Perkins, and Terrell. He'll make a picture-perfect Burgess Meredith to your Sylvester Stallone. Or would you prefer a Raging Bull to a Rocky?

Come to blows at McGarry's and, who knows, you or your child could get good enough to win the Golden Gloves, get a scholarship to college, medal in the Olympics, and turn pro—from tyro to title fight. And then you'll land all those lucrative product endorsements. George Foreman Grill, anyone? Yeah, oh yeah. You know, that's the thing about boxing, it makes you dream about being a contender.

THE PLAYBOY ADVISOR

68 North Lake Shore Drive
Chicago, IL 60611
www.playboyadvisor.com

"How can I enlarge my penis?" For women, that's a rhetorical question. For the advice columnists at *Playboy* magazine, however, it's their number one inquiry. If you've ever had a dad, a brother, or a boyfriend, or you went to parochial school, you know about *Playboy's* probers into priapic problems and their general discourse on intercourse. Since 1960, the Advisor has been answering readers' queries and offering "expertise about sex, relationships, and living the good life." And, along the way, they've become our nation's arbiters of sexual standards. (Question: Is it normal to masturbate with sandpaper?) Mike Ostrowski, one of three Advisor staffers—or, war correspondents, as he likes to say—said they receive over six hundred letters and e-mails a month. While the age range of all those "Signed: Dysfunctional in Dubuque" letters has remained constant (teenagers to seniors), what has changed is the male to female ratio:

now 30 to 40 percent of the questions are sent by women. (Q: How much are old *Playboy*s worth?) Is there something the Advisor hasn't been able to definitively answer . . . a Moby-Dick question? Mike says his "great white" is probably requests about the "G spot." (Is there one? Where is it? Do you have a printable map I can give my husband?) Whatever the question, the Advisor endeavors to answer each one seriously and with compassion, no matter how silly. (Q: Can a penis shrink?) You might be wondering, why write the Advisor when you can get self-gratification— to your question—by tapping into the library of libidinous information available on the Web? Because, Mike says, "people trust the *Playboy* name, it's like turning to an old friend." And about the answer to that number-one question? Well, Mike told us . . . aw, you'd better just write the Advisor.

POLE VAULTING CAMP

Air Time Pole Vault Club
(847) 392-7046
jlv56@attbi.com
Map: Suburban North
camp held at: Maine South High School
1111 South Dee Road
Park Ridge, IL 60068

You want to get high? Then go to *high* school. Grab a pole and vault on over to the practice camp at Maine South High School. During the summer months, the Air Time Pole Vault Club runs a pole-vaulting clinic at this suburban school. Besides being a smooth and graceful sport, it teaches you to convert the horizontal energy of a run to the vertical energy of going up and, inevitably, down, over a bar. (It's reckless fun *and* a science lesson, too.) There's a coach on-site to tweak the technique of the trained vaulter or help the novice take that first leap of faith. It's open to all, from pre–high school age to getting-ready-for-my-high-school-reunion age. Hey, as long as you can still get that pole up . . .

Coach Jim Lonergan says vaulters are considered the best athletes because "you need speed, you need to be quick and you need to be a little goofy." Yeah, you try dropping with decorum from 15 feet up. How thrilling is this sport? One "bounder" we met said his day job was as an air traffic controller at O'Hare. Another said he continues to vault because "chicks dig scars." O-Kay. Well, whether your motivation to vault is daring or dating, the Air Time Pole Vault Club takes care of your biggest expense by providing the poles. So, if like Macbeth, you have "vaulting ambition," hoist your petard (and pole) at this track for a midsummer's night scream.

ROPE WARRIOR
DAVID FISHER
(888) JMP-ROPE
www.ropewarrior.com

We figured that anyone who can jump rope with his butt deserves a place in this book. David Fisher calls himself the Rope Warrior, and since 1993 he's been doing stunts like "rump jumping"

(jumping rope from a seated position, using his rump rather than his legs) at school assemblies, public events, and private parties. His rare talents have taken him from Moscow to Malaysia and landed him on numerous national television shows, as well as the inaugural parades for both Clinton and Bush. He holds the Guinness World Record for rump jumps in one minute: 56.

Fisher calls his program RopeNastics and claims it's the best cardiovascular workout available. It combines jump rope, dance, rhythmic gymnastics, martial arts, and aerobics into a big ball of fun and exercise. David has parlayed his jump-roping jones into two workout videos, a play (*Rope: A New Twist*), and a series of children's books in which the Rope Warrior uses his trusty rope to fight the forces of evil.

SIEBEL INSTITUTE OF TECHNOLOGY

4055 West Peterson Avenue
Chicago, IL 60646
(773) 279-0966
www.siebelinstitute.com
Map: Chicago North

Every year people from all over the world descend on a plain-looking building in the Sauganash neighborhood to learn the intricacies of hops, barley, and malt. The Siebel Institute opened its doors in 1866, making it one of the oldest brewery schools in the world. It offers four courses ranging from two to twelve weeks in duration, and its students include neophytes who want to learn how to brew beer in their basement and professional brewmasters who hope to pick up some new techniques.

The Institute provides the perfect environment for studying suds. It has a test brewery for trying out new recipes and a brew pub on the premises where

students can fulfill the beer-tasting part of the curriculum. The main challenge at the pub seemed to be tasting many beers in one sitting without getting totally blotto; we noticed a list of taxi companies on the wall for those who don't feel up to driving home from class. With all the nationalities represented (the first three students we met at the bar were from Mexico, Taiwan, and Brazil), there's some good-natured rivalry over where the world's best beer can be found, but there's also plenty of cross-pollination of ideas on what creates good taste and a thick head. All in all, we were impressed with the amount of serious thought going into the beer going into our mouths. Keep up the good work, Mr. Siebel, and please call us a cab.

WINDY CITY PRO WRESTLING

P.O. Box 170048
Chicago, IL 60617
(312) 409-WCPW
(773) 978-7317
www.windycityprowrestling.com

So you say you want to be a pro wrestler with a fancy nickname and your very own submission hold? Well there's a place nearby where you can learn the ropes, but be warned: This is not a sport for the weak of spine. Windy City Pro Wrestling trains would-be grapplers in the finer points of the Pile Driver, the Sleeper Hold, and the Flying Anatomizer (OK, we made that last one up). The place is run by a former AWA wrestler named Sam De Cero, who used to go by SuperMax of the Max Brothers. Each training session starts with warm-up drills where the students bounce off the ropes and hit the mat to get their blood flowing and their muscles loose. After that, Sam starts pairing up wrestlers and coaching them through some simulated matches. That's when all the throwing, punching, and kicking starts in earnest. From our vantage point it all looked alarmingly unfake, except for the referee's uncanny ability to be looking the other way when the worst transgressions were committed.

The ultimate goal of most of these guys is to make the big bucks in the WWE (World Wrestling Entertainment) or some other organized league. Windy City itself has a pro wrestling arm that puts on live events across seven states; their training facility even doubles as a TV studio so they can televise matches for cable. If you do well in class Sam might let you wrestle for the WCPW, which is certainly a start. Just promise you won't belly-ache the first time you get a knee to the groin or a chair to the head—you see, as long as the ref doesn't see it, it's perfectly legal!

MORE INSTRUCTION & SELF-IMPROVEMENT

CENTER FOR UFO STUDIES (CUFOS)
2457 West Peterson Avenue
Chicago, IL 60659
(773) 271-3611
www.cufos.org
Map: Chicago North
Clearinghouse for extraterrestrial sightings and theories.

CHICAGO FIRE ACADEMY
558 West DeKoven Street
Chicago, IL 60607
(312) 477-7239
www.cityofchicago.org
Map: Chicago South
Chicago's future firefighters train at the site of the 1871 Great Chicago Fire flash point.

GREAT LAKES NAVAL TRAINING CENTER

Great Lakes, IL 60088
www.ntcgl.navy.mil
Map: Suburban North
If you enlist, you'll train here (and don't skip Disaster Control School).

ILLINOIS INSTITUTE OF ART

350 North Orleans Street
Chicago, IL 60654
(312) 280-3500
www.ilia.aii.edu
Map: Downtown
Training ground for future animators and those with other artistic pursuits.

SPECIAL MUSIC BY SPECIAL PEOPLE

Chicago Park District Therapeutic
Recreation
2333 West Sunnyside Avenue
Chicago, IL 60625
(312) 742-7511
www.specialmusic.org
Map: Chicago North
Music program for students with developmental disabilities; concerts given regularly.

TRAPEZE CLASSES

Broadway Armory Park
5917 North Broadway
Chicago, IL 60660
(312) 742-8259
Map: Chicago North
Learn the art of swinging—literally.

MAGNIFICENT OBSESSIONS

QUIRKY HOBBIES AND
OFFBEAT SOCIAL GROUPS

CHICAGO AREA LACE GUILD

www.chicagoarealaceguild.com

This might be the most esoteric entry in this book: people who make lace. Lace making is the craft of looping, knotting, and stitching an openwork fabric or trim out of thread or yarn. Back in the sixteenth century, lace was such a highly prized commodity that the artists who created this "woven gold" were often restricted from leaving their towns. Then came the industrial revolution, and you know, if you stayed awake in class, that handmade gave way to machine manufactured. This guild is a collection of "thread-heads" who meet to learn, exchange, and preserve lace-making techniques. Creating lace is, to say the least, labor-intensive. One woman showed us a collar that took her 250 hours to complete. The guild meets only five times a year—maybe because it takes so long to make something for show-and-tell—where they have speakers lecturing on the latest news in lace and focus on a type of lace, like tatting, Battenberg, or bobbin. The guild was formed, one member told us, because "lace makers got lonely." (Hey, don't they know the travel restrictions have been lifted?) You won't have to pull some threads to get into one of their meetings; visitors are welcome, free. Go, and then you can get started on a basic project like trimming a handkerchief. Remember, though, after all your work, that hankie, as one member said, is "not for blow, it's only for show."

CHICAGO SUN CLUB NUDE RECREATION

George Morrison
(630) 377-3719
www.midwestsun.com/csc.html

Hey, get your mind out of the Dumpster, nude recreation is not about *that*. Yes, it *is* about a group of people who are nude and do engage in stimulating activity, but we're talking *bowling* here. If you think you'll bowl better with a bare body, then join the Chicago Sun Club. This nudist group organizes a chance to skittle without your Skivvies once a month. They rent out lanes so they can hit the alleys au naturel. And it's private. There won't be some fabric-covered family from Freeport saying, "Mommy, who's that cheeky chap in lane 10?" If playing tenpins topless (and bottomless) isn't your thing, the CSC also schedules nights out at a health club and the theater.

During the summer months, this coterie of the unclad joins other Midwest and national chapters at resorts, just in case you feel more comfortable doffing your duds in Duluth and not Downers Grove. There's mud wraps, music, portrait painting, and sports. "Clothing Optional" is the rule here, but if you don't divest yourself of your vest, and everything else, you might be labeled a "Textile." Check the Web site for upcoming absence-of-attire events and scholarship info. (You can actually study to be nude.) If the appeal of being unappareled is unavoidable for you, then don't forget to pack plenty of sunscreen. Oh, and maybe a fanny pack. Otherwise, just where would you keep your keys?

CHI-TOWN SQUARES

Ebenezer Church Community Center
1640 West Foster Avenue
Chicago, IL 60640
www.iagsdc.org/chi-townsquares
Map: Chicago North

There's nothing square about dancing with the Chi-Town square dancers. Before you even square off to swing yer partner, you have to decide which way you and your partner "swing." Members of this gay and lesbian group are allowed to choose whether they want to dance as a boy or a girl, to lead or to follow. Even if you don't know which way you want your sex, you still have to settle on which sex you want. Y'see, the dance of the square is predicated on the dancers responding to cues given by the caller. The cues tell the couples how to move as a group, as couples or as belles and beaus, so you gotta know which way you do-si-do. You won't need to bring a partner—there's always a spare hen or rooster around—and the dress code is casual. If you think you'd like to give it a go, step 'n slide up to the Web site. You can find out about the Squares' next dance or when they'll appear at special events, such as the annual Gay Pride Parade. If you're not proud enough to promenade in front of people, take a class. The Chi-Town twirlers offer all levels in modern and chal-

lenge square dance. If you're not gay or lesbian, don't worry, the Chi-Towners aren't biased about their membership—they'll allemande with anyone. In fact, not being gay or lesbian has an advantage. "They have a lot more fun," says one member. "Our club is a lot more high-energy than a lot of the straight clubs."

CIVIL WAR REENACTMENT

The Grove
1421 Milwaukee Avenue
Glenview, IL 60025
(847) 299-6096
www.glenviewparkdist.org
Map: Suburban North

Once a year a group of avid Civil War aficionados descends on The Grove in Glenview to reenact a battle from that historic conflict, much to the delight of the crowds that come to watch. The participants pitch tents, start campfires, and generally immerse themselves in the glory of being a Union or Confederate soldier. Most bring their own weapons, many of them authentic muskets from the mid-1800s. And the guns aren't the only thing that's period—we saw plenty of carefully groomed whiskers that led us to believe their owners had done some research and shaved accordingly.

As for the battle itself, it is no free-for-all but instead is meticulously choreographed like a daylong pageant, with each soldier playing his part. Everyone strives for realism. When a combatant is "hit," he not only goes down, he often writhes and moans quite convincingly. There's little or no danger of any real casualties occurring, since the guns use only black powder and most shots are fired well over the heads of the enemy as an added precaution. It can get pretty loud, though, with actual cannons adding their roar to the short blasts of the muskets.

After the battle, spectators are guided to the makeshift hospital tent to view the struggle's aftermath. Wounded soldiers plead for help while doctors covered in (fake) blood perform very rudimentary surgeries, often involving mock amputation. For any youthful onlookers who found the battle a stitch, it's only funny 'til somebody loses a limb.

CRITICAL MASS

Daley Plaza
Washington & Dearborn Streets
Chicago
www.chicagocriticalmass.org
Map: Downtown

On the last Friday of every month, an intrepid gathering of bicyclists takes to the streets in order to take *back* the streets from the four wheeled monster. Critical Mass started in San Francisco in 1992 as a way to build awareness of the bicycle as a cleaner and healthier alternative to the automobile. It has since burgeoned into an international phenomenon, with Critical Masses taking place from Toronto to Tel Aviv,

bringing pedaling to the people globally on the same day each month.

The Chicago convergence begins at Daley Plaza at about 5:00 P.M., where anybody with a pedal-powered vehicle is welcome to join the throng. Several possible routes for the hour-long ride are suggested and voted on, at which point the mass becomes mobile. Now, when you have up to three hundred bikes traveling together on public streets, the rules of the road get a little hazy. Stoplights are often ignored for the sake of cohesiveness, and roadways are frequently obstructed to other traffic. This has led to an occasional brush with the law—more than thirty arrests in the Eighteenth Police District alone. And if the Critical Mass masses aim to win over motorists to their gas-free world, their methods sometimes seem to have the opposite effect; there was plenty of honking the day we joined the ride, and we're pretty sure it wasn't meant as encouragement. It didn't put a dent in the convivial attitudes of the riders, though, who chatted amiably with whomever happened to be next to them and waved happily at the grim-faced car and SUV folk. Thus was the uneasy truce between the two-wheeled and four-wheeled maintained—at least until the next month.

G.I. JOE COLLECTORS CLUB

Kevin Bolger
(847) 577-8437
gijoe@core.com

Here's a group of men who are firmly in touch with their inner children. They'd have to be to spend so much time dressing up dolls to show them off, play with them, or trade them. Actually, don't ever call G.I. Joe a doll around these guys or they might pelt you with plastic accessories. No, Ken may be a doll, but G.I. Joe is an "action figure." It was 1964 when Hasbro created the square-jawed hero, and a lot of the club members purchased their first Joe around then. They've apparently been hoarding their toy soldiers ever since: Attend one of the group's periodic get-togethers and you'll see tables and tables of miniature militia, along with their tanks, amphibious jeeps, and other paraphernalia. The plucky G.I.s will often be placed in dangerous scenarios by their owners; in one we witnessed, a band of Navy Seals, their faces blackened for concealment, stormed the beach in an inflatable boat while the enemy awaited them behind a wall of tiny sandbags. Hey, wait a minute . . . those enemy soldiers are G.I. Joes, too! What's going on here?!

Some club members enjoy customizing their action figures, giving one Sean Connery's head, another the body of the Incredible Hulk. Others prefer their G.I. Joe as is, with the manly scar on his right cheek, the dog tag around his neck, and the upside-down thumb. Say what? Yes, apparently Hasbro, as a means of trademarking its creation, gave him a thumb with the nail on the wrong side, which means that while G.I. Joe may not be a pansy like Ken, he is somewhat of a freak.

GREAT LAKES MODEL HORSE CONGRESS

(630) 262-8323
www.greatlakescongress.com
Map: Suburban West

The only way to have a horse show at a Holiday Inn is if the horses are small and plastic. At the Great Lakes Model Horse Congress in Bolingbrook, Illinois, competitors mimic in miniature everything equine—except, of course, the manure. In categories like Western Riding, Cutting/Roping, and Dressage, entries are judged on how close they look to the real thing. A fence post out of place or a bridle askew can be the difference between a blue ribbon and a red flag.

A lot of the mostly women who collect and trade these plastic beauties grew up wanting a living, breathing horse but couldn't afford the money or the hassle. The models are certainly a step down, but they don't buck or bite, and you don't have to feed or clean up after them. That doesn't mean there's not a lot of time and effort that goes into this hobby. Hours and hours (and dollars and dollars) are spent customizing the store-bought models to make them life-like. Then there's the accessorizing, finding just the right saddle or boots for the horse, the right garb for its rider.

Entrants are also responsible for constructing the scenario that will serve as the backdrop for their stallion or mare, such as an obstacle on a steeplechase course or a babbling brook in the countryside. With all this preparation, it's easy to understand some of the overzealous behavior displayed at the Congress. We overheard comments like "She's trotting quite nicely," and "That horse is shying from that bridge!" Unfortunately, our helpful reminder that *"they're only plastic"* was greeted with some very icy stares.

INKIN' LINCOLN TATTOO & PIERCING JAMBOREE
Freebird
(630) 552-3465
www.tattooshow.com

There are those who consider the body not a temple, but a canvas, fit to be dyed. Once a year they descend on a suburban hotel for the Inkin' Lincoln Tattoo Jamboree. Imagine, if you will, tattooing booths as far as the eye can see, filling several huge banquet halls; that gives you some idea of what organizers "Freebird" and "Booger" hath wrought. People come from all over Illinois to either get a new tattoo or show off the ones they've already got. Contests are held in categories such as "Mythical," "Floral," and "Extra Large." The year we attended, the winner of the "Extensive" category was actually covered from neck to toe with tattoos (we'd call that "Very Extensive"!), and he told us it took three hours every week *for five and a half years* to complete. Our favorite category was "Likeness," in which contestants have to bring in photos of the people pictured on their flesh so that they can be judged for accuracy. We saw the Three Stooges on an arm, Vivian Leigh on a shoulder, and a self-portrait adorning a belly (no picture

required). One woman even had her whole family tree pictured on her thigh. Now there's a conversation starter!

Wander around the jamboree and you'll witness numerous tattoos in progress, as well as the occasional piercing. Hey, as long as you're beautifying your body with art, why not decorate it with some hardware? There was one woman sporting jewelry on tongue, lip, and bridge of nose, and she assured us her nipples and nether regions would also set off a metal detector. It seems that both piercings and tattoos are like potato chips—you can't stop with just one!

INVENTOR BEN SKORA

ben@adamflowers.com

If Rube Goldberg and Thomas Edison had had a child together, it would have been (besides a big headline in the *National Enquirer*) Ben Skora. This inventor has spent more than thirty years outfitting his home with electric doodads designed to stun, startle, and amuse. From wheel-mounted chairs capable of cutting figure eights to an electrified store mannequin, this house is wired for wonderment. Want to freshen your drink while on the patio? No problem. Press a button and both you and the patio revolve inside while the living room comes outside. The bathroom is a magnet for his creativity. A vertically retracting shower curtain, soap "handed" to you from a hidden arm, and a toilet—wait, where *is* the toilet? A huge flowerpot reveals the concealed commode. And all of these delightful devices are run by relays, receivers, and remotes. Though he never studied to be a whimsical engineer, Ben says the knack for electronics "sort of comes to me; I really believe it's from another incarnation." Take a tour of his house and you'll be greeted by AROK the robot. AROK is Ben's automaton emissary. He's allowed to leave the animated abode and make appearances at museums and mall openings. Why, he has even carried a bride down the aisle. If you have an idea for a commission or want AROK to give you away—maximum bride load 115 pounds—give Ben a buzz, or a jolt, or push a button, or, geez, just grab a remote and press.

KLINGON ARMADA INTERNATIONAL

www.klingonarmadainternational.org

We all know about those avid *Star Trek* enthusiasts known as "trekkies." Well, it turns out that there is a subset of this gung-ho group that has devoted itself exclusively to the enemy camp. They're called the Klingon Armada International, and they take their alternate world very seriously. If you attend a meeting, you will see them dressed in full Klingon regalia and hear them addressing each other by their official Klingon names ("Karza Torg, I want you to meet Captain Tosach Sutei Nuack"). There are actually two types of Klingons coexisting peacefully within the armada: The "Next Generation" version, based on the *Next Generation Star Trek* series, has long flowing locks and what looks like a mountain range of lumps along their forehead, and the "classic Klingon," based on the original 1960s TV show, looks pretty much like a human, only with large, funky eyebrows.

The Chicago chapter of these kooky curmudgeons meets regularly and will often appear at various fund-raisers and community events. We crossed paths with them at the Villa Park Public Library, where they held a makeup demonstration and a trivia contest—who knew that Klingons eat live worms for dinner and value chocolate as an aphrodisiac? It's really cool when they start talking in the guttural language of their adopted planet, which we can't hope to re-create here, other than to wish our readers well with a hearty "Kaplah!"

LANAHOLICS

www.lanaholics.com

"Hello, I'm Steve."

"Hello, Steve."

"And I am a lanaholic."

This is a true story. His name has not been changed to protect his innocent pursuit of the fastest network connection. Steve's drug of choice is the multiplayer computer game—fifty to sixty gamers playing at the same server connection speed. To achieve his maxi-mbps (megabytes per second) fix, Steve and fellow 'holic Wally—yes, they met on the Internet—organize a LAN (local area network) party for a weekend of gaming. Every six weeks, gamers gather their sleeping bags, computers, and caffeinated drinks and settle in for a serious frag fest (*Frag,* in the gaming argot, means "kill"). The games played here are on the first-person shooter order, so, leave the *Pokémon* at home. You're probably wondering why you should sit next to someone for forty-eight hours who's probably not bathing. Well, in gaming, the faster the network connection, or *ping,* the quicker your reaction time, or your ability to annihilate your opponent. With a LAN, the network is a few feet of cable away from your PC, giving you a jackrabbit ping of 5 or 6. Play at home over a dial-up modem and your ping will be around 300. (Whoa, that's deader than Ping Crosby.) Plus, a LAN party offers you the chance to meet the players you've only known by their screen noms de guerre. A virtual community turns into a real community. And isn't it always nicer to see the face of the person you're fragging? If you lust for less lag time and wish to lay waste with your Luger, then pack a power strip, breath mints, and a thirst to conquer the continents.

MIDWEST MODEL T FORD CLUB

www.modelt.org/midwest

You know about a chop shop, where they take a car apart? This antique car club does it in reverse. They set up shop, put the parts together, and do it chop-chop. These Model T collectors perform their "Take-A-Part Car" event in competition and for exhibition. Five guys take the guts of a Model T—frame, motor, tank, axles, etc.—and try to assemble and drive it off in the quickest time. The contest started as a commemorative to Ford's invention of the assembly line to produce autos like the Model T and Model A. (Henry Ford: clever with building, not so hot with naming.) The current world record of one minute and twelve seconds is held by the fast

flivver fixers of the Midwest Chapter. To find out how you can witness this moment of manic manpower, or to request the group's participation at one of your events, drive to its Web site. There you can learn about the club and upcoming activities. Come to the annual Breakfast Run in June or Parts Swap in September, and you'll find a park dotted with black cars, like poppy seeds on a bun. Ford was the man who said, "The customer can have any color he wants, so long as it's black." (Henry Ford: an ocean of ideas, a wet rag with color.) You won't need to own one of these jet jalopies to join the club, all other cars are acceptable as long as they're collectible. And, if you decide to buy a Model T? "Don't," advises one member, "they're addictive." You can get a metal monkey on your back for as little as $1,500. 'Course, it'll probably take you more than 1:12 to restore it.

MODEL A FORD CLUB MANIFOLD COOKING

Salt Creek Chapter
www.mafca.com
modela_m38_jim@msn.com
Map: Suburban West

Come to this car club's annual picnic, where the preparation takes seventy years—not the food but the Ford it's prepared on. The Salt Creek charioteers drive to their outing in Model A's with their meals cooking on the manifold. With the food foil-wrapped and strapped to the pipe, this culinary caravan travels out, stopping halfway to flip the fricassee. Don't ask about cooking temperature, ask about how many miles per hour. These 4-cylinder, 40-horsepower Webers-on-Wheels sputter along at around 20 mph. A two-hour trip is enough to prepare decidedly offbeat fare: Pothole Burgers, Asphalt Fritters, Roadkill Stew, even Franks on the 'Fold.

There are a few drawbacks to Model A menu making. The food occasionally gets burned (hey, just like home), and placing the foil too close to the

spark plugs will short out the car and give you a nice jolt, too. A real thrill grill. Whereas the food may turn out toasted, the cars look terrific when the owners drive them in and line them all up in a row, just like cakes at the county fair. The group is very talkative—there's a lot of history in a seventy-year-old car—and you can learn all about Henry Ford's metallic marvels. The club members might even ask you to partake in their movable feast.

So, the next time you're looking for good food around the 'hood, try looking *under* the hood. Don't knock it till you drive it.

MOUNTAIN BUILDER JOHN VAN BARRIGER

Route 30
Big Rock, IL 60511
Map: Suburban West

There just aren't that many mountains in our neck of the woods, and to John Van Barriger that seemed like a pretty good reason to build his own. "I've been trying to get out west and never made it," he told us, "so I decided to bring the West here." Mount Barriger (John claims a neighbor gave it its name) majestically sits at the edge of John's thirty-two-acre property in Big Rock, Illinois, about a hundred yards away from the putting green he's working on. From a distance it doesn't look like much more than a small hill, but up close, with the 50-foot precipice looming over you, it makes quite an impression. The mountain consists of bricks, stone, and sand reinforced by rebar metal and stabilized by a wire mesh, with the final layer being sculpted cement. The crest is dotted with various

types of man-made cacti, and there are several rock formations evident that are almost worthy of Monument Valley. He even has a "gorge" that runs between the two highest peaks—though he insists it's not called Barriger Gorge.

John faced some stiff opposition from local bureaucrats when he started to build his Western landscape. Apparently, his property wasn't zoned for a man-made mountain, and they insisted he needed a permit. But John stubbornly faced down the paper-pushing varmints, and his mountain became, to his mind, a testament to freedom and the American way. Now those of us who yearn for a taste of the West can find it in our own backyard—well, actually it's Barriger's backyard, but you get the point.

 # BEHIND THE SCENES

We're not sure if John Van Barriger ever finished his putting-green-in-progress, but we did hear that since our visit he has built *another mountain*. The new one is called Mount Derick after John's grandson ("Barriger II" was apparently never considered), and it features a formation that John calls Turtlehead Rock. And there's more: atop Turtlehead Rock sits Van Barriger's version of an Indian chief named, appropriately, Chief Turtlehead.

Our question is, how many more mountains will the Man from Big Rock have to build before it qualifies as a range?

MUSHROOM HUNTERS
Illinois Mycological Association
(847) 432-8255
www.ilmyco.gen.chicago.il.us

Don't be fooled by their gentle exterior. The mushroom hunters must be fearless in the face of possibly poisonous fungi and the constant challenge of finding their way back to the car. The Illinois Mycological Association (IMA) has been proving that there is "fungus among us" since the mid-1970s. That's when the club members began their forays into Chicagoland's many wooded areas in search of their sometimes elusive prey. Many of their finds will wind up in the members' kitchens as part of some tasty dish, while other more rare varieties will be diverted to the Field Museum's collection. That's because the Field's Greg Mueller is the IMA's scientific adviser and usually accompanies them on their excursions.

He's able to identify some of the more obscure mushrooms and prevent any igno-rant 'shroomers from eating the wrong ones and taking a premature dirt nap.

Yes, make no mistake, this is a potentially fatal hobby if you munch on the wrong mush. As Mueller is fond of saying, "You'll meet old mushroom hunters and bold mushroom hunters, but never old, bold mushroom hunters." There are between fifteen and twenty thousand mycological species world-wide, over a thousand in Chicago alone, and the FMA has discovered a few that have never been seen *anywhere* else before. Even the more common species have some excellent nicknames, like the black Dead Man's Finger, the glow-in-the-dark Jack-o-Lantern, the Hen of the Woods (good for soup!), and the Puffball, which when squeezed shoots out a cloud of spores. *Danger:* the spores can cause an asthmatic reaction, yet another looming threat to these intrepid fungus foragers.

NAKUPUNA UKULELE CLUB
Japanese American Service Center
4427 North Clark Street
Chicago, IL 60640
(773) 275-7212
Map: Chicago North

*N*aKupuna means "elder" or "senior citizen" in Hawaiian, which is fairly descriptive of this particular ukulele club. The median age of the members is around sixty-five, and they rehearse at the Jap-anese American Service Center—did we mention that 90 percent of the club is Japanese American? Apparently Hawaiian music is huge back in Japan (there are approximately 10,000 hula schools there), so you could say that these NaKupunans, strumming "Tiny Bubbles" in their Hawaiian shirts and leis, were an inevitability. It didn't seem that way in 1997, though, when none of these folks had even touched a uke. Then someone happened

to bring one to the center one day, and it looked like such a hoot that soon nearly everyone had a pint-sized four-string. The club took shape after the strummers found a Hawaiian ukulele instructor and began learning the subtleties of their instruments, and it was only a matter of time before they added singing to the strumming. Although they don't understand many of the Hawaiian words coming out of their own mouths, it doesn't prevent them from vocalizing with gusto.

The NaKupuna Club is now about fifty members strong, and they've performed all over Chicagoland and as far away as Washington, D.C. They've long since discarded their cheap, plastic ukuleles (which they called "Taiwan Specials") in favor of the wooden variety. Their instructor told us that they're as good as any uke group from the islands, so save that airfare to Oahu and catch one of the NaKupunans' concerts. If you know how to hula, bring your grass skirt!

NATIONAL WOODIE CLUB

Lincoln Log Riders, Midwest Chapter
www.nationalwoodieclub.com
Map: Suburban West

If you like your women high maintenance and on the older side, then attend this pageant of wood-clad, mid-century beauties at their annual picnic. More than thirty owner-members pack a wooden basket *and* a car to match when they convene at their Log Jam. You'll find Buicks, Fords, and Chryslers, all with their hoods up and their trunks down, ready for your inspection and interest, from the top-of-the-line 1948 Chrysler Town and Country (nicknamed the Land Yacht) to a street-rod Woodie, where

the engine's been upgraded. There are plenty of "in progress" cars, as well—old Jan-and-Dean–type surfer wagons that'll cost more than a song to restore.

You'll find many owners have multiple Woodies, but of course they always remember their first Woodie. The wood is ash and mahogany, though those made by Ford used maple because Henry Ford owned acres of it up in Michigan's Upper Peninsula. It's a good thing these guys love playing with their Woodies 'cause this wood takes work. It needs constant varnishing and checking for woodborers. It'll help if you're more carpenter than mechanic. And though the originals can get up to 90 or 100 mph, with no air bags or seat belts, if you get into a wreck, you'll be, as one owner said, "picking toothpicks out of your butt."

Of the many pleasures of having one of these maple-and-mahogany madeleines, the sweetest one, owners say, is seeing complete strangers smile and wave when they whip out their Woodie.

PARAMOUNT TALL CLUB

P.O. Box 661182
Chicago, IL 60666-1182
(312) 853-0183
www.tallclubchicago.org

Imagine a life where every single day you are asked, "How's the weather up there?" A life where, day in and day out, you must endlessly repeat to complete strangers, "No, I *didn't* buy my shoes at a boat shop." Solely because you are of above-average height, yours is a life where you were never a cheerleader, never asked to dance, and always accused of being too big to be out trick-or-treating. When life is short and you're not, what do you do? Well, you find other vertically endowed people, form a club, and start acting like teenagers. The Paramount Tall Club is into serious socializing. They like to say "Activities are the lifeblood of Paramount," and they're pumping the plasma with parties, picnics, dances, happy hours, and kaffeeklatsches. They meet once a month to discuss their social calendar and to introduce new members—they have to introduce the new members because they don't stand out in this crowd. The remaining twenty-nine or thirty days of the month, this elevated group is going off to concerts, attending the theater, canoeing, camping, bowling, and playing volleyball. To join, you must be at least twenty-one years of age and meet the height requirements of 6 feet, 2 inches for men or 5 feet, 10 inches for women, in your stocking feet, of course. If you're a small fry, don't cry, you can still join their obelisk outings. Just grab a tall person by the, let's see, thigh, and make them bring you. But if you go, a word of warning: Don't call anybody "Stretch" or "Tall Drink of Water" or "Amazon" or "Mastodon," and never, ever ask, "When did you get that tall?"

PUG CRAWL

www.pugparty.com
Map: Chicago North

You might want to lie doggo at this event unless you own one of the wrinkle-faced, short-bodied, curly-tailed canines called pugs. Two to three times a year, Midwest pug owners will meet on the street and dogleg it from bar to bar for some socializing and marking of territory. (Who you calling pug-nosed, you mangy mutt!) There is a dress code—no, not for people, for the pugs. The dogs are draped with scarves, jewelry, and hats; some curs are even costumed to resemble celebrities. And while *you're* allowed to beat your dogs (i.e., your feet), you won't find many owners letting their dog pound the

pavement. Most are carried or conveyed in carriages, strollers, or well-festooned wagons. Ahh, a dog's life.

This pooch procession is breeding. The Pug Crawl started with just a couple of pugs showing up, but now there are over two hundred. We hope they'll bring plenty of plastic bags. Check the Web site for upcoming dog days and to submit a pinup of your precious pug for their pictorial. Concerning this puppy parade, let me leave you with this bit of doggerel: "Put on the dog and go to the dogs, it's a whelping good time."

SINGLE GOURMET

2920 West Grand, Suite 100
Chicago, IL 60622
(773) 772-3535
www.singlegourmetchicago.com
Map: Chicago West

We know you. You work hard. In fact, you live for your job. You spend so much time there, the nighttime cleaning crew knows you snore. A social life? Ha! When was the last time you went out? Been a while? Like, what, are we talking geologic time? Well, get out of the Pleistocene and into the pleasure scene when you join the Single Gourmet dining club. Once or twice a week, including weekends, they get a singular selection of fifty or so people together at a different restaurant. The evenings are arranged to provide general mixing and small-group conversation. The club insists it's not a dating service but merely a "nonthreatening" way to meet new people and enjoy fine dining. We insist that when you get fifty singles together for a night of food and drink, there's bound to be a little romance over the romaine. Sure enough, the club says there's a handful of marriages every year. The Single Gourmet is open to all, and the average age is between thirty and fifty. If your social life's a desert, why not join them for a dessert? What have you got to lose? As Maya Angelou said, "Life is a glorious banquet." Graze with this group and you know you'll be served a delectable buffet, meet a smorgasbord of people and, perhaps, have a feast of flirting. And your tablemates might even let you talk about work.

SOCIETY FOR CREATIVE ANACHRONISM

Shire of Grey Gargoyles
www.sca.org, www.midrealm.org
Map: Chicago South

They say you shouldn't live in the past, but don't tell that to the lords and ladies of the Society for Creative Anachronism, especially the ones with broadswords. The society is devoted to re-creating the world of the Middle

Ages (except, of course, for the plague), and they're impressively thorough. Attend one of their gatherings and you'll find people in period dress going by names like "Sir

Johnathan the Ospry" involved in every medieval activity under the sun: woodworking, sewing, calligraphy, madrigals singing, group dancing (great way to meet medieval chicks), and of course, plenty of ale-drinking.

Our favorite part of the festivities was the fighting, and we don't mean over who gets the last ale. Using blunted rapiers, broadswords, axes, and any other weapon common to the time, the combatants engage in surprisingly brutal "fights to the death," death being a head or body shot. Take a blow to the arm and you must pretend to have lost the arm, just as a blow to the leg brings you to your knees. As a spectator, we couldn't help but be reminded of the beleaguered knight in *Monty Python and the Holy Grail*, down to just a torso but still battling.

So whether you decide to join as a member or simply attend as an onlooker, the Society for Creative Anachronism provides a pleasant diversion from the twenty-first century. You may even find yourself wishing that you could live back in the Middle Ages when times were simpler and the cleavage barer. Most of us, however, will stick with plumbing.

SQUIRREL LOVER'S CLUB

318 West Fremont Avenue
Elmhurst, IL 60126
(630) 833-1117
www.thesquirreloversclub.com
Map: Suburban West

The title says it all, you nut! These are people proud to proclaim their unabashed affection for the noble rodent. They'll spend hours watching the frisky antics of these bushy-tailed rascals, give book reports on squirrelly themed literature, dream about *Rocky*

& Bullwinkle film fests. Founder Gregg Bassett has trained his wild backyard buddies to hotfoot it up his leg and take food out of his mouth. He gives them names, does impressions, and has a license plate that reads SQRL NUT. This Saint Francis of the furball has such an affinity for squirrels that club members

"swear Gregg wears peanut butter aftershave." If you want to share your adoration for these arboreal imps, then join the other nutcases by becoming a member of the Squirrel Lover's Club. The members take field trips to squirrel-saturated areas, and you'll receive copies of "In A Nutshell," their bimonthly newsletter. (They'd probably publish more often, but they forget where they bury them.) If you're not quite ready to make a pilgrimage to Frostbite Falls, Minnesota, at least become more aware of the squirrels in your neighborhood. Y'see, you, or rather your car, is a squirrel's number one unnatural predator. The club wishes to remind you that squirrels also travel down our streets but "they don't have crossing guards." The good news is that the SLC has a large network of vets and rehab hospitals, just in case you do flatten one of these pelted pixies with your Ford.

STITCH 'N' BITCH
www.stitchnbitch.org

Every Tuesday night a group of determined women do their best to bring the art of knitting and kvetching bravely into the twenty-first century. They call themselves Stitch 'n' Bitch, and their meeting place is usually a cozy north side coffeehouse. (Location varies—check Web site). Their queen bee is Brenda, who, after many nights in her living room knitting alone, decided to search out some kindred spirits. One e-mail later and Stitch 'n' Bitch was born, with 130 members and their own logo.

Not everybody shows up each week, but the sampling we met was certainly a lively bunch and represented all levels of knitting expertise. We saw hats, scarves, and crocheted bikinis being stitched, and as for the bitching, the most common topic was (surprise!) men. One member warned her fellow bitchers to never knit a long-sleeved sweater for someone you're dating: "It will inevitably end up sleeveless when the relationship is finished before the sweater."

THINK SMALL BY ROSEBUD DOLLHOUSES

3209 North Clark Street
Chicago, IL 60657
(773) 477-1920
thinksmallrose@aol.com
Map: Chicago North

If you have château taste in housing but a bungalow budget, forget the mortgage and buy or build your dream house at Rosebud. The only catch is you'll have to duck your head to get into it. Think Small is a miniature-dollhouse store and workshop. Design and build your own little lodge in their not-so-miniature basement. They have everything you need: saws, drills, paint, and guidance. They even have an on-site electrician to wire your new compact Colonial. And you'll meet plenty of new neighbors down there; at any given time you'll find more than forty people—

moms, dads, and kids—working on *their* scale-model mansions. Which means you'll have to keep up with forty other "Joneses."

If you don't have time to build your own petite palace—some spend years on them—Think Small offers a selection of completed dwarfed dwellings. Already have a dollhouse? Why not rehab your miniscule manse with something from their extensive line of decorations and furniture? Chaises, Chippendale chairs, and Swarovski crystal chandeliers will add the finishing touches to your tiny Tudor (son of four-door and wagon). Don't forget to raid their larder of faux food miniatures; set your teeny table with turkey and all the trimmings. The best part is no calories, ahhh. At Rosebud, unlike the namesake sled, you *can* go home again. And again and again and again.

VALLEY VIEW MODEL RAILROAD

Ted Voss
17108 Highbridge Road
Union, IL 60180
(815) 923-4135
Map: Suburban North

Ted Voss is a modern George Pullman. He owns and operates everything in this town. The transportation, the people, the pigeons. You could say he built it . . . 'cause he did. In the hayloft of his converted barn, Mr. Voss has constructed the largest privately owned model railroad in northern Illinois. His engineered empire is a re-creation of the Chicago & Northwestern line from the northwest suburbs to downtown Chicago. It's a twenty-two-train, two-level layout that transits over 9 scale miles of track and takes 10,000 feet of wire to juice. What really separates Trainman Ted's diminutive domain from other model railroads is the detailing. The Lilliputian Loop has auto traffic, pedestrians, signage, even smoke emanating from factory stacks.  Look anywhere in his miniature model of our world and you'll see scenes mimicking daily life: firefighters responding to a burning building, meat packers preparing cattle carcasses, a cop pulling over a motorist—yep, just like scenes from daily life. And it's all open. This petite Pleasantville isn't covered in Plexiglas; you can get close enough to see the rust painted on the sides of the track or the dirt smudging the hobo's coat. Like Mussolini, the trains run on time—Ted's time. If you can't make it to the station during his slender business hours, Mr. Voss will accommodate groups during off-hours and off-seasons. For larger loads of locomotive action, drive down the street and visit the Illinois Railway Museum.

WHEATON COMMUNITY RADIO AMATEURS

(630) 924-1600
www.qsl.net/wcra
Map: Suburban West

They're just hams—ham operators, that is, and you can watch them showing off their abilities during the country's largest annual radio event. On Field Day, local clubs like Wheaton's will test their capacity to set up emergency communication equipment in case of a disaster. They'll commandeer a local park, pitch their tents, and for a period of twenty-four hours try to contact as many hams as they can from around the nation. How important is this exercise? In  1990, more than two hundred Chicago-area hams were called in to keep the information flowing during the Plainfield tornado. (And you thought ham operators only stayed in their basements "rag chewing" with somebody from Butte.)

The Wheaton club also helps people who want to train for this high-tech hobby. Starting off is relatively affordable. You can get a nice setup for your workbench or dining room table for around $200. If you study for your license, then you can legitimately spend as many hours as you want in the basement talking to people in Montana because you'll be a hero in waiting. Plus, you'll get to drive around with those snazzy HAM OPERATOR license plates. At the very least, come out and see the radio amateurs on Field Day. It *is* the one day of the year these guys get out of the house.

WHIZZERS CLUB
Ray Spangler
(847) 891-4716

It used to be kids could attach a motor kit to their bicycles and have something called a Whizzer, and though the company stopped production fifty years ago, there is a small group of hardcore Whizzerheads who keep the dream alive. They've formed a club that gets together periodically to drive down country roads in a pack and roar through small towns. Rarely do they strike fear into the local populace, however, since forty middle-aged guys on bicycles are not exactly Marlon Brando and the Wild Ones.

The Whizzer first came into use in 1938, and its heyday was during World War II. Back then they went for around $250, but now these rare antiques can fetch about $4,000. The kit's engine nestles between the two wheels of a bike, and the accelerator is on one of the handles. You pedal to get started, and when the engine turns over, you can coast at speeds of up to 40 mph (downhill, soaking wet). There are about a thousand Whizzer owners nationwide, and approximately four hundred of them belong to the Whizzer Club. These motorized maniacs are clearly filled with nostalgia for the days when they defied their mothers' wishes by turning their bicycles into speed machines. If you have a sentimental streak for a Whizzer from your own childhood or simply relish the idea of riding in a pack, we encourage you to take a "whiz."

YASUKUNAI BONSAI GARDEN
6061 Dempster Street
Morton Grove, IL 60053
(847) 966-5142
Map: Suburban North

Bonsai means "tray grow," and you'll be tres chic if you dig with these doyens of dirt at Yasukunai, Chicago's only full-service bonsai shop. The idea behind bonsai (pronounced "bone-sigh") is to create, through pruning and wiring, the ideal tree in miniature. If disciplining a dwarf sounds good to you, then sign up for a class. Ivan Watters, proprietor of Yasukunai (which translates as "not cheap or shoddy") can teach you the art of trimming and bracing the branches of junipers, spruces, and elms. Like braces for teeth, this arboreal orthodontia takes time. One student told us she was looking at three to five years to grow her bonsai to cascade correctly. Bonsai not only teaches you patience, but it also relieves stress. Ivan adds, "It's a great hobby if you're a control freak." Though it takes years to see results, bonsai need daily maintenance. They have to be watered often. "They're like kids, you can't neglect them," Ivan says. "The big difference, kids leave home when they grow up. The bonsai never grow up." If you own a pint-sized pine, or other bonsai, Yasukunai offers a boarding greenhouse. And, if you don't think you have the time it takes to torture topiary, then buy one here. Like Yasukunai's name, bonsai is not cheap. The prices—up over $1,000— reflect generational tending and artistry; these trees can live hundreds of years.

Come to Yasukunai just to look at the display. You won't find such a concentration anywhere else. This horticultural haven might even inspire you to answer the sylvan siren's call and take up the reflective art of bonsai.

MORE MAGNIFICENT OBSESSIONS

CHICAGO SCOOTER RALLIES
www.2strokebuzz.com
Originators of Death Scoot 2000 and other small-scooter rallies.

HOVERCRAFTING
Goldstein Hovercraft, LLC
www.gohover.com,
www.chicagohovercraft.com
Travel on a bed of air over land and water.

INTERNATIONAL TAROT SOCIETY
P. O. Box 1475
Morton Grove, IL 60053
(847) 965-9916
www.tarotsociety.org
World Tarot Congress (always held in Chicago area); annual get-together of tarot card enthusiasts.

LEAPING LESBIANS
www.leapinglesbians.org
Women's skydiving club.

MICROCAR AND MINICAR CLUB
(630) MICRO-CA(R)
www.microcar.org
Car collectors who like their autos tiny but drivable.

NORTHWEST TURNERS BINGO
6625 West Belmont Avenue
Chicago, IL 60634
(773) 777-9290
Map: Chicago West
Thousands of dollars awarded at these weekly Wednesday night bingo games.

PSYCHOTRONIC FILM SOCIETY

www.psychotronic.com
B-movie and cult classic worshipers.

REVOLUTIONARY WAR REENACTORS

Northwest Territory Alliance
www.nwta.com
*Re-creating battles and culture of
the American Revolution,
1775–1783.*

"UFO GUY" CHESTER TUSZYNSKI

Universe-O' System
P. O. Box 205
Rensselaer, IN 47978
(219) 866-3828
*Amateur inventor (of a flying saucer)
and published author.*

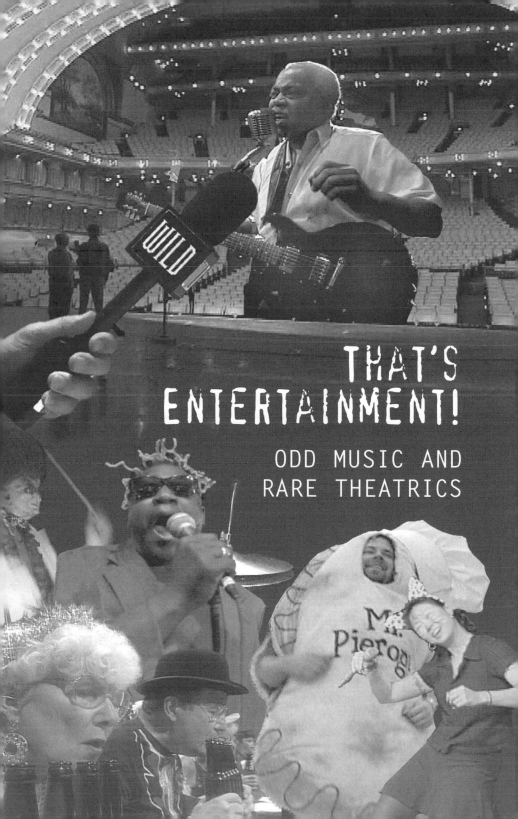

THAT'S ENTERTAINMENT!

ODD MUSIC AND RARE THEATRICS

BABY DOLL POLKA CLUB

6102 South Central Avenue
Chicago, IL 60638
(773) 582-9706 Baby Doll
(773) 586-3719 Eddie Korosa
and the Boys from Illinois
ekbabydoll@aol.com
Map: Chicago South

You certainly don't have to be Polish to enjoy the polka, and if you've got a pulse you're going to love the Baby Doll, where bouncy music and fancy dancing combine to make this one of the most convivial spots in town. Its location right across the street from Midway Airport sometimes proves challenging, but no amount of airplane noise can drown out this music, or the forty pairs of feet doing the Polish hop. And if you don't dance, just sit back and watch the wide variety of polka proficiency on display, from the deadly earnest couples who don't miss a step to the inebriated neophytes just trying not to injure themselves.

It's more fun when there's a live band (and thus a bigger crowd), so it might be a good idea to call ahead to find out if there's one playing. Whatever night you go, we guarantee your mood will be elevated. As the saying goes, "Polka music is happiness."

BIG C JAMBOREE

Martyrs'
3855 North Lincoln Avenue
Chicago, IL 60613
(773) 404-9494
www.martyrslive.com
Map: Chicago North

Rockabilly isn't just a type of music, man, it's a way of life, at least for its purveyors and fans. If you want proof, just walk into Martyrs' on the first Thursday of any month. That's when the Big C Jamboree takes over this North Side bar and shakes, rattles, or rolls anyone in the vicinity. The first thing you'll notice is the hair—pompadours and sideburns for the men, plenty of Aqua Net on many of the women. Then check out the threads: sharkskin suits and vintage bowling shirts, poodle skirts, and angora sweaters; these folks know how to dress! As for the music, think Elvis during his early Sun Records years, played by a roster of bands with names like the Venus Flycats, the Moondogs, and HiFi and the Roadrunners. Of the occasional girl bands, we're always partial to the Menstruators.

There's always a featured group, but mostly it's an open mike—guitars and attitudes welcome. And that rockabilly music has such an infectious, impulsive sound, even the most dance-shy couples will be forced to swivel a hip.

BLUES MUSICIAN JIMMY BURNS

www.delmark.com

Jimmy Burns was born in the Mississippi Delta in 1943, the youngest of eleven children, and his first instrument was a broom wire that he nailed to the wall and played with a bottle. He was raised on the blues, but it was singing with a doo-wop group called the Medallionaires in Chicago (where he'd moved at age twelve) that got his musical career started in earnest. After that, Burns made the transition into singing soul and R&B as a solo recording artist, and it wasn't until he was in his forties, after an extended hiatus to open a barbecue joint, that he returned to his first love, the blues. Since then he has been playing and singing it with a vengeance, mixing his original songs with covers. He has long since

graduated from one string to six, and he plays a mean harmonica as well. But it's that sweet voice of his that really enables Jimmy's music to get under your skin and why his first blues CD, *Leave Here Walking*, won Independent Record of the Year from the Association for Independent Music.

Burns is backed by a tight band and these days can be found playing blues clubs as close as North Halsted Street and as far away as Tokyo, Japan. He still manages to run the west-side barbecue place he calls Uncle Mickey's (why it's not Uncle Jimmy's is a mystery to us) and promises that he'll keep playing his music "till the good Lord calls me." Here's hoping the line is busy for a long time.

CHIC-A-GO-GO

Chicago Access Network Television
Channel 19
Studios at 322 South Green Street
Chicago, IL 60607
www.cantv.org, www.roctober.com
Map: Chicago West

It's a rare thing when one TV show recommends that you watch another, but that is just what's about to happen! *Chic-A-Go-Go* is a locally produced dance party that airs on Chicago's Cable Access Channel 19 at 8:30 P.M. Tuesday and 3:30 P.M. Wednesday. Its two hosts, a spunky rock drummer named Miss Mia and a wisecracking rat puppet predictably named Ratso, are delightfully underrehearsed and surrounded by a

group of volunteer dancers who are gleefully untrained. There are also appearances
by local bands, who lip-synch their lyrics
and pretend to play their instruments. And
not just any local bands—*Chic-A-Go-Go* is a
magnet for a weird array of musicians, with
names like Velcro Lewis and His 100 Proof
Band and Gravy Train.

The whole shebang is run by creators
Jackie Stuart and her husband, Jake Austin
(who doubles as the puppeteer and voice of
Ratso). They manage to keep things fluid
and upbeat with segments like the Fantasy
Dance, where the dancers take turns
gyrating in front of a music video projected

onto a huge screen. It all makes for some entertaining viewing, but if you want
to do more than just watch, you're welcome to come down to the studio and
become part of the show (all ages welcome). Check the Web site on when to
show up, and then just go-go.

FILMMAKER DAVID "THE ROCK" NELSON
www.psychotronic.com

Film director David "The Rock"
Nelson has been called "the Ed Wood
of the '90s" and indeed, he actually managed to snag one of Wood's former actors,
Conrad Brooks of *Plan Nine from Outer
Space*, for one of his own movies
(*Frankenstein vs. Dracula*). "The Rock" gives new meaning to the term *low-budget*,
using himself and his friends as actors and keeping the special effects very rudimentary—you *will* believe your eyes when a flapping bat on a string instantly trans-
forms into Nelson as Dracula, frantically flapping his cape. He often uses his parents'
yard for the set, and the costumes look like they came from a bad Halloween party.

The films (actually shot on video) have such memorable names as *Devil
Ant, Werewolf's Revenge,* and *Dinosaur Woman* (Nelson's version of *Jurassic
Park,* complete with an obviously Styrofoam egg). Despite critics calling his cin-
ematic efforts "garbage," Nelson vows to keep cranking them out, and we certainly hope he does. With their convoluted plots, ripe dialogue, and

preposterous performances, these are, in our opinion, some of the most entertaining movies in existence. Show one at your next party and we guarantee it will be the hit of the night. And as for whether David Nelson is in on the joke, that may forever remain a mystery.

FREE ASSOCIATES THEATRE COMPANY

Royal George Theatre Center
1641 North Halsted Street
Chicago, IL 60614
(312) 255-1674 office
(312) 988-9000 box office
www.thefreeassociates.com
Map: Chicago North

Chicago has been a hotbed of improvisational comedy since Second City opened its doors in the 1960s, and these days it seems like every week a new improv show is opening at a theater near you. Just when it seems that nothing new can be done with the art of taking audience suggestions and making something up, along comes a company like the Free Associates to give it an inventive new twist. The group improvises full-length plays based on famous literature, movies, and TV shows. Maybe you've heard some of their memorable titles: *As We Like It* (their Shakespeare takeoff), *Alfred Hitchcock Resents*, *Blithering Heights*, or *Charlie and the Fiction Factory*. Their detective-novel spoof let the audience choose among such heroes as Nancy Drew and Phillip Marlowe for that night's detective and was mischievously called *Pick a Dick*.

It all started back in 1991 when founder Mark Gagné came up with the idea for an improvised Tennessee Williams play; *Cast and a Hot Tin Roof* ended up running for six years and is an annual hit at the Tennessee Williams/New Orleans Literary Festival. The Free Associates have since racked up 2,500 performances of their various takeoffs for an estimated 125,000 people (their popular *ER* spoof *BS* recently celebrated its one-thousandth episode). For each show the cast studies up on the subject matter either by reading the author or playwright or by watching a particular film genre or TV series. When you see the result of all that homework, you may be tempted to think it's pre-scripted. Nope, it's Free Association!

HARVEY FINKLESTEIN'S INSTITUTE OF WHIMSICAL, FANTASTICAL, AND MARVELOUS PUPPET MASTERAGE

(312) 458-9135
www.harveyfinklestein.com
Map: Chicago North

Ishtar, Battlefield Earth, Heaven's Gate. In an orchard abundant with bad films, which one is ripe enough for parody? If you're this puppet troupe, you choose the over-ripe and early-rotted *Showgirls,* Paul Verhoeven's 1995 movie about Las Vegas dancers. Harvey Finkle-stein's Institute has mercifully con-densed the film's original running time of 131 minutes down to 30. But they didn't hack away at any of the things that made the movie infamous. There's still plenty of the film's rank dialogue and endless nudity. Not that you'll see nudity, per se, onstage. These are puppets, after all, sock puppets—long, white tube socks that have undergone sox-surgery to display breasts the size of parade floats. (Don't plan on bringing any of the little Buster Browns in your family to this show.) You can increase your enjoyment of the play if you view the film beforehand. As with all parodies, the audience should have a base knowledge of the material—or is that a knowledge of the base material? We're only sorry for the embarrassment you'll risk by requesting *Showgirls* at your neighborhood Blockbuster. The puppet show has legs—and feet—and could become a long-running hit. If it's closed by the time you read this, however, no problem—there's a surplus of movie-to-sock-plays that Finklestein and company can get their hands into. Our only regret about seeing *Showgirls* is we'll never be able to look at Jocko, our Red Heel sock monkey doll, the same way ever again.

HOWL AT THE MOON

26 West Hubbard Street
Chicago, IL 60610
(312) 863-7424
www.howlatthemoon.com
Map: Chicago North

Used to be your average piano bar would have a tuxedoed fellow behind the keys playing Gershwin or Sondheim to a cocktail-sipping clientele. Well, the folks at Howl at the Moon had a different idea. For one thing, there are two piano players working the room, and for another, they ain't playin' show tunes. The music here is unadulterated rock and roll, with the two performers trading vocals and banging their baby grands with joyful abandon. This piano bar trades sophistication for frat-party frenzy, and the crowd seems to love it. Every song is a sing-along here, with most of them being requests from the audience. The musicians who work the Moon have to have a huge repertoire to cover all the numbers they might have to play, and what they don't know, they'll usually try to fake.

Between songs, they keep up a steady repartee with each other and the crowd, occasionally pointing a high-powered flashlight at a table of revelers and engaging them in some playful two-way heckling. Howl at the Moon is a popular destination for bachelor and bachelorette parties, and sometimes the rowdy joie de vivre can become a little exhausting. In that case, you may want to retreat to the Zebra Lounge for a martini and some music from *Cats*.

LIGHTNING AND THUNDER

(877) 4 NEIL 99
www.lightning-thunder.com

Take Neil Diamond, throw in a little ABBA, and then pipe in some background music and what have you got? Lightning and Thunder, that's what. This husband-and-wife team has been making the rounds of Chicago nightclubs with their own brand of crowd-pleasing camp for over a decade. Lightning is the Diamond stand-in, and he's definitely got the growling voice and bushy sideburns down to a T. Thunder provides a compendium of other recording artists, with the aforementioned ABBA as her specialty. Their musical instrument is a machine, but don't call them a karaoke act. "We're an entertainment vocal duo in a Las Vegas style!" insists Thunder.

Whatever it is, it's packing them in at places like Hog Head McDunna's on the north side, where they have a devoted following of second-generation Neil and ABBA fans. The audience demographic seems to be about twenty-one to thirty-five, and these kids squeal and sing along as if the real stars were onstage. Clearly there is a curiosity factor involved; Lightning's resemblance to an economy-size Neil Diamond is kind of weird, and Thunder, who lost a leg in a freak accident, actually performs from a wheelchair. There's also the cheesiness factor, what with Lighting baring his puny chest at every opportunity and constantly directing pelvic thrusts toward the crowd. As Thunder bluntly put it, "Some people come to our show because they think it's idiotic." Hey, whatever works.

LIMA LIMA FLIGHT TEAM
www.limalima.com

L ima Lima is the only six-aircraft civilian precision air team in the world. Its members are mostly former or current pilots in commercial aviation, and with a few exceptions they're somewhat long in the tooth. But their age doesn't seem to affect their abilities in the air, where they calmly execute aerobatics worthy of the Thunderbirds or the Blue Angels. Neither has it prevented them from giving each other cool nicknames like Bullet, Quick, and, yes, Cool. Their airplane of choice is the Beechcraft T-34 Mentor from the 1950s, painted bright yellow with their signature black stripe on the tail. The origin of the team name comes from the FAA designator for their home airfield, LL—the letter L in the phonetic alphabet is Lima.

These aging flyboys put on quite a show, complete with daring aerial stunts and streaming aerial smoke. It's no surprise that they've performed at air shows coast to coast in front of (or above) over one hundred million spectators. Since their inception in 1975, they've had only one fatality: pilot Keith Evans perished in a training exercise over Oswego, Illinois, in 1999. To this day, Lima Lima always ends its show with a "missing man" formation in his honor.

MAGIC INCORPORATED
5082 North Lincoln Avenue
Chicago, IL 60625
(773) 334-2855
www.magicinc.net
Map: Chicago North

M agic Incorporated has been catering to aspiring illusionists since 1926 and has more than four thousand tricks for sale. Its owner is the dean of American magic, Jay Marshall, a former vaudevillian who has fourteen appearances on the *Ed Sullivan Show* to his credit. He's the guy with the eye patch behind the counter—it's not a showbiz affectation, he really lost the eye a few years ago and now has ten minutes of "one-eye" jokes in his repertoire. Jay has staffed the place with magicians almost as good as he is, who are only too willing to demonstrate any trick on the shelf. For the really ambitious, they offer private lessons on the premises, and there's also an occasional magic show in the back room.

Even if there's no show scheduled, you might ask to check out that back room anyway, since the walls are covered with old publicity photos and classic posters touting acts like Kon Mi, who apparently would swallow a loaded gun and shoot crackers off a man's head. Speaking of great acts, among the books for sale is the biography of Le Petomaine, a French performer who used flatulence to make music and blow out candles from 10 feet away. Seriously.

MARVIN TATE'S D-SETTLEMENT

Adam Conway
(773) 276-7476
www.d-settlement.com

You are a multifaceted person. You appreciate music, adore being politically challenged, crave the spoken word. Then catching a performance by Marvin Tate's D-Settlement will appeal to your diamondlike desires. These vocalists and musicians call their music style "urban collision." It combines poetry with "various influences: rock, funk, jazz, gospel, R&B, opera, reggae." (If you're looking for mariachi, hit the road, bub.) This group features a playlist that takes you on a fun-house ride careening from comedy to sober social commentary, from rockin' nocturne to mad madrigal, from symphony to antiphony. It's all very theatrical,

right down to the wardrobe. Founder and performance poet Marvin Tate wears what look like orange pipe cleaners in his hair—he calls them "Kraft Macaroni and Cheese." And while Mr. Tate's tresses may tickle you, the group's avant-garde (and unguarded) lyrics will catch you off guard in a song such as "N-Word." The group might also surprise you by directly engaging you. Members will jump off the stage to verbally and physically interact with the audience. About their exuberant performance style, the Settlement says, "To be in your face and to bring it to you, it's like, you made the decision to come here. So be prepared for what you get." You'll be prepared to take the heat . . . you're a diamond, remember?

MENTALIST CHRIS CARTER

(847) 783-5191
www.mindcramp.com

Chicago area native Chris Carter does not claim to have psychic powers, but he will play with your mind if you give him half the chance. Carter is hardly what you'd expect a mentalist to be like; this is no brooding Uri Geller but a congenial guy-next-door who happens to know some phenomenal head games. The primary fun of attending his show is trying to figure out "How'd he do that?"—like when he turns on a lightbulb or speeds up a watch using only "brain waves." At one point, Carter, with his eyes taped shut, manages to identify random items collected by a helper from audience members (the night we attended, these included a piece of chewing gum from the mouth of a wiseass college student). His most impressive trick is when he asks the crowd to think of a number, then brings onstage the person who matches the one that he has written down. A cassette tape that has been sealed hours

before is subsequently played for the audience, who listen in amazement as Chris's voice describes in detail the person who stands before them. How'd he do *that*?

Carter mostly plays the college circuit, though he occasionally settles in for a run at a local Chicago theater. His presentation employs plenty of volunteers—usually, it

seems, the prettiest women in the audience. And while his purported telekinetic power can sometimes creep people out, he always leavens the festivities with humor. We witnessed him solicit written questions that he proceeded to draw from a hat while blindfolded and attempt to answer (think Carnak the Magnificent); when Carter spoke the name "John Larson," a fellow piped up, "That's me!"

Carter: "Now tell the audience your question."

Larson: "Who is the most gullible person in this room?"

MEXICAN RODEO

Plaza Garibaldi
Across from Twenty-sixth
and California Avenue
Chicago, IL
(312) 421-5272
www.cfevents.com
Map: Chicago West

If you yearn to see an authentic Mexican rodeo, there's no need to go south of the border, just go south of Cermak Road. That's where you'll find Plaza Garibaldi, which plays host to a Mexican rodeo every Sunday during the summer months. The festivities get started at around 4:00 P.M. and last well into the evening. If you're one of those people with a short attention span who needs to have constant action for your entertainment dollar, you'll need to check that attitude at the door. Everything happens at a very leisurely pace here, with large chunks of downtime between events. A parade of horses, their riders dressed in impossibly colorful costumes, will circle the arena, and then perhaps forty minutes will pass before some tricks with a lasso are performed. It might be another hour later that a *chiarro* enters the ring on a bucking bronco or an angry bull.

The mostly Mexican American audience is just fine with the long lulls punctuated by bursts of action. After all, food and drinks are available at nearby booths, and a group of musicians keeps up a constant barrage of sound from the bandstand. The looseness of the schedule also allows for plenty of socializing with good friends and total strangers. As for the rodeo itself, if you watch closely, you'll notice a subtle difference in methodology between Mexican broncobusters and their American counterparts: while the American cowboy holds on with one hand, the Mexican *chiarro* uses two. The end result, however, is usually the same, with the rider's posterior making a hard landing in the dirt. Not to worry—he'll probably have at least an hour to recuperate before it's bull-riding time.

MORNING POLKA PARTY FOR SENIORS

Major Hall
5660 West Grand Avenue
Chicago, IL 60639
(773) 237-8089
Map: Chicago West

It's suds, sausage, and swaying when seniors take to the floor for a morning of polka partying. Every Tuesday Major Hall opens at 8:00 A.M. and turns its banquet room into a mature dance club. For $2.00, white-haired, gray-haired, and blue-haired men and women meet to beat their feet for a five-hour marathon of Bohemian dancing. Music is provided by the Pension-Aires, a group composed of players who've performed in professional polka bands since the 1940s. Couples lick their lips to the opening riffs of polka hits like *Love You Girl Polka, Don't Go Mary Polka,* and *Going to War Polka.* (There's a lot of "declarations" in polka.) A hall spokesman told us that the party's a great way for people to dance their way to good health, and you'll see some healthy ballroom bustling as seniors polka-dot the floor doing the familiar "hop-step-close-step" dance. A late-morning lunch break is scheduled so the polkaholics can catch their breath and take a bite of the Polish sausage. Food prices range from $2.00 to $3.00, depending on what's being served. Folks, *this* is the real early-bird special. To slake their thirst, the hall has a cash bar. You can just imagine that at the end of the party, everybody raises their beer and lighters as the Pension-Aires lead them out with an encore of the *No Beer in Heaven Polka.* If you don't find it disturbing to picture your Grandma doin' the bump and drinkin' a Bud at 8:00 A.M., then hustle her over to Major Hall for a morning of movement and music.

NEO-FUTURISTS

5153 North Ashland Avenue
Chicago, IL 60640
(773) 275-5255 show hotline
(773) 878-4557 office
www.neofuturists.org
Map: Chicago North

The Neo-Futurarium is situated above a funeral home in Andersonville, where its denizens have been producing mind-bending theater since 1987. Their signature production is *Too Much Light Makes the Baby Go Blind*, which promises to give you "thirty plays in sixty minutes." Don't like the plot? Wait a minute or two and there'll be a new one. These pint-sized plays, performed by a merry band of actor-playwrights, are usually quite funny and often thought-provoking. And each week they replace a few of them, so if you go back a month later, you're liable to see a whole new show!

The entertainment starts before you've even sat down. You're greeted at the door by one of the performers, who hands you half of a pair of dice that you then roll to determine your ticket price—five dollars plus whatever's on the one die. That's bargain enough, but if they sell out, they order pizza for the whole audience!) Then you proceed inside, where you're given a name tag with your new Neo-Futurist moniker (for example, Billiard Ball or Heartbreak Soup) and a menu listing the thirty possible plays for that night. Once everyone is seated, the audience is encouraged to shout out a number, and the first one the cast hears, they perform (as soon as the clock starts). When each play ends, more shouting. You'd be surprised how quickly the sixty minutes go by, but it's rare that they don't get in the full thirty plays. You leave knowing you've gotten your money's worth—especially if you rolled a one!

 ## BEHIND THE SCENES

Because the Neo-Futurarium asks its performers to create their own plays, it has become a launching pad for several actors-turned-playwrights. Founder Greg Allen has had a number of his plays produced locally, as have alums David Kodeski and Sean Benjamin. But perhaps the biggest success story is Greg Kotis, who coauthored the hit Broadway musical *Urinetown* and put fellow Neo-Futurist Spencer Kayden in a starring role.

NEW DUNCAN IMPERIALS

www.newduncanimperials.com

This three-man group named after a yo-yo has fashioned itself into one of Chicago's premier party bands. Goodtime, Skipper, and Pigtail have built a reputation for putting on quite a show, complete with smoke effects, explosions, party favors, and hard-driving rock and roll. The evening usually begins with the boys, dressed in straw hats, tuxedo shirts, and large bow ties, entering through the crowd to great fanfare; Beethoven's Fifth blasts from the sound system and Pigtail pounds the bass drum he's carrying, while Skipper and Goodtime hand out sparklers to the crowd. Once on the stage (which is festooned with bras and other bizarre decorations) they launch into a rock song about scrapple ("covered with pink crapple") or perhaps the unforgettable "I'm Schizophrenic, No I'm Not." Their music tends toward power pop accompanying hilariously juvenile lyrics, such as these from "White Trash Boogie":

Well I used to date my mother,
But my momma ran off with my brother.
Now I'll have to find myself some other,
'Cuz my dad has got my girlfriend covered!

Admittedly the musicianship sometimes takes a backseat to all the crazy the-

atrics, but when you've got a gadget that can blow toilet paper all over the band and the crowd in midsong, why not use it? And the scantily clad, gyrating ladies who occasionally sing backup provide ample distraction if you get tired of the Imperials' antics. As you can imagine, this stuff strongly appeals to all those American males still in touch with their inner adolescent, but we saw plenty of women in the audience, too. When we asked the band whether they had a name for their rabid following, à la Jimmy Buffet's Parrot Heads, Skipper chimed in, "Yeah, we call them 'Morons.'"

PIEROGI FEST

Whiting/Robertsdale Chamber of Commerce
(877) 659-0292
www.whitingindiana.com
Map: Multistate

Ah, my little dumpling, come to the love-in that honors this short, chubby pasty. The pierogi—for those of you not current with culinary parlance—is a boiled and buttered, itty-bitty, filled pie. Once a year, Whiting, Indiana, rolls out the doughy doormat and stuffs itself (and you) with all things pierogi. Why Whiting? It gives them a chance to celebrate their Eastern European heritage, of which the porky pierogi is part. On the last full weekend of July, they kill the fatted pie with pierogi eating, tossing, and tasting—and even a musical pierogi-oke. On Friday night the parade kicks off with its leader, Mr. Pierogi, followed by the Pierogi Queen and the Pieroguettes—Misses Potato, Cheese, Mushroom, Berry, Beef, and sassy Sauerkraut. They're joined by the Twirling Babushka Brigade and the La-Z-Boy float. It's

the kind of parade where the city puts its spiffy fire truck on display with lights flashing. For those not passionate about pierogi, there are still plenty of things to do with a "p" in them: polka, play Eastern Block Jeopardy, pant during the 5K run, or watch the Precision Lawn Mower Drill Team performance. Why not spend the weekend in Whiting? Only a few miles beyond the Illinois–Indiana border, Whiting has beautiful architecture and a lovely lakefront. That way, you can *really* indulge in the goodies at this glutinous gala. About activities at the fest, one participant told us, "We just drink, drink, drink, come up for pierogi, then we drink, drink, drink some more." Oh, there *is* one more thing to do with a "p" in it: get pickled.

PUPPET PARLOR

1922 West Montrose Avenue
Chicago, IL 60613
(773) 774-2919
Map: Chicago North

If you saw the movie *Being John Malkovich* and marveled at John Cusack's puppetry, we've got a guy who does this stuff for real. Ralph Kipnis has been a master puppeteer for nearly forty years, and he's the proud owner-operator of the Puppet Parlor on Montrose Avenue. The Parlor is about the only place left that puts on puppet shows year-round, and Ralph and his assistants make sure their patrons are treated to a rich theatrical experience. A plush red curtain rises to reveal the intricate stage setting while in "the pit" a puppet orchestra plays the overture. Don't think this is exclusively a "take the kids" outing; the Puppet Parlor also offers an adults-only show, *Le Petite Follies*, complete with some marionette nudity!

Ralph creates many of the puppets himself using clay and plaster casts, and the marionettes have seventeen separate parts attached to seventeen separate strings, allowing a skilled puppeteer to make their movements surprisingly lifelike. Where can you learn such skills yourself? Why, at the Puppet Parlor, of course, where Kipnis offers an array of illuminating classes. So go for the education, go for the gratuitous nudity, but just go!

REDMOON THEATER
2936 North Southport Avenue
Chicago, IL 60657
(773) 388-9031
www.redmoon.org
Map: Chicago North

The Redmoon Theater is known for making a spectacle of itself. Whether it be in a local theater or on the street in front of the Museum of Contemporary Art, this company pulls out all the stops to create vital and visually exciting theatrical events. The company is primarily known for combining puppetry with live actors, and its puppets often transcend any preconceptions you might have of this childlike art form. One show featured a 30-foot caterpillar that shed its cocoon to reveal an enormous butterfly with a wingspan that practically covered the stage and surrounding audience. The actors who work for Redmoon often erase their individuality behind masks or garish makeup, in a way rendering themselves just as puppetlike as the "constructed" performers with whom they share the limelight.

The performers' home base is Logan Square, where each year they put on an outdoor Halloween extravaganza and an indoor Christmas pageant. Both employ the services of neighborhood children and teens, who help out with the creation of the puppets as well as the actual puppeteering and performing. Redmoon's first production was in 1989 and was provocatively titled *You Hold My Heart between Your Teeth*. The company has since done a series of plays adapted from other sources, such as *The Hunchback of Notre Dame*, *Moby Dick*, and *The Old Man and the Sea*. In each case, the featured character was portrayed by a life-size marionette, though sometimes the puppet had to share the part with a human actor made to look identical. The audience would sometimes lose track of which one was which—and that's just the way Redmoon likes it.

SHOWMAN MILT TRENIER
www.rockabilly.net/milttrenier

Milt Trenier's nightclub closed its door several years ago, but Milt himself is still going strong, and after more than fifty years in show business, you better believe he can work a room. He got his start with his brothers in the legendary Vegas act The Treniers back in the 1950s. He left the act in 1959 to go solo, eventually landing in the thriving nightclub scene here in Chicago. In 1977 he opened Trenier's, but after one too many nights of looking over his shoulder while onstage to make sure table number 3 got their drinks, he closed the place and went freelance.

Milt, now in his seventies, remains the consummate showman; he sings, he dances, he cracks jokes and does impressions, making it all look pretty darn easy. He's usually backed up by his three-man combo, who are more than capable of keeping up with the tireless Trenier. He'll bandy some ribald repartee with them, then wade into the crowd to exchange lyrics with delighted audience members. On one such foray we watched him lasciviously sing, "I'm a sixty-minute man!" then shove the microphone in front of a nearby male patron. "I'm an all-night man!" declared the inebriated fellow, but when his date labeled him an "8½-minute man," Milt turned to the guy and said, "That means you did the rest of the night by yourself!"

SINGER/GUITARIST PAT MCCURDY
www.patmccurdy.com

Singer/guitarist Pat McCurdy has been a fixture on the Chicago music scene for over a decade, and the reason is simple: this guy can flat out work a crowd. With a boffo catalog of original songs combined with a voluminous array of covers, McCurdy has plenty of ammunition, but it's his showmanship that's created a cult following here (and all over the Midwest). Called "Patheads" or "Pataholics," these rabid fans rarely miss a show and know all the words to McCurdy's songs, which is a good thing, since Pat peppers the show with sing-alongs and will often grab somebody out of the audience to share the onstage vocals.

Don't think you have to be a regular to enjoy the evening, Pat aims to please everybody. He's been known to stop a song in midverse, if he senses the crowd losing interest, and then take a request. And believe us, if you shout it, he probably knows it. As for his original songs, they all sport great pop hooks and hilarious lyrics, which are often not meant for the easily offended. Take this little ditty, for instance:

> *My little soldier is standing at attention,*
> *My little Jack has jumped out of the box,*
> *My little key is looking for a keyhole,*
> *And I'll be there when opportunity knocks!*

You gotta love this guy.

SOUTH SHORE DRILL TEAM

Arthur Robertson, director
7705 South Cottage Grove Avenue
Chicago, IL 60619
(773) 651-0220
Map: Chicago South

If you've seen them strut their stuff in a local parade, you know that South Shore is not your average drill team. Oh, they can twirl and toss those fake rifles with the best of 'em, but it's what they're doing *while* they're twirling and tossing that has earned this African American squad eight state championships. To put it simply, when the rifles go up, the South Shore Team is getting down (with its bad self). These kids' moves would make James Brown proud, and it's no coincidence that the music they usually "march" to is not Sousa but soul.

Founder and director Arthur Robertson wanted to develop a program that would keep kids off the street and doing something constructive. He welcomes boys and girls of all ages under twenty-one to join, as long as they're willing to work hard: Arthur rehearses his team three nights a week (and sometimes weekends). The kids themselves come up with some of the fancy steps, though their director will sometimes tone down the more suggestive pelvic maneuvers. South Shore doesn't go in for the military-style uniforms of the normal drill teams—one year they dawned brightly colored double-breasted suits over black silk shirts!

All the hard work and sartorial splendor definitely pays off. When you see thirty to forty youngsters dressed to the nines and doing precisely coordinated, funked-up choreography, all the while manipulating wooden rifles, you'll never think of drill teams quite the same way again.

ST. LUKE'S BOTTLE BAND

Paul Phillips, conductor
(708) 366-1379
www.stlukespr.org/bottleband.html
Map: Suburban North

Since 1979 the St. Luke's Bottle Band has been proving that partially filled glass containers can be music to the ears—that is, if someone blows into them, plucks them with a wet finger, or clinks them with a small mallet. Those are the methods employed by the St. Luke's band to create music, and it's gotten them all the way to the *Late Show with David Letterman.* But never forget that their first television appearance was on *Wild Chicago* back in 1993, when they showcased a repertoire that ranged from the sublime to the ridiculous.

The note that the bottle makes depends on the amount of fluid inside it, and founder and conductor Paul Phillips personally tunes all bottles before each concert, since such things as evaporation or excessive drooling can make a bottle go off-key. The twenty-five band members are an eclectic mix culled from the church's congregation. Their bottles of choice are Leinenkugels because, as Paul tells the audience, "They had the best tone of the hundreds of brands that we tested."

When the whole band gets to blowing, plucking, and clinking (occasionally joined by a kazoo or violin), it's a truly joyous sound, and audiences simply go nuts for it. If you don't believe us, book them for your next block party or ice-cream social, and if they're not doing a national television show, they will rock your world.

WEEDS

1555 North Dayton Street
Chicago, IL 60622
(773) 943-7815
www.geocities.com/weedspoetry
Map: Chicago North

Weeds bar made an appearance on *Wild Chicago's* very first episode, and we're pleased to say that they're still going strong. This watering hole-in-the-wall has been owned and operated by the Martinez Family for more than forty years. Since 1984 it has been presided over by the gruff but gregarious Sergio, who tends bar, collects donations for the band, and amiably berates his customers. He's also in the habit of doing a shot of tequila with anyone in his presence celebrating a milestone—it could be a birthday, anniversary, or new toupee.

The now famous Poetry Slam had its origins here, and Weeds still devotes Monday nights to poetry reading. The live music (Wednesday through Saturday) never has a cover charge, but has to compete for the audience's attention with the TV behind the bar. That's where Sergio airs videotapes of previous evenings at Weeds, and regulars sometimes prefer seeing themselves to the entertainment onstage. P.S. Don't miss the bra collection on the ceiling and the lifelike bust of Sergio near the bandstand.

MORE ENTERTAINMENT

AC ROCK
www.acrock.com
A cappella rock from four guys in colorful suits.

BILL O'CONNELL'S SKYLINERS BIG BAND
www.chicagoskylinersbigband.com
Playing the best of the big bands from Basie to Kenton.

BOPOLOGY
www.bopology.com
Six-piece jazz combo featuring Sinatra standards and Ellington arrangements.

CHECKERBOARD LOUNGE
425 East Forty-third Street
Chicago, IL 60653
(773) 624–3240
Map: Chicago South
A legendary South Side blues bar that's played host to most of the greats.

CIRCUS BOY BOBBY HUNT
www.circusboy.com
A one-man variety show, capable of some truly impressive tricks.

CLEANING LADYS
(708) 352–0050
www.cleaningladys.com
Prolific local rock band whose public appearances are rare but memorable.

DEAF ELVIS

www.members.aol.com/DeafElvis
Profoundly deaf Elvis interpreter performs using American Sign Language—a Graceland favorite.

EDDIE KOROSA AND THE BOYS FROM ILLINOIS

(773) 586-3719
Polka band that can often be found at the Baby Doll Polka Club.

FAMOUS BROTHERS HYSTERICAL BLUEGRASS

www.famousbrothers.com
A comedy bluegrass act featuring three inbred brothers from Monkey's Crevice, West Virginia.

FITZGERALD'S

6615 Roosevelt Road
Berwyn, IL 60402
(708) 788-2118
www.fitzgeraldsnightclub.com
Map: Suburban West
Roadhouse tavern that showcases some of the best roots music in America.

FOUR CHARMS

www.fourcharms.com
Jumpin' jive music performed with energy and style; regulars at the Green Mill jazz club.

GIGOLO JOHNNY

www.gigolojohnny.com
Comedic crooner who specializes in Sinatra tunes.

GREEN E, THE ENVIRONMENTAL ELVIS

(312) 933-7953
www.greenelvis.com
Elvis with a message delivers parodies of the King's hits, with an environmental theme—for example, "Are You Recycling Tonight?" and "Hunka Hunka Burnin' Sludge."

GREEN MILL POETRY SLAM

4802 North Broadway
Chicago, IL 60640
(773) 878-5552
www.slampapi.com
Map: Chicago North
The often imitated but never duplicated original poetry slam.

HOT HOUSE

31 East Balbo Drive
Chicago, IL 60605
(312) 362-9707
www.hothouse.net
Map: Downtown
The best venue in Chicago to hear world music.

LIGHT OPERA WORKS

www.light-opera-works.org
Map: Suburban North
Lavish musical theater from American, British, Viennese, and French operettas.

MASS ENSEMBLE

www.massensemble.com
Beautiful and hypnotic sounds played on enormous stringed instruments.

MAXWELL STREET KLEZMER BAND

www.klezmerband.com
Eastern European jazzy Yiddish band.

MOJO AND THE BAYOU GYPSIES

www.redhotmojo.com
They're loud, they're exciting, and they'll get you on your feet.

NEW TRADITION CHORUS

(800) 746-9246
www.newtradition.org
Popular song interpretations in barbershop harmony by a north suburban chorus.

POLKAHOLICS

(773) 278-4383
www.thepolkaholics.com
Polka with a rock and roll attitude.

ROCKEFELLER CHAPEL CARILLON

Rockefeller Memorial Chapel
5850 South Woodlawn
Chicago, IL 60637
(773) 702-2100
rockefeller.uchicago.edu/carillon.html
The second-largest carillon in the world. (The largest is in the tower of the Riverside Church in New York City.)

ROTC, RIGHTEOUSLY OUTRAGEOUS TWIRLING CORPS

www.geocities.com/rotc_chicago
Gay men's rifle twirling team.

SAMBA BAMBA!

(773) 525-5404
www.twigs.com/sambabamba
Sergio Mendes meets the B-52's.

THOSE DARN ACCORDIONS

www.thosedarnaccordions.com
All-accordion rock band (OK, there's also a drummer).

WILD CHICAGO REVUE

Carmel Music & Entertainment
(847) 869-5969
carmelme.com/wildchicago
Yes, you can hire Will and some of the novelty acts listed in this book in a package of unusual and outrageous entertainment for your next corporate event.

WM. DARKE PSYCHOCIRCUS AND FREAK SHOW SPECTACULAR

www.darkeshows.com
Disturbing variety show featuring some alarming and sometimes dangerous acts.

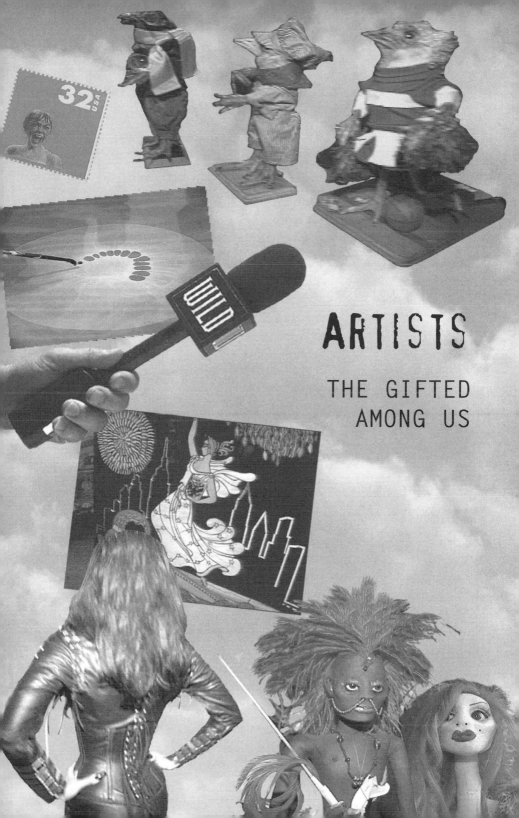

ARTISTS

THE GIFTED
AMONG US

GEOFF BINNS-CALVEY

(708) 366-0171
gidc@attbi.com

Artists often work from a model, but how many work right *on* the model? Geoff Binns-Calvey's specialty is what he calls "life-casts"—a similar idea to death masks, only done while the subject is very much alive. They're created by combining a goop derived from seaweed with plaster of paris and pouring it on part of the (normally) nude body of a male or (usually) female subject. The cast, once dry, will be used as a mold to create bronze wall sculptures that can be found in galleries and private homes all over Chicago. Geoff seems partial to torsos and rear ends, but he does do the occasional face, in which case he provides straws strategically placed so that the model can breathe during the procedure.

If you're looking for that offbeat gift idea, Binns-Calvey often does commissioned work for people who want to surprise that special someone with a lifecast of their own torso or other body parts. (And who wouldn't want a bronze replica of his or her lover's butt above the fireplace?) You may never have considered your physique to be a work of art, but just wait until Geoff gets through with you!

 BEHIND THE SCENES

This is the only segment about an artist who casts body parts to be *broadcast* on *Wild Chicago*, but not the only one we shot. In 1996 we profiled Cynthia Plaster Caster, the rock and roll groupie whose hobby of casting the genitalia of her favorite male rock stars has garnered her some celebrity of her own. But though we kept the "members" of her collection discreetly covered with fabric, WTTW refused to air the piece, the only segment of our show ever to be pulled.

KEN ELLIS

Rainbo Club
1150 North Damen Avenue
Chicago, IL 60622
(773) 489-5999
Map: Chicago North

These are not the kind of quilts you throw on a bed, unless you like sleeping with a skinhead. Artist Ken Ellis eschews (*Gesundheit!*) traditional quilt patterns for turbulent historical tableaus. His padded pix depict the Klan, neo-Nazis, Al Capone, JFK's assassination, and Hitler—

certainly agitating stuffing. These are hard images reinterpreted through a soft medium. There's something disturbingly compelling about seeing Kennedy's brain "blossoming" over the bullet's impact (cruel work rendered in crewelwork). Like Lot's wife, you've got to look at it.

Speaking of splattered blood, Ellis marks the back of his works with drops of his own. (In theater lore, if an actor's costume is marked with the blood of the seamstress, it will bring him good luck. Perhaps owning an Ellis will bring its buyer the same.) To achieve his embroidered pictures, Ken copies photos onto fabric, applies paint and dyes (and his DNA), adds batting, and sews. His nifty needlework can be seen in galleries and clubs around the city, and he also considers commissions. If you do decide to snuggle under one of Ellis's "uncomforting comforters," choose one with Al Capone—he was known for making people sleep for a very long time.

MIKE ENGLEHARDT
15 Crooked Creek Drive
Yorkville, IL 60560
Map: Suburban West

Mike Engelhardt is a licensed taxidermist with a peculiar specialty: give him the head of a turkey and a few doll clothes and he'll give you a *Poultry Personality*. It all started over twenty years ago, when Engelhardt was helping out on a local turkey farm. When he saw the heads being discarded, he began retrieving them, stuffing them, and then attaching turkey claws for the arms and legs. The coup de grâce was to dress them up in the clothes from his daughter's old doll collection. That same daughter printed up some brochures, and Engelhardt found

himself with a new side business, selling his turkey works to customers from as far away as Scotland and Jamaica for as much as $200 apiece.

The whole process of creation—including treating the stuffed heads with formaldehyde, inserting glass turkey eyes, finding the right outfit, and then posing and mounting it on a pedestal—takes about six months from start to finish. The final result might be a cheerleader, a World War II flyboy, quarterback Joe Montana, even a bewigged lady of the evening. It's not unusual for Mike to grow attached to his Poultry Personalities (which he calls "my little people") and not want to part with them. Actually that *is* unusual, but Engelhardt makes no apologies for his sideline. He has since branched out to other animals: a football-playing pheasant, a Mexican duck, and a patriotic groundhog. Where does he procure *these* nonturkey creatures? Well, to be honest, they're usually roadkill that he scraped off the pavement or, in one case, pulled off the grill of his car. Why waste a good model?

FEITIÇO GALLERY

1821 West North Avenue
Chicago, IL 60622
(773) 384-0586
www.feitico.com
Map: Chicago North

Hot, carnal, spicy, voluptuous. Are these titillating terms turning you on? Then see them made flesh when you cross through the portal of a gallery dedicated to the delectable. Co-owner Ms. Marilyn, a dominatrix, says, "We're trying to promote sensuality in art." You said it, sister. Through paintings, photography, sculpture, and film, Feitiço celebrates the body: bare, bondaged, or big-breasted. Specifically, the gallery addresses—or, rather, undresses—the needs of the fetishist. Here, you can feed your fantasy of the human form by peeping at works done by leading erotic artists including Liz Walters, Chris Bonk, and Woody. Come to one of their openings where you'll have a chance to have intercourse—the social kind—with the artists or to mingle with the devotees of their delicious art. Co-owner Kurt Wright says, "anybody who comes in here can be themselves," so don't expect your typical gallerygoers.

These are sensualists with a proclivity toward wearing corsets, cat suits, and complex leather clothes with chains. They make Lady Chatterley look like Pippi Longstocking and border on upstaging the artwork. Perhaps you prefer not to watch, but to do? Then sign up for Feitiço's Erotic Life Drawing class. You'll be drawing from models that are outfitted in fetishwear. Boy, it sure beats having to ask your mom to pose for you.

MICHAEL HERNANDEZ DE LUNA

P.O. Box 08282
Chicago, IL 60608
(312) 563-0554
www.badpressbooks.com

This Pilsen artist breaks the law every time he creates his art, and even if you find his work offensive, you have to admire his chutzpah. Michael Hernandez De Luna's canvas is the size of a postage stamp—oh wait, it *is* a postage stamp! He claims that fake philately is an old and established art form, but he has given it a decidedly modern twist. Seeking out pictures from other sources such as magazines and posters (he calls himself a "garbage recycler of images"), De Luna incorporates them into a provocative stamp design. Once the actual stamps are produced, he has his phony postage mailed to himself; friends who are traveling send a bunch of his envelopes from their destination in the hopes that at least one will get past the postmaster.

Considering that the stamps are often large and quite subversive, it's astounding that so many *do* get through. But there they are, postmarked envelopes at a gallery near you with depictions of nude women, urinating men, a marijuana plant—whatever strikes De Luna's fancy.

The stamps often have a political bent: There's a picture of the revolutionary Zapatistas that was mailed from Mexico, an image of JFK smoking a cigar that got past the Cuban post office, and a portrait of Monica Lewinsky postmarked in Washington, D.C. Sometimes the stamps' contents seem like no more than a juvenile prank, such as the one titled "Just Horsin' Around Doggy Style" that shows one horse mounting another. Whatever his motives, De Luna seems totally fearless in flouting the authorities. He has received a cease and desist letter from the postal inspector (which he promptly had mounted and framed), but when we asked whether he had ceased and desisted, he smiled and referred us to his lawyer.

JO-JO'S CLOSET

1579 North Milwaukee Avenue,
Suite 311
Chicago, IL 60622
(773) 862-5656
www.jojochicago.com
Map: Chicago North

Jo-Jo's Closet may be small, but his dreams are very big, as are some of the vaguely disturbing creations that surround him. See, Jo-Jo makes dolls, a few of them life-size and all of them anatomically correct. If you're put off by seeing genitalia on a doll (or by a male artist who prefers to dress as a woman), best to avoid this tiny studio in the Flatiron Building. But we warn you, you'll be missing a truly memorable experience.

Jo-Jo studied doll making under the late Greer Langton, a member of Andy Warhol's Factory and onetime employee of Jim Henson and the Muppets. The dolls on display at the Closet are provided with armature (interior boning), which allows them to stand and be posed. If they seem lifelike, it may be because Jo-Jo uses real dentures for teeth and antique glass eyes that have, in some cases, served prior duty in human eye sockets. The dolls are often stuffed with human hair, which Jo-Jo has access to in his/her other job as a hair salon artist.

Customers who purchase a Jo-Jo creation will see a sign on their way out: YOU ARE NOW COMING OUT OF THE CLOSET.

WAYNE KUSY
(773) 784-3379
www.enteract.com/~kusy

Wayne Kusy has taken model shipbuilding to new lengths—25 feet, to be exact. But that's not even the most remarkable thing about this man's hobby, because Kusy builds his model ships with *toothpicks*. In a meticulous process that takes years (and several gallons of Elmer's glue) to complete one vessel, he painstakingly constructs the ship's skeleton and then adds the hull and deck plating, the superstructure, and finally the detail work, all with his little slivers of wood. His first model was the *Titanic*, which came to 8 feet long and 75,000 toothpicks. The next one he finished was the 16-foot *Lusitania* (160,000 picks), built in two pieces so he could get it out of his apartment. His latest creation is the *St. Mary*, 25 feet long, 3 feet wide, and 7 feet tall; there are now two million more toothpicks that will go unchewed.

Kusy works from blueprints, pictures, descriptions from books, sometimes even smaller plastic models of the same ship. To replicate things like the smokestacks and the lifeboats, he must bend his toothpicks and cut them to size. The portholes are done with a drill and a prayer. Wayne's models can periodically be seen in local art galleries and museums, and they are all for sale. But if you buy one of these spectacular toothpick ships, don't attempt to see if it'll float: Elmer's glue is water-soluble.

GRETCHEN MCCARTHY

115 Scottswood Road
Riverside, IL 60546
(708) 447-2674
www.littlehomemaker.com

I magine finding a sweet, petite lady in your neighborhood yelling, "Your house is just screaming to be sculpted!" Evidently she hears voices you can't if you haven't had Gretchen McCarthy make a model of your home in clay. She says sometimes she'll be driving home and she'll spot a house that just "screams" to be sculpted. Gretchen even screams on her Web site: "Artist Gretchen McCarthy sculpts your house in miniature!" (OK, she's not actually screaming on the site, but the exclamation point at the end looks like she raised her voice.) Anyway, since 1990 she's been sculpting minimodels of businesses, historic buildings, and regular old houses like ours. She starts the process with photos of your soon-to-be-memorialized home, and then, using a sculpting material, she carves them and pops them in the oven to bake. While she stresses that her works are artistic interpretations rather than architectural replicas, you'll be delighted by her detailing, right down to the lawn ornaments and streetlamps. Prices to have Gretchen "remodel" your home start at $300. Having a compact, clay copy of a house is a pleasant way to remember a childhood home or to give as a gift to that friend who's particularly house-proud. Employers, how about skipping that big, fat bonus check this year and giving your employees a model of the company they love and adore.

There is a good way for you to find out if your home deserves to be sculpted. Go outside right now, stand on the lawn, and see if it screams.

PACIFIC TALL SHIPS

106 Stephen Street, Suite 100
Lemont, IL 60439
(630) 243-1277
www.pacific-tall-ships.com
Map: Suburban South

Pacific Tall Ships in downtown Lemont sells museum-quality model ships ranging in size from 15 to 50 inches. Most are miniatures of those grand old galleons with the intricate rigging, rows of gun ports, and handsomely carved (and usually seminude) women on their bows. Master builder Bill Hartman designs the models or modifies existing kits and then farms out most of the work to a thirty-eight-man crew that he's trained in the Philippines. Around a thousand man-hours go into the bigger models, and it shows—to fully appreciate each carefully rendered detail of just one vessel would take hours. That's, of course, reflected in the prices, which are mostly in the $15,000 to $50,000 range.

When asked who the clientele is for these nautical gems, colorful owner Dennis Egan answers, "People who have money!" That includes about two dozen current or former world leaders, with Queen Elizabeth and Bill Clinton topping the list. Many of the models on display are replicas of specific ships from history, for example, the English fighting vessel *Sovereign of the Seas* and the famous slave ship *Amistad*. Others simply mimic a type of seagoing craft such as a Chinese junk or a Greek galley boat. Each one is a feast for the eyes, so if you can't

afford to buy, feel free to stop by and ogle. As for those models that don't come out to Bill Hartman's liking, he has a simple solution: " I stomp it."

CHAIM PINKHASIK

Agudas Achim Synagogue
5029 North Kenmore Avenue
Chicago, IL 60640
(773) 784-4453
Map: Chicago North

Russian immigrant Chaim Pinkhasik can do some amazing things with stained glass, though that's not what he calls it. His "mosaics" are not the same as stained-glass windows, in that they are unleaded—meaning there is no lead between the pieces of glass. He has developed his process over the last fifty years or so, and the results are a banquet for the eye: wildly colorful images that contain hundreds, sometimes thousands, of intricately placed segments. Chaim works alone, tracing the picture he wants to create, then cutting the glass and gluing it into place. His hands are testament to his dedication: They are covered with tiny scars from where the glass pieces have cut him.

Pinkhasik's studio is in a local synagogue, from which he also sells his mosaics. Visit him in person and you'll find that he's quite passionate (and voluble) about his work. "This is fine art, one of a kind!" he exclaimed to us at one point. "It's washable, it's durable, it's beautiful!" Chaim's subject matter usually springs from his imagination. He also accepts commissioned work, taking photos and drawings and re-creating them in stained glass. One client wanted a mosaic of the Blues Brothers, and, not having heard of the musical duo, Pinkhasik was confused about their name. His solution? A strikingly faithful portrait of John Belushi and Dan Aykroyd—except for their bright blue skin.

AMY LEE SEGAMI

Segami Studios
P.O. Box 408500
Chicago, IL 60640
(312) 635-3800 by appointment
www.segami.com

Suminagashi is an art form that was created in China two thousand years ago and practiced by Japanese Shinto priests in the twelfth century. It has been brought into the twenty-first century by a woman whose last name spelled backward is *images* (Harry Caray would have loved that, eh?). Amy Lee Segami was a graduate of Illinois Institute of Technology and a successful engineer when she experienced a

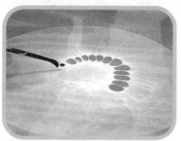

midlife crisis. It led her to take up the ancient art of her ancestors, suminagashi, which, roughly translated, means "painting on water." In her studio sits a wooden tray, 4 feet square and 2 inches deep, that holds fifteen gallons of water mixed with a seaweed extract. Segami painstakingly drips her paint one drop at a time onto the water's surface with a pointed brush and allows the paint to spread. She'll occasionally spray color onto her liquid canvas using a toothbrush—an instrument that was obviously not at the Shinto priests' disposal.

Once she's created her desired image, she places onto the water a piece of thick paper, which absorbs the paint on contact.

After it dries, it's framed and there you have it: a new piece of suminagashi. The finished pictures, with names such as "Floating Dream" and "Forever Dragon," can be wildly diverse in appearance; due to the fluid nature of the process, Segami admits that she does not have complete control over the final image. She doesn't see that as a drawback, though. "People think of chaos as a turbulent, negative thing," she told us, "but I think you can order chaos so that it can become beautiful." After seeing some of her work, we wholeheartedly agree.

DALE SINDERSON
Chemung Tech
24201 Route 173
Harvard, IL 60033
(815) 943-7100
www.webpages.charter.net/chemungtech
Map: Suburban North

We happened to be driving near Harvard, Illinois, when we stumbled upon the amazing roadside art studio of one Dale Sinderson. It's called Chemung Tech, being as it's located in the tiny town of Chemung and Dale employs some rudimentary technology in his art—some of it moves, makes noise, and/or lights up. It all started when Sinderson was taking the same drive we did and spotted a two-room shanty sitting on an otherwise vacant piece of land. He decided

it would be the perfect place to exercise his artistic talents, and since then he has covered the property inside and out with his wildly inventive creations. The place kind of resembles a giant pop-up book: Adjacent to the studio is a small town in miniature, complete with general store, radio station, and a Denny's. (Actually, it's not *that* miniature: the bank building looks to be about 10 feet tall.) Then there's what Dale calls his "robots," flat wooden figures with garish faces that are motion-activated to talk, wave, or shine their lightbulb eyes at you. As you enter the studio, for instance, a 2D fellow with big glasses and loud trousers begins braying, "Hey, you got a customer here!" while behind the counter a yellow-haired character with bad teeth bleats, "Hello, would you like to buy something?"

All the taped voices are Sinderson's, and as to what allows these robots to talk while their jaws move or their heads nod, it seems to have a lot to do with rubber bands and wooden spools. Dale's dad owned a junkyard, and he claims that's where he learned how to make things work. Some of his stuff is for his own amusement, but most of it has a price tag. Ask Sinderson what inspires his artwork and he'll say, "I'm just following my brain around." If you're anywhere near Harvard, you'll definitely want to stop by and find out where it leads him.

CHARLES SMITH

African American Heritage Museum
and Black Veterans Archive
126 North Kendall
Aurora, IL 60505
(815) 968-9770 Jessie Bates, agent
Map: Suburban West

Drive by the home of Dr. Charles Smith in Aurora and you will almost certainly find yourself slowing down to get a better look. This Vietnam veteran and part-time preacher has found his true calling in sculpture, and he's turned his front yard into a jaw-dropping open-air museum. He calls it the African American Heritage Museum and Black Veterans Archive, which is quite a mouthful but still doesn't do justice to the place. Smith has created more than thirteen hundred pieces of folk art depicting African American history and culture, and they're all crammed into the plot of land that surrounds his house. Vying for your attention are sculptures of such notables as Crispus Attucks, Duke Ellington, Harold Washington, and the Harlem Globetrotters. Much of Smith's subject matter is deeply affecting, such as the sculpture of a seated slave, red wounds from a whip visible on his back, solemnly reading the Emancipation Proclamation; or the representation of James Bird Jr., who was dragged by racists from a car and then decapitated—you can see where the head has been broken off and reattached.

The doctor's raw material is wood that he takes from the trees on his property. Once a sculpture is done, he paints it using a substance that, along with providing color, takes on a rubberized form that will protect the piece from the elements. Smith gets great pleasure from guiding wide-eyed visitors around the crowded museum, and with his background in preaching he's never at a loss for words. When asked about the project's beginnings, he told us, "This started by way of divine intervention of information seeking God for help against issues I was personally facing." Doctor Smith, whatever your inspiration is, it's working!

THRIFT STORE ART

www.thriftstoreart.com

I f you want to start collecting art, why not begin in the basement—the bargain basement, that is—by acquiring thrift store art? You've seen this stuff: peculiar paintings collecting dust at the Salvation Army store or donated to the church bazaar, self-taught or "naive" or just plain bad art. Painted at an early stage (or the only stage) of the artist's career, these crimes, sorry canvases can be had for a few bucks. But where to begin your collection? Do you start with an unnaturally rendered still life or with a grotesque nude? If you don't think you have enough good sense of bad taste, start your education at Paul B's on-line gallery. Here you'll find dozens of deeply shallow pieces from the collection he houses at his subterranean salon (okay, his basement) and others donated virtually. Whether these works are samples of faux primitivism or faux pas, Peggy Guggenheim would gag. You'll find *Grumpy Cigar Smoking Man with Velvet Crown* next to *Portrait of a Man with White Beard, Thick Glasses and Embroidered Shirt* (no confusing titles here), painting after painting done by hobbyists not hobbled by restrictions of color, composition, or technique. The provenance of each work is listed, when known. Surprisingly, some of these assassinations in acrylic are unsigned.

Paul says he could never part with one of his paintings; it would be "like selling your children." Indeed, getting cash for your kids is a barbaric thought in today's enlightened age. But one look at *Grumpy Man* and you'll think maybe we've progressed too far.

STEVE WOLF

(847) 821-0656
www.majorleaguemodels.com
Murphy's Bleachers
3655 North Sheffield Avenue
Chicago, IL 60613
(773) 281-5356
Map: Chicago North

W alk to the back of Murphy's Bleachers in Wrigleyville and you will find a baseball fan's impressive tribute to the stadium across the street. Steve Wolf took the better part of a year to build a miniature version of Wrigley Field. It's actually not that miniature—at ⅛-inch scale, the model comes to about 6½ square feet in area. Wolf worked from blueprints, photos, and many visits to the old ballpark; among his materials were several types of wood, Plexiglas, aluminum, glue, and some really tiny bulbs for Wrigley's controversial lights. The final result is delightfully detailed, down to the numbers on the scoreboard and the team banners flying from the flagpole. It rests

under a glass case at Murphy's, but at one point it looked like the model would never leave Steve's house. After he finished it in his second-floor workroom, the darn thing wouldn't fit down the stairs, and he had to rip out some bay windows in order to lower it to a waiting truck. That makes him either a dedicated artist or an irresponsible homeowner.

Wolf is now working on a gorgeous replica of Boston's Fenway Park, and he already has a massive model of Chicago's old Comiskey Park that takes up his whole garage. All his masterpieces are for sale, and he does do commission work (he's got a Yankee Stadium and a smaller Wrigley on order right now). By the way, there's one detail in his Friendly Confines miniature that some cynical fans might call inaccurate: On the scoreboard, the Cubs are winning.

MORE ARTISTS

PATTY CARROLL
2505 West Chicago Avenue
Chicago, IL 60622
(773) 342-0707
www.pattycarroll.com,
www.elimpersonators.com
Elvis-themed photography specializing in the fantasies of American culture.

ED FRUH
efruh@aol.com
Miniature models of Chicago's favorite amusement park, Riverview Park.

KATHERINE HILDEN
(847) 475-2954
www.khilden.com
"The line that draws a crowd" is this caricaturist's motto.

ROY KOERNER
www.bananaboyroy.com
Appealing artist celebrates the banana skin in sculpture.

GEOFFREY MAC

1932 South Halsted Street, No. 301
Chicago, IL 60608
(312) 733-9128
www.geoffreymac.com
Map: Chicago South
Slinky and sexy latex fashions for the daring.

GREG MARTIN

(630) 736-6201
www.chameleonartist.com
Custom made, delicate carvings of ostrich, emu, and rhea eggs.

GISELE PERREAULT

Artisans 21
5225 South Harper Avenue
Chicago, IL 60615
(773) 288-7450
www.giseleart.com
Map: Chicago South
Extraordinary masks for feline fanciers.

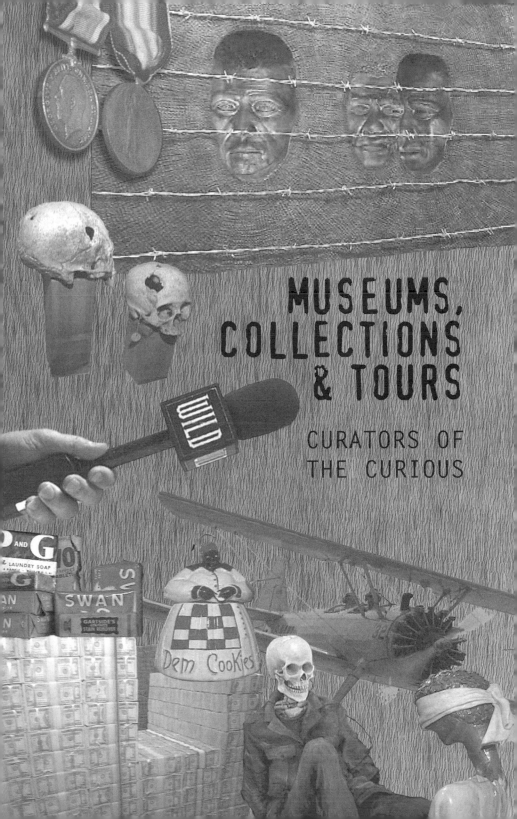

MUSEUMS,
COLLECTIONS
& TOURS

CURATORS OF
THE CURIOUS

AIR CLASSICS MUSEUM OF AVIATION

Aurora Municipal Airport
43 W636 U.S. Route 30
Sugar Grove, IL 60554
www.auroraairport.com/museum
Map: Suburban West

Don't miss the Air Classics Museum of Aviation in Sugar Grove, where the only thing as old as the planes are the folks that fly them. The tour guides are quite often pilots who are veterans from World War II and the Korean War, and they're some of the feistiest octogenarians you're ever going to meet. The museum, which spills out of a hangar at the Aurora Municipal Airport, has accumulated an amazing array of vintage military aircraft. Most of them have been loaned or donated, and all of them are capable of going airborne.

Our tour guide was one Nick "The Ripper" Cardella, a World War II veteran with thirty-three missions over Germany, and his in-depth knowledge about each and every plane he showed us was impressive. We were sad to hear that Nick has since passed away, but we'll always remember him describing the workings of a jet that draws in air through a large opening in the nose, then blasts it out the other end. With a mischievous glint in his eye, Nick told us this one was called a "Suck and Blow."

ANTIQUE FABRICARE MUSEUM

Pert Cleaners
4213 West Irving Park Road
Chicago, IL 60141
(773) 282-6216
Map: Chicago West

There's been a war going on. For hundreds of years, battles have been staged in tailor shops and laundry rooms around the country. It's the dirty war to disinfect and discipline our clothes. Here's your chance to view the machines, implements, and Rube Goldberg–type contraptions that have been conscripted into the campaign to keep what we wear smooth and spotless. Curator Tony Lupo has amassed more than three hundred irons, washing machines and boards, solvents, and suds makers for his Antique Fabricare Museum. You'll see old Lux and Duz detergent packages and a hand-cranking washing machine. Among the assortment of irons are the humble sad iron (which happily sat on the stove to get heated), a natural gas–fueled iron, and the iron maiden of irons (a

coal-stuffed Big Bertha that weighs twenty pounds).

Come to this museum to see the fallen fabricare heroes—casualties in the constant battle to keep our frockery looking fabulous. Salute them . . . and then take off your pants. Why? Because this museum is housed in a working dry cleaners. That means you can look over the collection while you take advantage of its one-hour cleaning service. Clever, huh? Hey, you think the Field Museum will starch your shirt while you stroll around looking at Sue the Dinosaur? We don't think so.

AWARD COLLECTION

Jeffrey Schramek
P.O. Box 300791
Chicago, IL 60630
(773) 539-5751
www.collectnobel.com

We found a guy who has more medals and prizes than he knows what to do with, and he didn't win any of them! Jeffrey Schramek collects awards given to significant historical figures, and the magnitude of some of his possessions is astounding. He is the proud owner of the Order of Isabelle the Catholic that was presented to Evita Peron by Spanish dictator Francisco Franco back in 1947. If that doesn't impress you, how about the 1936 Nobel Prize given to Sir James Chadwick, who discovered the neutron? Schramek graciously honored us with the Order of Merit of the British Monarchy from King George VI, but only for about two minutes—then it went right back into its case.

Before you deduce that Jeffrey Schramek must be some wealthy dilettante with money to burn, you should know that he is actually an aviation police officer at O'Hare who shares a modest bungalow with his dad. Needless to say, the lion's share of his disposable income goes into buying other people's medals,

most of which he acquires at British auctions (he bids over the phone). That would explain the large number of United Kingdom–related awards, like the beautiful gold stall plate meant for the Chapel of the Order of the Bath in Westminster Abbey (apparently they ran out of stalls—sorry, Sir George Cook!) or the posthumous medal given to English suffragette Emily Wilding Davison, who died at the racetrack after throwing herself in front of the king's horse.

Schramek has been known to present his collection at libraries and private functions, and he's always looking for new sources, so if you've got a line on a Nobel Prize, give him a ring. That old bowling trophy in the attic won't be of much use to him, though, unless it's Henry Kissinger's.

CHESTER GOULD MUSEUM

101 North Johnson Street
Woodstock, IL 60098
(815) 338-8281
www.dicktracymuseum.org
Map: Suburban North

Woodstock, Illinois, is the hometown of comic strip artist Chester Gould and also home to the museum that honors his most famous creation. You know who we're taking about, right? Yellow fedora, squarest jaw in Christendom, cheated on Tess Trueheart with Madonna? That's right, Dick Tracy, the detective you can still read about in the morning paper after seventy years.

The museum is located in the old courthouse building right on Woodstock's beautiful main square (which you may recognize from the movie *Groundhog Day*). It's jam-packed with Tracy and Gould paraphernalia, including the drawing board on which Dick first took shape and some original versions of the popular strip. There's a fascinating display of the research and crime technology used by Tracy that proves Chester Gould was way ahead of his time: Some of these gadgets weren't used by actual police until years later. All those freakish-looking villains are in evidence, with life-size models of several of them staring down at passersby. One look at criminals like Prune Face, Flat Top, or Wormy will convince you that crime doesn't only not pay, it can be seriously detrimental to your personal appearance.

COOKIE JAR MUSEUM

111 Stephen Street
Lemont, IL 60439
(630) 257-5012
Map: Suburban South

Browse, buy, or swap at this necropolis of cookie jars. With more than two thousand of them—squeezed onto every surface—you're sure to see one just like the one that sat so tantalizingly out of reach above Grandma's fridge. (And you wonder why you've got that sugar jones today.) It's a carnival of deliriously colored ceramics—genies, elves, pumpkins, pigs, pandas, and clowns both happy and, of course, sad. There are old soldiers, too,

in this cemetery of gallon-size jars—Aunt Jemimas, Howdy Doodys, and McCoys worth thousands of dollars. Stroll down one aisle to see the silly (a tepee jar), sensational (a NASA commemorative), and strange (a disturbing, dissipated man's head. *That'll* keep your hand out of the cookie jar). Some pieces are not priced, so be prepared to bargain with the owner, Lucille Bromberek, a sort of Cerberus to this collection. This creative crockery is worth the look, if only for the nostalgia factor. Buy one and you'll knock decades off your life. Open one and you might just hear the echo of children's squeals over the exhaustless riches it once contained.

CURT TEICH POSTCARD ARCHIVES

Lake County Discovery Museum
27277 Forest Preserve Drive
Wauconda, IL 60084
(847) 968-3381
www.teicharchives.org,
www.digitalpast.org
Map: Suburban North

If you thought postcards were just meaningless missives from semiexotic locales to be put on the fridge and then discarded, you may be surprised to hear that there's a museum devoted solely to the postcard. It's the Curt Teich Postcard Archives, and it's well worth the short road trip to Wauconda to see it. It's got cards dating back to the late 1800s, when the Curt Teich Company of Chicago first started sending photographers across the country to preserve landmarks for postcard posterity. Curt's minions were amazingly thorough—no matter how small your hometown, it's liable to make an appearance in the archives. The images arrayed here can provide an intriguing glimpse into our past; before TV, postcards were often the first view people got of major events and important personages, and now they qualify as pictures of history.

Visit the public exhibit and we're afraid you'll just see the tip of a very large iceberg. The bulk of the collection is stored in drawers at a whole other building, so if you want to research some family history or just find a nice picture of the Mitchell Corn Palace in South Dakota, you'll have to make an appointment. The original postcards aren't for sale, but you're welcome to purchase a reproduction or two. Helpful hint: If you visit, be sure to make time for a walk around the beautiful and expansive park that surrounds the museum.

FEDERAL RESERVE BANK

230 South LaSalle Street
Chicago, IL 60604
(312) 322-2400
www.chicagofed.org
Map: Downtown

Right near where LaSalle Street comes to an abrupt halt at the Board of Trade, you'll find a stone fortress fronted by imposing Roman pillars. The Federal Reserve Bank's exterior clearly discourages horseplay, which is one reason there's been not one attempted robbery since its doors opened in 1922. The interior is just as majestic and well worth a visit, but don't try to cash a check. The Federal Reserve is really a bank for banks: Cash flows through, counterfeit and unfit bills are weeded out and shredded (to the tune of $30 million a day!), and good cash is then distributed to regular banks which, we hope, distribute it to people like us.

While folks at the Fed won't give you change for a twenty, they will give you a tour, which includes a mini-money museum just off the main lobby. Here you can see what one million dollars looks like inside a big glass case and try your hand at picking out counterfeit bills. You'll also get a gander at early American currency, back in the day when each bank printed its own money. Just don't get any ideas when the tour passes all that shredded cash, even if you have a whole lot of free time and plenty of Scotch tape.

FIELD MUSEUM CATACOMBS

1400 South Lake Shore Drive
Chicago, IL 60605
(312) 922-9410 general info
(312) 665-7700 membership info
www.fieldmuseum.org
Map: Downtown

Any visitor to the Field Museum has probably heard about Sue the Dinosaur, but have you heard of Lou the Snail? Ever been in a room full of flesh-eating beetles or held a piranha in your own two hands? You'd be able to answer "Yes!" to these questions if you'd ever been invited deep into the museum's catacombs. The only way for us nonscientists to get that invitation is to become a member of the Field and attend one of its Member Nights. Those who do will discover that the museum does much more than exhibit dinosaur skeletons and Egyptian mummies to the public. In the laboratories and

storage rooms that the tourists never see, the museum's staff is methodically archiving the world's creatures, great and small. Their efforts will enable the scientists of today and tomorrow to study any species their heart desires, even if it's extinct.

For us average folks, it's just a kick to share a room with 450,000 (admittedly dead) birds from all over the world, some dating back to the 1860s. On Member Nights, the guides take groups into the bowels of the museum to visit a fish collection (very dead) so large that it's causing the building to sink a couple of inches a year. In the mammals department, they've got a whole floor devoted solely to rodents. That's also where you'll find the room full of carrion beetles, used to remove any remaining flesh from those darn mammal bones. And as for Lou the Snail, he's the Invertebrates staff's tongue-in-cheek answer to the greatly hyped Sue. He sits on a rock in their office and has his own soundtrack. Join now, before he slithers under the radiator.

50'S HOUSE

3100 Central Road
Rolling Meadows, IL 60008
(847) 577-7086
Map: Suburban North

Back in the early 1950s, a man named Kimball Hill pretty much built the town of Rolling Meadows from scratch, and to commemorate that accomplishment, the town Historical Society has replicated one of his houses. They haven't just copied the architecture and decor of those cozy one-story homes, they've filled the shelves, tabletops, and closets with actual items from the 1950s. Most are real artifacts while some are reproductions, and they leave it up to you to guess which is which. We particularly admired the "sip-n-smoke" set—a coaster and ashtray all in one!

The Historical Society has even given the house a pretend family: Fred, Mildred, and their three kids. When you come in, it's supposed to be as if they've all just stepped out; the kitchen counter is strewn with Mildred's cooking stuff, Fred's underwear drawer is ajar, and the TV is playing *I Love Lucy*. If you can overcome the feeling that you're trespassing (or that Fred and Mildred have come to a horrible end), a visit here can be like stepping back into a bygone era.

The consultants on the project were Rolling Meadows housewives who raised their kids in just such a domicile. One of them apologized to us that the black asphalt tile was 12 inches square instead of the original 8-by-8-inch size. You know, ma'am, we hadn't even noticed!

FRANK P. BURLA ANTIQUE PIPE AND TOBACCIANA MUSEUM

(630) 271-1317
members.aol.com/fpburla

What's a retired FBI man doing with a hookah in his condominium? If he's Frank Burla, it's just one item in an astounding assemblage of pipes and "tobacciana" (Frank swears that's a word). Burla can no longer live in this particular condo, since his museum takes up all four rooms and, it turns out, two full garages. Once you've entered his pipe-filled domain, you're greeted by Queen Mando, a 7½-foot bronze statue of a topless Cameroon monarch; she smokes a pipe whose bowl resembles a monkey's head. The proud owner and curator then guides you through the rest of the collection, giving you the historical and cultural background of the items on display. He'll show you one ornate pipe that turns out to be the last remaining symbol of freedom for Transylvania, with all its battles for independence depicted on the exterior. There's also a tomahawk that Native Americans could put tobacco in and smoke—presumably after they buried it in some enemy warrior's chest.

The oldest implement on display is a stone pipe from India, dated from around 200 B.C. Between that and the more current smoking paraphernalia from the 1970s, you will find a treasure trove of "tobaccianic" (is that a word?) curiosities. Don't miss the opium pipe from the Orient, or the Gambiar pipes that were carved in the likeness of the people buying them. Who knew that scrotal sacks of bulls were once used as tobacco pouches, or that clay pipes once provided smoke enemas to wary patients ("Hey, are you blowing smoke up my ass?!")? You might spot several somewhat pornographic pipes portraying such naughty activities as Leda being ravished by the Swan and Zeus protecting a vestal virgin. Burla insists these are mythological, not erotic. Whatever you say, Frank . . .

GHOST HUNTER RICHARD CROWE

P.O. Box 557544
Chicago, IL 60655
(708) 499-0300
www.ghosttours.com

Here's a letter we received from a *Wild Chicago* viewer: "I am sitting at the table, preparing to write down all the strange occurrences that have been happening in my house. I'd open a window and it would immediately slam shut. I'd pull the comforter up around my chinny-chin-chin and it would be yanked to the floor. And now, at my desk, I see my pen moving though I am not touching it. What spirit is pulling pranks on me? I must tell someone. I must tell a spectral detective like Richard T. Crowe. Mr. Crowe (Caw!) is Chicago's only full-time ghost hunter and spiritual tour guide. If you have a haunting, he wants to hear about it. He's checked into supernatural disturbances at cemeteries, murder sites, Indian burial grounds, and even private homes. Richard will—Wait! My pen! My pen is upright now and, and dancing on my desk! Damn this pixie! I can't concentrate. Where was I? Oh, yes. Richard then collects these tales of apparitions and manifestations and he will—and this is the really creepy part—Richard will lure people who have a love of the lore of the undead and get them onto buses or into restaurants where he then tells his ghost stories. Mr. Crowe (Caw!) pioneered the use of luxury buses and sightseeing boat tours to spin his narratives of the unnatural. I didn't hear that from a ghost, it's on Richard's Web site. At his site—Wait! My pen, it's up in the air! It's turning, it's, why, it's pointing at me. What the—Ahhhhhhh!! I've been stabbed! Oh, mother! The blood, the blood! My Casper's not so friendly now! Must tell my tale . . . Richard! Mr. Crowe (Caw!)! Get your . . . bus . . . here soon . . . must . . . tell . . . them . . . Caw! Ca—"

HARLAN J. BERK GALLERIES

31 North Clark Street
Chicago, IL 60602
(312) 609-0016
www.harlanjberk.com
Map: Downtown

Enter through the revolving doors of the Harlan J. Berk Galleries and you're immediately greeted by a 7-foot stone statue of a Roman senator from the days of Caligula. You've stumbled onto one of the most amazing privately owned collections on the continent, of which the proud and erudite owner is only too willing to remind you. Harlan Berk's taste in belongings is usually expensive, always refined, and incredibly eclectic. At his gallery you will find Egyptian burial artifacts, letters signed by world figures such as JFK, Malcolm X, and

Napoleon, autographed photos of Bela Lugosi and the Marx Brothers, even an autographed baseball from the 1923 Cubs. He once had some Egyptian mummies on the premises that none other than pop star Michael Jackson inquired about buying (he didn't).

That's right, everything has a price tag, though you'd think a lot of this stuff belongs in a museum. But before you assume that you could never afford to shop here, look closer. Sure, there's the coin with an Egyptian queen on it for $100,000, but there are also Roman coins for as low as $15. Keep in mind that not everything mentioned here will still be on display when you visit—some reclusive pop star might have beaten you to it.

HARTUNG MUSEUM

3623 West Lake Street
Glenview, IL 60025
(847) 724-4354
Map: Suburban North

This is a museum dedicated to automobilia and memorabilia. It's a warehouse filled with vintage cars and motorcycles, tractors, toys, police badges, license plates, dolls, electric trains, and baby carriages. Unlike most museums, however, where you walk through and passively experience the collection, here you'll feel like you walked into a production of *Our Town*. As you recall from Thornton Wilder's play, the Stage Manager character addresses the audience and describes the people and events in his small American town. Well, cast Lee Roy Hartung in the lead, substitute Glenview for Grover's Corners and get ready to encounter a living museum. Y'see, Mr. Hartung has amassed his collection with items he's acquired locally, within about a 15-mile radius. So he not only knows the original owners, he also knows their kids, parents, and grandparents. He'll tell you tales of the town as viewed through their property, like the story behind the 1934 bike. The child who owned this item received it after winning the essay contest "Why Mom Wants Me to Eat Quaker Oats." Lee says the kid was so very proud of that prize that "he kept it in his bedroom with a sheet over it." It's intimate details like these that will have you feeling like you know these people, as surely as you come to know George Gibbs and Emily Webb in the play. Because, really, what is a life but the adding up of simple moments and details? Oh, and just like a real play, you'll need to make reservations. Tours for Hartung's repository of memories are by appointment only.

HEMINGWAY'S APARTMENT

1239 North Dearborn Street
Chicago, IL 60610
(312) 944-7368
Map: Chicago North

No, this is not about the museum dedicated to author Ernest Hemingway in Oak Park. This is about a Chicago apartment that gets its Warholian fifteen minutes because Hemingway lived there for approximately four months in 1921. Mark Weyermuller, who now lives in the apartment, found out that Ernest had holed up there briefly before moving to Paris. While maybe not enough to inspire a doctoral thesis, Mark has taken this tidbit and turned it into a lifelong "school" project. He has decorated the hallway with a harvest of Hemingway memorabilia. You'll see *Life* and *Time* magazine covers, news clippings, photos, and a taxidermic marlin. Mark also displays what are claimed to be Hemingway's typewriter and fishing pole. They're not really Ernie's, Mark admits, but

he has created histories about them to tell guests just the same. He does a better snow job than the one on Kilimanjaro. He also has constructed little dioramas depicting pivotal moments in the writer's life. One, titled *Mayo Clinic 1961,* has a gurney-strapped G.I. Joe doll standing in (or rather, lying down) for the author while Dr. Ken and Nurse Barbie administer electroshock therapy. There's even a button so visitors can give Hemingway's head a jolt. Wait a second—we had to read *A Farewell to Arms* in high school, let us at it! Drive by the building and you might see a pic of Papa staring down at you. 'Course, after the electroshock, that's pretty much all he could do. Call Mark to schedule an appointment to tour his immovable feast of the fiction writer's life.

INTERNATIONAL MUSEUM OF SURGICAL SCIENCE

1524 North Lake Shore Drive
Chicago, IL 60610
(312) 642-6502
www.imss.org
Map: Chicago North

Located in a large stone building across from Oak Street Beach, this museum houses some of the most gruesome exhibits you're ever likely to see. No matter how you slice it, surgery ain't pretty, which we think is what Max Thorek set out to prove when he founded this place back in 1954. The history of the surgical sciences certainly illustrates that we've come a long way, baby. What medical school did early

Peruvians attend when they learned that cracking skulls open with a spike would relieve a headache? And whose idea was it to rejuvenate an ill patient by pumping the blood of a mule into his veins (almost always fatal)? You'll view paintings and sculptures portraying horrific maladies and their more horrific treatments. We will never forget the image of a man suffering from elephantiasis of the scrotum—the angry look on his face makes us think he just heard the words "Turn your head and cough."

There's a surgical kit from the nineteenth century on display, complete with hacksaw, that would strike fear into any breast, and something called the "bone crusher" designed to straighten bowed legs by breaking them (actually the before and after pictures indicate that it may have worked!). It's no surprise that practicing sadomasochists are frequent patrons of this museum and have attempted to purchase some of the items on display. But even *they* blanch at the sight of the "Kidney Stones and Gallstones" exhibit. Ewwwww!

JOHN DILLINGER MUSEUM
7770 Corrinne Drive
Hammond, IN 46323
(800) ALL-LAKE
www.johndillingermuseum.com
Map: Multistate

Just across the Illinois state line in Indiana you'll find the John Dillinger Museum, housed in a futuristic-looking building that turns out to be the Lake County Visitors Bureau. It's an appropriate location if you consider that Dillinger's most famous escape occurred in Lake County at the jail in Crown Point. The museum is made up of a plethora of interactive exhibits revolving around the famous bank robber's life and times. You can spend a few minutes stewing in a jail cell like the ones Dillinger was so fond of exiting or saunter into a bank in the middle of a holdup—don't fret, it may *look* like Dillinger's gang, but they're really just mannequins in period dress.

You can test your crime-fighting instincts in one area, your knowledge of Dillinger trivia in another. The curator assured us that the museum had numerous belongings of the desperado in its possession, but it turns out they're all in a vault somewhere; the letters home, tommy guns, and family pictures you see on display are only replicas. You'll still probably enjoy this place, and if not, there's an easy escape route: right through the gift shop!

KENOSHA MILITARY MUSEUM

11114 120th Avenue
Pleasant Prairie, WI 53159
(262) 857-3418
www.kenoshamilitarymuseum.com
Map: Multistate

Better knock off those cheesehead jokes, because it looks like Wisconsin is ready for war! Or at least that's the way it seems when you first lay eyes on the Kenosha Military Museum. If you've ever taken I-94 across the state line, you must have seen it: over a hundred pieces of military hardware sitting in an open field. Owner and curator Mark Sonday is an Air Force veteran who's been collecting military equipment since he was a kid. He goes to government surplus sales (foreign and domestic) and base closings, where this stuff is sold by the ton. The museum has on display any

number of planes, helicopters, tanks, personnel carriers, jeeps, and cannons that Sonday basically rescued from becoming scrap metal.

The museum tour has plenty of highlights. There's a 40-foot-long missile that looks like the one Slim Pickens rode to oblivion in *Dr. Strangelove*. Don't miss the Huey helicopters from the Vietnam era, or the Sikorsky Sky Crane that can lift its weight—twenty thousand pounds. If nature calls, stop by the World War II army latrine that remains in working order. And that's not the only thing that works; several of the aircraft still fly, and Mark has been known to take his M-60 tank for an occasional joyride along the Wisconsin-Illinois border—just in case the Land of Lincoln gets any bright ideas . . .

MUSEUM OF ANESTHESIOLOGY

520 North Northwest Highway
Park Ridge, IL 60068
(847) 825-5586
www.asahq.org/wlm
Map: Suburban North

If you're the kind of person who needs to be put under for a simple teeth cleaning, you'll want to make a beeline for the Museum of Anesthesiology in Park Ridge, where you'll find a bizarre array of contraptions devoted to knocking people out, from the primitive to the quite advanced. There are tours offered, some by the founder of the museum himself, Dr. George Bause. All the folks who work here take their subject very seriously; in fact, when we visited, the receptionist definitely seemed sedated.

The museum covers anesthesiology of every variety: general, local and yes, deadly (their display of blowguns with darts dipped in curare was our favorite part of the exhibit). The main purpose of medical anesthesia is, of course, to prevent the patient from moving during surgery, or, as our guide explained, "The doctor can't let you wiggle while he works." It's alarming to discover that after all the time and effort spent on refining the art of anesthetizing a body, they still aren't exactly sure how it works. Makes you almost long for the Neanderthal days when all they needed was a large rock.

NATIONAL VIETNAM VETERANS ART MUSEUM

1801 South Indiana Avenue
Chicago, IL 60616
(312) 326-0270
www.nvvam.org
Map: Downtown

It's the only museum of its kind in the world: a collection of art whose subject is a war, its artists the combatants of that war. To have your work exhibited here, you have to have fought in Vietnam, on *either* side. It's the brainchild of three Vietnam veterans who found themselves in art school together after they'd returned to the States. They decided to seek out other vets with artwork on the subject of Vietnam, and judging by the museum's two floors of memorable paintings, photographs, and sculptures, their search was a pretty big success.

When you walk into the NVVAM, the first thing you should do is look straight up. That's where you'll see the *Above and Beyond* installation, a 10-by-40-foot rectangle of shimmering silver that turns out to be the dog tags for every American killed in the Vietnam War—58,226 and counting. Go farther inside and you will find works of art that powerfully evoke the horror,

anguish, courage, and even humor that came with being a soldier in this conflict. There is a harrowing sculpture of a blindfolded prisoner of war, a drawing taken off the body of a dead North Vietnamese soldier, and a series of cartoons sketched on the envelopes of a GI's letters home. We especially admired a series of pictures that were created with the only materials the soldier had on hand: C-ration coffee and paper.

At some point in your visit you may hear a soft jingling sound; it's an eddy of air passing through those thousands of dog tags.

NORTHERN ILLINOIS POLICE CRIME LABORATORY

1677 Old Deerfield Road
Highland Park, IL 60035
(847) 432-8160
Map: Suburban North

Are you thinking of committing the perfect crime? Well, know this: After you perpetrate your act of lawbreaking, there'll be a posse of people breaking their necks trying to nail you. The forensic investigators up in Highland Park are such a group. They handle and evaluate evidence from a crime, including the one *you're* contemplating. If you've ever seen an episode of *CSI*, the lab here is relatively similar, except on the television show the lighting is more attractive and so are the scientists. (Sorry, guys, but they're actors.) They've got all those high-tech devices and gadgetry that'll examine, extract, dissect, and detect; enough to send the perp to the big house. They can check for DNA (better wear a hair net at your crime), handwriting analysis (scratch out forgery for you), and shoe impressions (Can you commit your felony walking on your hands? Nope, forget it. They've got a great fingerprint department). You don't even want to know what they store in their refrigerator. If you have questions concerning crime solving, give them a call. Or, schedule a group tour of the lab. Seeing, firsthand, the extent of the tests they can do to evidence will have you reconsidering that perfect crime, although it might just inspire you to *write* about one. Make sure you thank the lab on the acknowledgments page of your best-seller.

OLD CHICAGO GOLF SHOP

4977 Arquilla Drive
Richton Park, IL 60471
(708) 747-1045
www.oldgolf.com
Map: Suburban South

Niblicks, long-noses, mashies, cleeks—if you're golf enthusiast Leo Kelley, these are a few of your favorite words. Leo has amassed a diverse and quite valuable collection of golf-related items and with it has managed to turn his hobby into his vocation. The basement of his home has been converted into a museum and shop (by appointment only, please), and he also has a thriving mail-order business. Both feature an array of rare golf memorabilia that would make any duffer drool. The first matched set of metal woods ever produced is here as well as the largest collection of giant niblicks in the world *(giant niblick [noun]: iron with a round, thin head used to hop ball over opponent's ball on the green; predates "marking").* Kelley's oldest club is an 1820 bunker iron made by a blacksmith in England, and there's a driver on display that could measure the distance of your drive with a little meter on the bottom. Unfortunately, it didn't tell you where the heck the ball went.

Leo's also got a full line of vintage golf togs that includes hats, argyle socks, and knickers (Kelley has to have his own knickers custom-made, as he's a "56 portly"). There's also a slot machine that spits out golf balls if you win, and a small selection of golfing literature; our favorite title was *Golf and Be Damned.*

If you choose to visit the Old Chicago Golf Shop in person, Leo is a convivial host and may even take you out to the homemade putting green and sand trap in the backyard. It's a good place to try out your cleek *(cleek [noun]: We're not sure, ask Leo).*

POLKA MUSIC HALL OF FAME AND MUSEUM

4608 South Archer Avenue
Chicago, IL 60632
(800) TO-POLKA
www.internationalpolka.com
Map: Chicago South

"Polka is happiness." That's what our tour guide told us when we visited this museum dedicated to Bohemian music. Your depression will surely lift when you giddily waltz through their collection of polka sheet music, recordings, artifacts, and memorabilia. They've got the pictures and paraphernalia of all the players that have pumped pleasure into the hearts and feet of polka-loving Chicagoans. See Joe Paterek's famous World War II accordion that's colored red, white, and blue. Read Governor Jimmy Carter's letter concerning the proclamation of January as National Polka Music Month. Gaze at the photos of some of the people behind this vivacious music: Dave "Scrubby" Seweryniak, Sylvester "Shep" Wolan, and "Whoopee John" Wilfhart. The museum's mission is to "bestow proper honor and recognition to performers, deejays, and others who have rendered years of faithful service to the polka entertainment industry." If you've already created a temple to these "tempo-makers," what else is there? You throw them an awards banquet. Go on-line to check out how you can get tickets to see such polka legends as Frankie Yankovic and Lenny Gomulka receive their due. Find out, too, where the museum is currently located. As of this review, it was looking for a permanent home. Then, come ready to swing!

RICOBENE'S CLASSIC CAR MUSEUM

928 West 38th Place
Chicago, IL 60608
(773) 847-5740
Map: Chicago South

Hidden in a nondescript neighborhood on the South Side is a jewel of a museum. It houses Frank Ricobene's car collection, and if you recognize that name, it's because Frank also has a chain of self-titled restaurants. (How do you think he pays for the cars?) Before Ricobene thought of selling sandwiches, he was a teenager trying to keep a series of $50 junk cars running, and thus was born his hobby of restoring automobiles to pristine condition. Another of Frank's pastimes

was illegal drag racing in the Back of the Yards, sort of Chicago's version of *The Fast and the Furious*. That probably explains the predominant number of muscle cars in his museum, *muscle* denoting a big engine in a relatively light chassis. Those that aren't built for speed are clearly meant to be shown, like the '58 Impala with power everything or the '64 Thunderbird convertible with the movable steering wheel to allow for easy entrance. The criteria for being displayed here clearly do not include economy or fuel efficiency.

   The oldest car in the lot is a beautiful '49 Cadillac convertible, lovingly detailed inside and out just like the rest of the forty-some cars in residence. Pop any hood and you'll find an engine that sparkles, with nary a hint of grease. But don't think for a moment that excellent form equals lack of function—these show-pieces are all still quite drivable, and Ricobene was even racing one of them in the old neighborhood fairly recently. Don't tell the police, though, or Frank will have to sell a bunch of sandwiches to pay the fines.

SCHOLL FEET FIRST MUSEUM

3333 Green Bay Road
North Chicago, Il 60064
(847) 578-8417
www.finchcms.edu/scpm/feetfirst
Map: Suburban North

Dr. Scholl's foot museum is going to put all those small-town foot museums out of business. Most people don't even look at their feet because, well, they're so far away. Dr. William M. Scholl practically set up shop down there. At the College of Podiatric Medicine is an exhibit dedicated to the man of the ubiquitous corn pad and contour wooden sandal fame. The first gallery in this little shop of heels (and toes) is where they insist you MEET YOUR FEET. Hello. Whoa. You are assaulted by a gargantuan skeletal model of the foot. If we are going to be forced with an introduction to our foot, we cannot believe it is this colossal clodhopper. Surely someone stole this from the T Rex exhibit at

the Field Museum? No, the college maintains, it's just not to scale. If you don't trip over your feet, you'll see displays on the walking process (in the average life, we walk 100,000 miles), foot surgeries (bunions and hammertoes are the most popular ailments), and plaster casts of the various types of arches (fallen, high, and golden). They even have the world's largest

shoe, size 35. This tank-with-a-heel came from a Mr. Wadlow, a downstate boy from the apparently bigfoot town of Alton. We think he donated the shoe after being forced to close his own foot museum. The second gallery is a celebration of Dr. Scholl's fancy footwork during his long career of foot-care education and innovation. He created and cleverly marketed thousands of "pod" products, and you'll find many of them here.

We don't think we could walk in Dr. Scholl's shoes . . . we tried. Falling out of one of those wooden sandals is a killer.

VOLO AUTO MUSEUM

27582 Volo Village Road
Volo, IL 60073
(815) 385-3644
www.volocars.com
Map: Suburban North

Here's a museum where not only can you browse through the antique and classic cars but you can buy them. Owner Greg Grams has amassed a display and "for pay" collection of over 250 vintage autos in the tiny, northwest town of Volo. (How tiny? The cars outnumber the people.) Step into one of the four "showrooms" and you'll be astounded by the ice floe of autos—row after row of Cadillacs, Fords, Chevys, Woodies, "muscle" cars, Model A's, foreign roadsters, and street rods. You'll find more Mustangs here than there are out in the wild. And, unlike most museums, this one lets you handle the displays. You can slide behind the wheel of a '57 T-Bird or poke your head under the hood of a '70 Roadrunner. Even better, serious buyers can take the cars out for a drive. What drives people to purchase these old autos? One customer told us because "they increase in value, 18 percent a year." Greg thinks it's because newer cars are homogenized: "To me, they're like jelly beans. When you go down the highway, I can't tell one from another." However, cruise around in a GTO or a Fleetwood and "I guarantee, going down, you'll have everybody stopping and looking at it." Remember, though, that beauty has a price—and don't we know it. These pre–energy-enlightened cars are fuel hogs. The trade-off is cheaper insurance. Greg says that thieves don't want to steal the classic cars because "It's like a neon light going down the road."

WATER RIDERS

(312) 953-WATR
www.wateriders.com
Map: Downtown

There are many ways to tour the Chicago River, but few give you as good a workout or put you as close to the aqua as Water Riders Adventure Agents. That's because water rider = kayak, and kayak = strenuous exercise and potential wetness. But for you hardy souls who find those big tour boats much too comfortable, this might be right up your estuary.

Water Riders usually start their tours on the docks behind the East Bank Club downtown. They provide the kayaks (though you're welcome to bring your own), and for people whose paddling skills are rusty, there's a quick refresher course before touring commences. Once under way, participants are faced with a number of challenges, not the least of which is dodging the much larger traffic going up and down the river—kayaks are clearly small fry among the Wendellas

of the world. Then there's the pressing task of staying close enough to the tour guide's vessel to hear all the scintillating narration that's being provided; Water Riders offers a choice of theme tours to its clients on such topics as "Chicago History" and "Gangland Lore." You may find your mind wandering as you take in the sheer beauty of the city viewed from water level. That's okay, as long as you're not daydreaming in the path of an oncoming barge.

MORE MUSEUMS, COLLECTIONS & TOURS

BALZEKAS MUSEUM OF LITHUANIAN CULTURE
6500 South Pulaski Road
Chicago, IL 60629
(773) 582-6500
www.lithaz.org/museums/balzekas
Map: Chicago South
Southwest side shrine preserving Lithuanian history and culture.

CUFFLINK COLLECTOR EUGENE KLOMPAS
P.O. Box 5970
Vernon Hills, IL 60061
(847) 816-0035
www.justcufflinks.com
Map: Suburban North
This guy has thousands of pairs of historic and significant cufflinks.

DAVE'S DOWN TO EARTH ROCK SHOP AND THE PREHISTORIC LIFE MUSEUM
704 Main Street
Evanston, IL 60202
(847) 866-7374
www.davesdowntoearthrockshop.com
Map: Suburban North
Fantastic fossil collection and the world's largest carnivorous dinosaur egg.

GAS MASK COLLECTOR BART WILKUS
www.nofuture.com
A gas mask connoisseur who markets his collection to the paranoid among us.

J. FRED MACDONALD FILM ARCHIVES

5660 North Jersey Avenue
Chicago, IL 60659
(773) 267-9899
www.macfilms.com
Map: Chicago North
Treasure trove of old films, for lease or sale.

MUSEUM OF HOLOGRAPHY

1134 West Washington Street
Chicago, IL 60607
(312) 226-1007
www.holographiccenter.com
Map: Chicago West
Extensive collection of art created by lasers.

NATIONAL ITALIAN-AMERICAN SPORTS HALL OF FAME

1431 West Taylor Street
Chicago, IL 60607
(312) 226-5566
www.niashf.org
Map: Chicago West
Honoring the contributions of Italian American athletes.

NOTRE DAME SHRINE

Fine Arts Building
410 South Michigan Avenue
Chicago, IL 60611
Map: Downtown
A tribute to the South Bend institution created by the building elevator operator and housed in the basement.

PEACE MUSEUM

100 North Central Park Avenue
Chicago, IL 60624
(773) 638-6450
www.peacemuseum.org
Map: Chicago West
Imagine world peace—they do.

TOBY JUG MUSEUM

917 Chicago Avenue
Evanston, IL 60202
(847) 570-4867
www.britishcollectibles.com
Map: Suburban North
World's largest private collection of ornamental English drinking mugs.

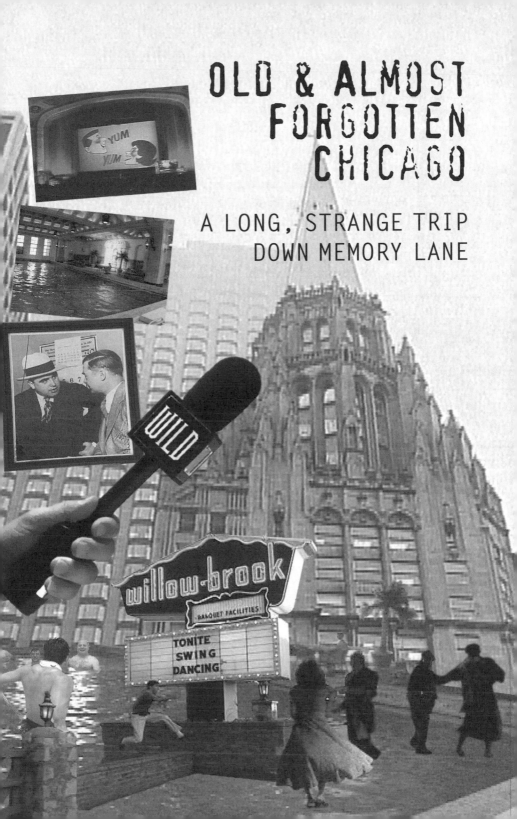

OLD & ALMOST FORGOTTEN CHICAGO

A LONG, STRANGE TRIP
DOWN MEMORY LANE

YUM
YUM

WILD

willow-brook

BANQUET FACILITIES

TONITE
SWING
DANCING

AUDITORIUM THEATRE

50 East Congress Parkway
Chicago, IL 60605
(312) 431-2389
www.auditoriumtheatre.org
Map: Downtown

The Auditorium Theatre has faced down the demolition squad on several occasions, and once you set eyes on this architectural gem, you'll be glad it was saved from the wrecking ball. The building was designed by Dankmar Adler and Louis Sullivan, with a little help from a young apprentice named Frank Lloyd Wright. It opened its doors in 1889 as the largest opera house in the world, with seating for 4,300. The theater was built to be flexible: When a temporary floor was installed over the seats, the first level could be transformed into a ballroom and was even used for indoor tennis and softball.

To fully appreciate the Auditorium's rich history and witness its many treasures, we highly recommend that you take the guided tour with resident historian Bart Swindall. He's a walking encyclopedia of knowledge, and he takes great pleasure in sharing it with anyone in his vicinity. He'll tell you, for instance, that by the end of World War II, the Auditorium had fallen on hard times and was actually used as a way station for returning soldiers, complete with a fourteen-lane bowling alley on the stage. In the 1970s, the theater took on rock shows that included Jimi Hendrix, Alice Cooper, and Styx. In recent years a concerted effort has been

made to bring the theater back to its former glory, and from the looks of it, the renovations are going quite well. Check out the restored painting above the proscenium depicting the cycle of life, or wander up to the mezzanine and experience the Whisper Gallery—the acoustics are so good that the faintest whisper can be clearly heard one hundred feet away.

Today the theater regularly houses plays, concerts, ballets, and the like. Why did attempts to demolish the Auditorium fail? Because it was so solidly built, it would have cost more to tear it down than the land was worth. Thank God for economics!

CAVALLONE'S WEST PIZZERIA

8933 South Archer Avenue
Willow Springs, IL 60480
(708) 839-5100
Map: Suburban South

Cavallone's West Pizzeria in Willow Springs was once a haven for gangsters, and if owner Rob Degan is to be believed, the place is lousy with spirits of the murdered and otherwise dead. Degan is proud to relate his building's colorful history, namely, that it used to be a speakeasy and brothel owned by none other than Al Capone. The first floor was for the liquor and illegal gambling, and the second floor was for the ladies of the evening. On his semiregular ghost tours, Degan claims that there are at least twenty-two "orbs" floating around the restaurant, some of them prostitutes killed by angry johns, others wise guys who met untimely ends. He delights in pointing out stains on the 1920s wallpaper upstairs that he says are dried blood from a knife fight, then guides you down to the basement where some bodies are purportedly buried. He'll also direct your attention to

several tunnels down there that he insists were escape routes for Capone's cronies, and a secret room behind the storage closet that may have been where the mobsters hid money, hooch, and themselves in case of a raid.

Rob has found a treasure trove of artifacts from the old speakeasy, including a "hidden gambling table" with a roulette wheel concealed beneath the tabletop and a painting with directions to a Capone hideaway scrawled on the back. If even half of this stuff is authentic and a third of Degan's ghost stories are true, Cavallone's West deserves a visit. Even if its checkered past doesn't appeal to you, the excellent Italian food probably will. Just hope a disgruntled poltergeist doesn't spit in it on its way to your table!

CHAPEL IN THE SKY

Chicago Temple of First
United Methodist Church
77 West Washington Street
Chicago, IL 60602
(312) 236-4548
www.chicagotemple.org
Map: Downtown

If you're standing in the Loop at Daley Plaza, follow the birds as they take flight from the Picasso sculpture. Up, up in the air (580 feet up, in fact), you'll notice a Gothic tower topped with a cross. This "vision" is the oh-so-appropriately named Chapel in the Sky. It's perched above the First United Methodist Church's Chicago

Temple. This high house of worship was built in 1952 in memory of Charles R. Walgreen (yes, the drugstore king) and it features beautiful woodwork and stained-glass windows. Sitting in here on a sunny day is like being inside an ecclesiastical kaleidoscope. The church says the chapel is popular for weddings (seats sixty) and the Easter sunrise

service is visually (and spiritually?) a knockout. This penthouse for prayer has even inspired fiction. Charles Merrill Smith's series of detective novels features Reverend Randollph, an ex-Rams quarterback turned clergyman, who tackles crime using humor and humility, much to the consternation of the pagan police. If you take the tour of the chapel, you, too, can be a detective. Try to spot the image buried somewhere in the stained glass that was placed with a wink to Mr. Walgreen's livelihood: a pharmacist's mortar.

DEARBORN OBSERVATORY

Northwestern University
2131 Sheridan Road
Evanston, IL 60208
(847) 491-7650
www.astro.nwu.edu
Map: Suburban North

"Giant Star Collapses!" Nah, this story is not about an overworked celebrity. In fact, it's not about people at all. It's about what happens "Out There Where Worlds Collide!" The Dearborn Observatory and its refracting telescope have been researching celestial phenomena since their dedication in 1888. Their astronomers have observed binary stars, done work to improve the accuracy of measurement within the solar system, and discovered that the Milky Way galaxy was not composed of chocolate and caramel. If you want a real "Oh, Henry" moment, check out the observatory's pedigree. The Dearborn building was designed by Henry Ives Cobb (who also designed the Newberry Library) and was named after a relative of the Revolutionary War hero Henry Dearborn (who, as you may recall, had a little fort in Chicago named after him). Today the telescope is used as a teaching instrument for the university's physics and astronomy students. Occasionally, a few astrology majors will slip in there, but as soon as they start talking about divining their love lives by determining the position of Venus, they're quickly detected and weeded out of the program. If you've got a black hole in your schedule, the observatory is open every Friday from 9:00 to 11:00 P.M. The entrance fee isn't astronomical, either—it's free. A maximum stargazing crowd of twenty is allowed, so reservations are required. If you've been using a home "tele" to scope out your neighbors, come to the observatory to increase the size of your playground by playing peekaboo with the planets.

DIVISION STREET RUSSIAN-TURKISH BATHHOUSE

1916 West Division Street
Chicago, IL 60622
(773) 384-9671
Map: Chicago West

You spend your whole work-week sweating over the little stuff. Now, come here to sweat for a little relaxation and, perhaps, better health. The Division Street Bathhouse is letting off steam for your physical pleasure. With an average temperature of 165 degrees Fahrenheit, the steam room's penetrating heat will melt your muscle tension and take the tartar off your teeth. It's *hot!* To attest to the therapeutic powers of a good steam, one customer said that "it's the only place

in the world for you to come when you've got arthritis or rheumatism and cold weather and damp weather." But, don't take his word for it, he was just some naked guy on a bench. A group of Japanese doctors determined that the heat can be beneficial to patients with cardiovascular disease—and they were dressed when they said that.

After you're through cooking, dip into the hot or cold pools, get a massage, or just nod off on one of the cots. Make sure you rehydrate with a beer or a fresh-squeezed juice at the bar.

When people think of a bathhouse, they picture portly old men with sagging breasts and flip-flops. And, while you will see a percentage of seniors, Division Street is attracting younger, firmer-bosomed bodies. Who's bared his butt here? Russell Crowe, Michael Jordan, and Denis Savard. Stop inside and you'll see an entire wall of celebrity photos. Sadly, females are not allowed. But, that's okay. Women see enough breasts as it is.

FRONCZAK'S HARDWARE

2606 West 47th Street
Chicago, IL 60632
(773) 847-3138
www.orderhardware.doitbest.com
Map: Chicago South

Fronczak's is stuffed to the gills with hardware and with Fronczaks. When we were there, we met Debra, Joe, Joe Jr., Maryann, Amy, Grandma, and baby Kylie Fronczak. How many Fronczaks work there? Joe said, "We all do. Sooner or later." Or, was it Joe Jr. who said that? Anyway, the shelves are chock-full of plumbing, electrical and woodworking supplies, tools, glass, and just about all the hardware you'll need to start or finish a job. They don't seem to waste much space. "No, we don't. We stack it high and tight," said Maryann . . . or was it Kylie? How do they compete with the big stores like Home Depot? First, since 1951 they've believed in service. *We* believe if one Fronczak can't help you, there's a boatload of others who can. Fronczaks were reared on hardware. They teethed on ball peen hammers. Second, "We're not just nuts and bolts" (and don't ask who said that, it was somebody tall). Sure, they carry all the basics, but Fronczak's inventory is deeper than Depot's. They cut keys but also carry old skeleton and skate keys. They offer so many screws, they have their own room, the Screw Room. They even carry beauty rings for a stovepipe. Carry stovepipes, too. If you don't know what these are, you don't need them. If you do, then it's good to know they are one of the few stores to stock them. For the true pipe aficionado, Fronczak's hand-crimps them. And if you need just one nail, they'll give it to you, free. Don't try abusing their generosity, though, or they'll "throw you out." Grandma Fronczak said that, we think, because she looks capable of tossing someone. She's got nice muscles from all that pipe crimping.

HOTEL INTERCONTINENTAL CHICAGO POOL

505 North Michigan Avenue
Chicago, IL 60611
(312) 321-8830
www.chicago.intercontinental.com
Map: Chicago North

The building that now houses the Hotel InterContinental on Michigan Avenue had a former life as the Medinah Athletic Club, owned and operated by the Shriners. There are very few fezzes to be seen anymore, but there is one very large vestige of the club in the fitness center between the hotel's eleventh and twelfth floors. I'm referring to what has been called one of the greatest hotel pools in the world.

The InterContinental pool boasts a luxurious swimming area with a lovingly preserved Venetian design. It was constructed in 1929 and features Spanish tiles imported from Majorca and an ornate "fountain of Neptune" adjacent to the pool itself. You'll find ample lounging space poolside and a great view of Michigan Avenue from the windows near the deep end. No wonder this place was once a frequent stop for big-name swimmers like Johnny ("Me Tarzan . . .") Weismuller.

To sample the pool's charms, you can either join the health club or spend a night at the Hotel InterContinental. We'd think twice about getting a room on the eleventh floor, though, unless you don't mind having 120,000 gallons of water directly over your head.

MARGIE'S CANDIES

1960 North Western Avenue
Chicago, IL 60647
(773) 384-1035
www.margiescandies.nv.switchboard.com
Map: Chicago West

Margie's has been "in tune with your taste since 1921," and this store knows your taste isn't singing the tune of liver and lima beans. They serve the seven deadly sins of sweets: sundaes, sodas, shakes, fudge, chocolates, and marzipan. Okay, that's only six, 'cause we ate the seventh, their four-scoop abomination of a creation called the "Eiffel Tower." You'll say "oui oui" to their homemade ice creams, which carry a jaw-dropping—and heart-throbbing—18 percent butterfat. Margie used to say about her ice cream, "It's good vitamins." *We* say Margie never heard the three words *cho les terol*. Make a bet with a friend (like, who'll pay the emergency-room bill) when you see who can finish the "World's Largest Sundae," which is mounded with a mammoth half-gallon of ice cream. For those who prefer a single scoop (haven't paid up your health insurance premium, huh?) check out their rainbow cones, which are caked in sugary sprinkles. Most of the other fountain creations are prettily presented like Venus on a half-shell–size bowl. What else is pretty? The price. A dozen of their Terrapins, chocolate-covered caramel and pecans, cost less than $10.

What also hasn't changed since 1921 is the decor. The booths are small and the place is covered—like a hot fudge sauce—with whatnots and knickknacks, including old newspaper clippings, a jukebox loaded with Bing Crosby and, inexplicably, stuffed animals. The food is available to go, so, you can sit outside and watch the world on wonderful Western Avenue. Or, stick it out inside and mingle with the clientele. As one server described Margie's patrons, "We have mostly regulars and then we have strangers."

MERZ APOTHECARY

4716 North Lincoln Avenue
Chicago, IL 60625
(773) 989-0900
www.merzapothecary.com
Map: Chicago North

If you have hemorrhoids, you don't have to take them sitting down. Merz Apothecary hand-mixes an ointment that's perfect for those pesky piles. Since 1875, Merz has been dispensing restoratives, nostrums, balms, preparations, and oils to remedy everything from acne to the aforementioned rear-end Vesuvius. If you're not finding a cure for your derriere dilemma or other ailment using over-the-counter correctives, give Merz a try. The apothecary focuses on herbal and homeopathic medicines using natural ingredients and traditional formulas. Even if you're not at death's door, come to this store for the decor. Merz has maintained the look of a nineteenth-century drugstore replete with herb-filled barrels, glass jars and vials, wood floors and exterior, and leaded glass windows. In a nod to the new, the shop also carries an extensive line of natural goods for the body, bath, and home, including Burt's Bees and Dr. Hauschka. Merz says it has become a Chicago landmark (tour buses make stops here) and "a mecca for people who want unique natural products for their bodies." And, it doesn't matter in what language you seek your salves and elixirs, their staff speaks seven of them. We asked, in English, one of their sage-looking pharmacists what he would recommend to treat a headache. He turned, and with a glint in his eye said, "The usual remedy is aspirin."

PATIO THEATER

6008 West Irving Park Road
Chicago, IL 60634
(773) 545-2006
Map: Chicago West

Ah, the movie palaces! They used to be a staple of Chicago entertainment— mammoth and ornate film venues that could seat, in some cases, up to four thousand people at a showing. Theaters like the Uptown, the Marbro, and the Paradise would surround their patrons with splendor, giving them a moviegoing experience to remember. Alex Kouvalis certainly

remembers, and when he found out that the Patio Theater (the neighborhood palace that he'd grown up going to) was in danger of being torn down to make room for a McDonald's, he took immediate action. Despite being a physicist and economist by trade, Alex bought the place and has managed to restore it to its former glory.

The Patio, like the better-known Music Box, is what's called an "environment" theater, so when the lights go down, make sure you look up. You'll experience the illusion of being out under the night sky, with stars twinkling and the occasional cloud seeming to float by. The organ up front is in fine working order and is given a periodic workout for special showings. We loved seeing the old-timey advertisements before the feature presentation, you know, the ones with the dancing hotdog and the talking box of popcorn. It all brings back what it used to be like to go to the movies, before all the cineplexes and multiplexes took over. Alex Kouvalis vows that there will be no 'plexes at the Patio, and here's hoping he can keep his promise.

ROSEHILL CEMETERY AND MAUSOLEUM

5800 North Ravenswood Avenue
Chicago, IL 60660
(773) 561-5940
Map: Chicago North

It is the oldest and largest cemetery in Chicago, with over three hundred thousand people buried there. Go on the guided tour and you'll discover that there's a tale behind just about every plot. Take, for instance, Charles Daniels, half of whom is buried here and the other half in the department store he had built in Denver, Colorado. Or what about the Hippach family? Its two children died in the Iroquois Theatre fire of 1903 and nine years later the parents went down with the *Titanic*—a classic case of being in the wrong place at the wrong time. Then there's Lillian Florence Jennings, who made the mistake of divorcing her vindictive husband and then dying before he did. He got his revenge by having a 16-foot monument that resembles a human phallus placed above her grave.

It could be argued that Graceland Cemetery has more famous residents within its walls, but Rosehill can still claim quite a few. Hot dog magnate Oscar Mayer has a tombstone here, as do Hinckley and Schmitt of bottled water fame.

Ironically, business rivals Richard Sears and Aaron Montgomery Ward are buried 30 feet away from each other in the mammoth mausoleum. You may not have heard of Frances Pearce and her infant daughter, who both died of tuberculosis in 1854, but they've gained a certain notoriety at Rosehill. It seems on certain evenings the glass case that covers the quite beautiful sculpture of their reclining bodies fills with a white glow, and the figures are seen to sit upright on their pedestal! Good Lord, *Noooo!*

SOUTHPORT LANES

3325 North Southport Avenue
Chicago, IL 60657
(773) 472-6600
Map: Chicago North

Southport Lanes has been a fixture on this "happening" avenue since well before there was anything "happening." One of the original Schlitz bars from the 1920s, it added bowling lanes in the mid-1930s, perhaps to distract law enforcement from the brothel and bookie joint upstairs. It's now the only Chicago bowling establishment where the pins are still set by hand. That's right, there's a couple of guys back there whose job description includes dodging your gutter balls (Jack be nimble, and he better be quick). But instead of trying to knock these pinsetters down along with the pins, try tipping them by slipping a 5-spot into one of your ball's finger holes before you bowl, and you might just find that the next 7–10 split disappears like magic.

The lanes here are pretty popular, so you may want to call ahead and reserve one. Get there a little early and you can sample the pretty good menu of burgers and the like. If bowling's not your thing, well, there are plenty of pool tables to go around. Sorry to disappoint you, but no, there's no guy under the table to help you rack the balls.

UNSHACKLED

Pacific Garden Mission
646 South State Street
Chicago, IL 60605
(312) 922-1462
www.pgm.org, www.unshackled.org
Map: Downtown

Chicago used to play host to numerous radio dramas that were sent out over the airwaves nationwide. Now there's pretty much just one—*Unshackled,* a Christian-themed program that's been on the air since 1950, making it the longest-running radio drama in history. It's taped at the Pacific Garden Mission on south State Street and goes out to nearly one

thousand stations all over the world. The true stories that are dramatized are usually (okay, always) tales of redemption involving someone who has seriously strayed
but eventually sees the light. The weekly production has all the elements of great
old-time radio: an impossibly deep-voiced announcer narrating the action, a cheesy
Hammond organ punctuating the actors' melodramatic dialogue, and, of course, an
incredibly agile sound-effects guy, slamming doors, throwing chairs, and running in
a box of gravel.

If all that doesn't hold your attention, check out the strange mix of audience
members around you—church groups are well-represented on one side, while
across the aisle are mostly denizens of the mission, street people who are
required to sit through the taping in order to get that day's free meal. One side
listens reverently, while the other side tries not to nod off. It all makes for a truly
unique Sunday afternoon.

WILLOWBROOK BALLROOM

8900 South Archer Avenue
Willow Springs, IL 60480
(708) 839-1000
www.willowbrookballroom.com
Map: Suburban South

I n the big-band era, the Willowbrook
Ballroom was the place to go for
hepcats in the know. It's now one of
only five bona fide ballrooms in the
entire country, and judging by the
schedule, the joint is still jumpin'.
Monday and Tuesday are for country-
and-western line dancing, Wednesday is
salsa, Friday is Singles Night, and Saturday is reserved for private parties. Sundays,
when we stopped by, there's ballroom dancing in the afternoon, then from 7:30 to 8:30
Willowbrook offers swing-dancing lessons. Later in the evening you can try out your
new steps to live music, and if you show up dressed in swing era threads, you get a

$2.00 discount. Such a deal!

The Verderbar family opened the
Willowbrook way back in 1921, and since
then it's estimated that close to 22 million
feet have twinkled their toes on the maple
wood floor. That floor is about 6,000 square
feet and holds up to eleven hundred
dancers. Much of the ballroom's decor dates
back to the 1930s, and it gives the place a genuine period feel, so even if you
don't want to cut the proverbial rug, it's worth a visit just to order a drink from

the magnificently long bar and soak in the ambience. Oh, and if you're wondering what goes on on Thursdays, the answer is absolutely nothing: They're closed.

MORE OLD & ALMOST FORGOTTEN CHICAGO

BERGHOFF RESTAURANT
17 West Adams Street
Chicago, IL 60603
(312) 427-3170
www.berghoff.com
Map: Downtown
Where locals have dined for more than a hundred years.

BIOGRAPH THEATER
2433 North Lincoln Avenue
Chicago, IL 60614
(773) 348-4123
Map: Chicago North
Watch a movie where Dillinger died. (He was killed in the alley next door.)

HOLLYWOOD ON LAKE MICHIGAN
www.lakeclaremont.com
Arnie Bernstein's comprehensive book on one hundred years of movie-making in Chicago.

MADE IN CHICAGO

WILD WARES FROM THE WINDY CITY

ADVERTISING FLAG COMPANY

3801 South Ashland Avenue
Chicago, IL 60609
(773) 523-3524
www.flagpro.com
Map: Chicago South

"Number 1 Mom." If you have a need to display the colors of your love, have a flag made by this company. Advertising Flag president Randy Smith says, "What we manufacture are custom-made flags and banners." They sell symbolic and sentimental streamers to individuals, industry, and governments. Whether you're looking for an insignia for your yacht (Jolly Rogers are their most popular) or a standard for a corporate event, contact Ad Flag and let them unfurl your idea. Their sewing department can create flags from a wide choice of fabrics: nylon, cotton, wool, and polyester. They'll appliqué, screen-print, and even color-match and dye. Then, they'll finish it off, ready for any installation or application. If you have a flag at home that's flagging, Ad Flag sells flagpoles and bracket sets, too. The company has made flags for the Smithsonian, the Art Institute, and the Latin Kings. "They were very happy with the work," says Randy. Go on-line to check out their selection of ready-made flags, including U.S., state, international, historical, and collectible flags.

Patriots looking for the perfect-size Stars and Stripes and potential potentates needing a flag for their new country, let Ad Flag be your Betsy Ross. Oh, and about that "Number 1 Mom" flag? That was available from the Web site's closeout section for just $14.95. Mom will never have to know that love is this cheap.

AMERICAN LAW LABELS

4135 South Pulaski Road
Chicago, Il 60632
(773) 523-2222 or (888) LAW-LABEL
www.americanlawlabel.com
Map: Chicago South

On a daily basis, the people at American Law Labels strike fear into the hearts of retailers and ignorant consumers alike. That's because they're the ones responsible for those tags affixed to stuffed articles like pillows, mattresses, and comforters that say DO NOT REMOVE UNDER PENALTY OF LAW. How many of us still have these mangy tags dangling from our stuffed goods in the hopes of avoiding hard time in the slammer? When if we'd read a little further, we'd see that the tag is not to be removed "except by consumer." It's actually there *for our benefit*, to certify the

materials used in stuffing that pillow or mattress. Less naive shoppers actually look at these things to make sure their comforter is filled with goose feathers and not old socks. It turns out the warning is for the retailer, who could be fined several thousand dollars for defying the terrible tag.

American Law Labels is owned and run by a no-nonsense father and son, both named Rocco Bruno. (It isn't a surprise that dad is a former boxer: "And in this corner, *Rocco Bruno!!*") They print their labels onto a hard-to-tear material called Tyvek, so even if you rip it off, you'll never rip it in half. When we asked the two Roccos if they'd ever considered producing something besides law labels, they proudly showed us their DO NOT REMOVE UNDER PENALTY OF LAW boxer shorts, designed to look as if they're covered with those famous tags. It might just be the perfect gift for a paranoid relative. Way to go, Rocco! You too, Rocco.

 BEHIND THE SCENES

With all the crazy stunts that Will Clinger has had to pull in the course of his tenure as *Wild Chicago*'s host, it might come as a surprise that the only serious injury he's suffered on the job occurred in the parking lot of American Law Labels. Will and producer Harvey Moshman were looking for an interesting way to get into the piece and decided to push Will into the camera's view on a sliding fence. Unfortunately, they didn't notice the

tracking system for the top of said fence until Will's hand went right into it, breaking the top of two fingers nearly off. Seventeen stitches and two splints later, he was as good as new and ready to jump right back on the fence—this time with his hands in a safer position.

FERRARA PAN CANDY COMPANY

7301 West Harrison
Forest Park, IL 60301
(708) 366-0500
www.ferrarapan.com
Map: Suburban West

Hey! Who you callin' a Lemonhead? *That* distinction belongs to one of the sons of the Ferrara Pan candy-making family. Legend has it that Mr. Ferrara named his company's best-selling citrusy-flavored candy after the birth of his child. It seems the boy was born with a head resembling the shape of a lemon. Fortunately, the young Ferrara grew out of his fruit head and developed into such an outrageously attractive man that he inspired the name of yet another FP product: the Red Hot (though it's believed they still post his baby picture up in the factory for Lemonhead quality control).

The Ferrara Pan company has been manufacturing its "heady" sweets in Chicago since 1908. If one of its rock-hard honeys hasn't touched your tongue, you've never been a kid. Besides making Lemonheads, the factory also turns out Atomic Fireballs, Jawbusters, and Boston Baked Beans—over 135 million pounds annually, and we've got the four cavities, two crowns, and a root canal to prove it. The *pan* in the company name comes from the method they use to make these candies. To view the process, visit the Web site, click on any of the candies, and take a virtual tour. Kids will love it. We did. Stay on-line and order some of the candy, in case you're not near a store that sells Ferrara Pan products, which, in this company's case, must mean you're living in Antarctica.

FILBERT'S SODA

3430 South Ashland Avenue
Chicago, IL 60608
(773) 847-1520
Map: Chicago South

Root beer consumption comprises only 3 percent of the soft drink market. But, boy, those 3 percent are diehards. Ask anyone who loves this original American drink made from roots and herbs and they'll quickly get all fuzzy-eyed just reminiscing about the fizzy drink. They recall black cows on the Fourth of July or misadventures guzzling gallons of the dark, frothy elixir in attempts to get drunk. Filbert's has been bottling its memorable soup-of-the-root since 1926. Karen and Ron Filbert are fourth-generation owners. It's a small operation—a mom-and-pop popper—that includes them, a sister, a couple of nephews, and a niece. Karen says, "We try to keep it in the family and keep the family in it." Root beer ... it's a bonding beverage. If your family's falling apart, come get the brew that could be the glue. And you will have to come because you won't find them at Jewel or Dominick's. All the

better to visit the factory, where you can watch the bottling process. In Filbert's Pop Shop, try some of their other sodas, including peach, raspberry, watermelon, and Mr. Newport (lemon-lime). Tap into the root beer at Filbert's and start creating memories of your own. Twenty-five years from now, your kids will fondly say, "I remember the whole family was loaded into the car to go pick up a case of Filbert's." 'Course, a quarter of a century later, they'll still be laughing about how you used to drive an SUV.

IMPRESSIVE CASKET

Factory Showroom
4200 Grove Avenue
Gurnee, IL 60031
(847) 662-4664
www.casketco.com
Map: Suburban North

Funeral expenses can be downright deadly, but we found a place to buy a casket that won't put you in the hole. You may have seen the company's sign while passing through Gurnee on Highway 41: CASKETS—SAVE UP TO 70%! Owner Maynard Cheris saw the need for more affordable funeral supplies and discovered that manufacturing coffins fit the machinery and equipment from his previous business of making automotive truck accessories. Thus began an "Impressive" success story. In the past, caskets were purchased exclusively through the funeral home, and funeral directors would routinely mark costs way up on their reliquaries; by selling direct to the public and skipping the mid-

dleman, Maynard has often saved customers *thousands* of dollars. His question to potential clients is simple: "Why bury your money?"

Impressive's product comes in a wide variety of woods and metals, and you can order your casket while among the living without paying any money in advance. (In a macabre way, it's sort of like "cash on delivery" . . . of a body!) The various coffin designs have such names as "the Precious," "the Homeward," and "the Angel" (sorry, no "Homeward Angel"). Prices start at around $647, and Impressive also has other funeral accessories available, including prayer cards and crucifixes. Cheris predicts that you'll eventually see caskets for sale in discount and department stores. We're impressed!

OPTIMO HATS

10215 South Western Avenue
Chicago, IL 60643
(773) 238-2999
www.optimohats.com
Map: Chicago South

Optimo Hats is one of the last haberdasheries around that custom-makes hats right on the premises. Personable owner Graham Thompson learned the chapeau craft from the previous owner of Optimo, and from the looks of it, he saved a lot of his predecessor's equipment. There are some great old contraptions behind the counter, including a mechanical hat blocker and something called "the Conformer," a metal-and-springs gadget that fits over the head to ascertain its shape and size—anything in a 7⅜" oval?

Graham prides himself on being able to find the ideal topper for a customer's face and personality, and he claims there's way less chance of "hat hair" when a hat is fitted to your particular head. Peruse the shelves and you'll see a wide and colorful array of Panamas, bowlers, porkpies, and fedoras, all created from the finest materials. Optimo has made hats for Buddy Guy and the late John Lee Hooker and provided the wide-brimmed beauty worn by Robert De Niro as Al Capone in *The Untouchables*.

Graham will sometimes travel to places like South America to purchase fine hats for his wealthier clients; he showed us one Panama that was worth over $6,000 and took more than eight months to weave. Most Optimos are much cheaper, but then again, how can you put a price on the absence of hat hair?

OXXFORD CLOTHES

1220 West Van Buren Street
Chicago, IL 60607
(312) 829-3600
www.oxxfordclothes.com
Map: Chicago West

They're the world's last remaining clothing manufacturer where the clothes are made totally by hand, so if they want to spell their name with two X's, that's just fine. Oxxford has been in business since 1913, and a lot of the employees have been working there for decades. Everything about the place is pure class—heck, even the elevator is pinstriped! They use only the finest materials, and an average of twenty-eight labor hours go into each suit produced. That could be why they charge so much (there's one suit listed at $14,000) and have had Al Capone, Elvis Presley, and several U.S. presidents on their client list.

Oxxford offers a guided tour (by appointment only) of its factory, and if you take it, be sure to ask about the kissing buttons and the lapels that have "memory." Then get the guide to show you the secret pocket sewn into the waistline of every suit. You also might be interested to learn that the jackets are usually only a quarter lined; our guide told us that full lining "hides the tailor's sins," the point being, we guess, that at Oxxford the workmanship is worth showing off.

STEWARTS PRIVATE BLEND COFFEE

4110 West Wrightwood Avenue
Chicago, IL 60639
(773) 489-2500
www.stewarts.com
Map: Chicago West

You put it in your mouth every day, don't you want to know how it's made? If you're a nipper of the nectar from the coffee plant, find out how your java's manufactured by visiting the factory. The Stewart family has been turning green beans into brown ambrosia since 1913. To make their coffee they'll "dump the green," roast 500 pounds at a time, precision-grind it, and pack it in their distinctive plaid cans. Stewarts says vacuum-packed cans are still the best way to keep the brew true and fresh. Loose beans sold from bins in the store expose the coffee to air, which can make it stale. And have you ever seen anybody

wash those bins? Director of Marketing Bob Tomkins says about the can that "it might be a bit uglier, but it's still very functional. It's kind of like the egg is the perfect container for right now." To taste some Stewarts, visit any major grocery chain. If they don't have it, dammit, demand it. If you haven't had your morning cup of mud and you're not quite ready to venture out, go on-line. There you'll find all their popular blends, in decaf and full-caf versions. If you're in food distribution and you're not already offering Stewarts swell joe to your customers, don't bother taking the tour—you'll probably be fired shortly, what with all the ruckus at your store caused by the crowds clamoring for Stewarts. For the rest of us, group tours are by appointment only. We're having a cup of the Red Eye Serious Brew right now. Hmm, robust and tasty, and boyohboywe'rereadytogogogogogo!

TEKKY TOYS

Orland Park, IL 60467
(708) 364-1520
www.tekkytoys.com,
www.getcoolstuff.com

Fart, fart, fart. Okay, that's out of the way. Remember the childhood prank involving the instruction to "pull my finger" which was then followed by the finger-pullee's releasing the excessive gas from his digestive tract (i.e., he farted)? Good. Well, three Chicago boys—or rather, men—have designed a line of toys celebrating the butt bugle. If you tug on the digit of their plush Pull My Finger Fred doll, Fred does indeed rip a rousing rump roar, shakes violently, and says, "Bombs away!" The addition of motion and speech to this gassy gag is a refreshing surprise. We're guessing your youthful pals didn't include *those* in their repertoire.

Smelling even greater opportunities to extend the fanny-firework franchise, the boys—sorry, men—created Squeezy Beans, soft-sculpture legumes (the original "party fuel") that when squeezed give a juicy toot and a tag line in character. After whistling through his britches, the Burgomaster bean, Cousin Cabbage, says "Mein-a heinie's on fire!" (Hmm, what would Goethe think?) Our clever hometown entrepreneurs are also making dolls outside the flatulence fest: There's the singing Hip Hop Teddy and Duelin' Banjo Buddies. It's good to know that Tekky Toys is constantly breaking wind in new directions.

WILLIAM HARRIS LEE VIOLINS

410 South Michigan Avenue
Chicago, IL 60605
(800) 447-4533
www.whlee.com
Map: Downtown

George Bernard Shaw said, "Music is the brandy of the damned." And you'll get pretty damn drunk with pleasure when you play one of the beautiful stringed instruments from this company. For over twenty years these artisans have been manufacturing violins, violas, and cellos in their multifloored workshop on Michigan Avenue. The process begins with mature North American woods that have been aged up to forty years. They even import soon-to-be-lyrical lumber from Italy—near where Antonio Stradivari lived. Then they craft each piece the traditional way, by hand—carving, assembling, and varnishing. The bows are strung with horsehair and curved over an open flame. Prices for these wooden wonders range from the "very affordable" to, probably, the "very affluent." But they're a great investment because each instrument can last hundreds of years. (Which, come to think of it, is longer than *you'll* last, so you might want to put it in your will.) And if you ever accidentally fracture your fiddle, don't worry, WHL also does repairs and restoration.

To see their homemade honeys in action, attend a performance of the Chicago Symphony Orchestra, where they have a large representation. Buy one and maybe the company will let you place your autographed photo on the wall with the others sent by pleased players. Bravo!

MORE MADE IN CHICAGO

FANNIE MAY FACTORY STORE
1101 West Jackson Boulevard
Chicago, IL 60607
(312) 432-3310
www.fanniemay.com
Map: Chicago West
Chocolates for sale from the factory next door.

LAKE MICHIGAN WINERY
816 119th Street
Whiting, IN 46394
(219) 659-9463 or (888) TNT-WINE
www.lakemichiganwinery.com
Map: Multistate
Southern Indiana grapes and Whiting, Indiana, waters combine for a very special vintage of wines.

LEO'S DANCEWEAR FACTORY OUTLET STORE
1900 North Narragansett Avenue
Chicago, IL 60639
(773) 889-7700
www.leosdancewear.com
Map: Chicago West
The place to go for dance outfits and accessories.

MAURICE LENNELL COOKYS COMPANY AND OUTLET STORE
4474 North Harlem Avenue
Norridge, IL 60706
(708) 456-6500
www.lenell.com
Map: Suburban West
Some of Chicagoland's tastiest cookies, just off the assembly line and often still warm.

NIGHTMARES, INC.

1985 Mannheim Road
Melrose Park, IL 60160
(708) 344-2084
www.dreamreapers.com
Map: Suburban West
Makers of incredibly creepy, terribly disturbing anatomical models.

REPLOGLE GLOBES

2801 South 25th Avenue
Broadview, IL 60155
(708) 343-0900
www.replogleglobes.com
Map: Suburban West
World's leading maker of geographic globes.

VIENNA BEEF FACTORY AND STORE

2501 North Damen Avenue
Chicago, IL 60647
(773) 278-7800
www.viennabeef.com
Map: Chicago North
The place to get a true Chicago hot dog (or other beef-related product) at its very source.

FOOD & DRINK

LIFT YOUR GLASS, FILL YOUR PLATE

A LA TURKA RESTAURANT

3134 North Lincoln Avenue
Chicago, IL 60657
(773) 935-6101
www.turkishkitchen.us
Map: Chicago North

If you sit down to a meal at A La Turka restaurant on a Friday or Saturday night, don't be surprised to find a gyrating navel inches from your face. That would be a belly dancer, one of several Turkish delights in this Lincoln Avenue eatery. There's also the delicious cuisine that features a plethora of kabobs with rice and a comfortable Mediterranean decor.

But let's get back to the belly dancers. There's usually two working the room, and as the dollars tucked into their costumes attest, tips are welcome.

Unlike the belly dancers we've seen in movies, who seem to have plenty of belly to dance with, the ones we saw at A La Turka had very tight abs, man. This sometimes makes it awkward for couples who dine here: The men find it hard not to ogle, and it soon dawns on the women that it's not the finger-cymbal playing that their dates are admiring. The situation is usually diffused, though, when the dancers coax some of the patrons into joining the gyrating. Some volunteers prove to be more limber-hipped than others, but it's always entertaining to see the varying attempts at sensuality made by the women (and men) who bravely participate. Some of us even wound up with a few dollars tucked into our belts!

BARNEY'S POPCORN

1110 West Wilson Avenue
Chicago, IL 60640
(773) 334-2603
Map: Chicago North

Shakespeare wrote, "If popcorn be the food of love, pop on." Okay, that's a lie. Shakespeare didn't write that. It's just that some people love popcorn enough to lie for it. Fortunately, there's no prevaricating needed when you purchase your corn delights at Barney's. If you think popcorn robed in caramel or drenched in cheese should be placed at the top of the food pyramid, then you'll find it conveniently located at the bottom of the L tracks at Wilson. You can stop off on your way to work or stop off on your way home from work. Hell, just stop off.

Speaking of hell, be prepared to hear some gospel tunes when you stop in. Barney is a singer who performs at local clubs and churches. He'll regularly break into a spiritual as he cooks up his confections. "I feel the Lord stretching out in me, stretching out in me," he sings. We sing back, "It's not the Lord stretching me, Mr. B., it's your damn popcorn." This stuff is good. To make caramel corn, he mixes two types of sugar, adds unconscionable amounts of butter, stirs the sauce in a copper kettle, and hand-tosses it, all the while singing, "I'm so tired Lord, my soul needs a restin'." (Yeah, sure, Barney, rest your soul, but keep your hands busy churning out the popcorn.) As for his cheese popcorn? Well, you'll just have to have that religious experience your-self. Y'know, popcorn could almost be a religion. It has its devoted followers, you turn to it for comfort and a kernel pops up into a starchy mass. (Mass. Get it? Ha, ha, ha.) Shakespeare did write, "If music be the food of love, play on." Play on, Barney.

CAL'S LIQUORS

400 South Wells Street
Chicago, IL 60607
(312) 922-6392
www.drinkatcalsbar.com
Map: Downtown

Cal's Liquors is a neighborhood liquor store and after-work watering hole that has been slinging drinks in the heart of the Loop since 1947. Brothers Cal and Fred hold court in the front room, where their ribald repartee with the customers is a show in itself, and if they can't find the beer, wine, or spirits you want, they'll damn well order it for next time. In back is the bar and grill, although to be honest the grill is actually just a hole in the wall to the restaurant next door.

The decor at Cal's hasn't changed much since the 1950s; as Fred puts it, "We don't believe in redecorating, just occasional cosmetic surgery." The clientele is an eclectic mix of characters from all walks of life—stockbrokers mix with bike messengers, and construction workers kibitz with corporate lawyers. Ladies, be warned (or excited): The male to female ratio in the bar-room is normally around 12 to 1. That doesn't stop Cal from showing off his "ginseng weed" floating in a bottle, which he claims is a potent aphrodisiac.

Put simply, the beer is cold, the music is loud, and the company is never dull. And if you want a hot dog, just shout through the hole!

DULCE LANDIA

5117 South Kedzie Avenue
Chicago, IL 60632
(773) 737-6585
www.dulcelandia.com
Map: Chicago South

¡Hola! It's Candyland, Candyland, Candyland! Stepping into Dulce Landia is like stepping onto a giant version of the childhood game's board. There are acres of candy. Hard candy, soft candy, candy that you suck, lick, chomp, or chew. They have over five hundred varieties of Mexican candies. If you've never tasted this candy, you're in for a surprise, either pleasant or puckering, depending on your palate. Y'see, the candy here is not divided into milk chocolate or semisweet, but rather into "hot" or "not." Eduardo Rodriguez, a member of this family-owned business, says about their product, "Chili powder is a candy in itself." (Glad we didn't stumble onto his house at Halloween.) Take the lollipops, called *paletas*. You'll find suckers of mango, pineapple, and watermelon, many of them covered in the

powder. It's an interesting mix of salty, sweet, and spicy. Brach's it's not. For the truly hot, try the "balls of fire" called Bolas de Fuego. (Warning: Don't *fuego* awaygo without a glass of *agua* nearby.) After you've picked your candy, pick out a place to pack it, a piñata. They have hundreds of them propped up like a sea of small people. Go to their Web site for store locations or to e-mail a suggestion. Here's our suggestion: try the Pollito Asado. It's a trompe l'oeil lollipop of a rotisserie chicken on a stick. Peach is the flavor and, that's right, it's peppered with chili powder.

GULLIVER'S RESTAURANT

2727 West Howard Street
Chicago, IL 60645
(773) 338-2166
Map: Chicago North

Get your hands on the food of Rome and roam your hands all over the sculpture at this North Side pizzeria. Owner Jerry Freeman says his passion is food and his avocation is antiques, and you'll see these demonstrated with a menu as big as the Roman Empire and a restaurant decorated with everything art nouveau and Victorian. This place is crammed with pieces: terra-cotta friezes and reliefs, stone intaglios, alabaster busts. Look up from your linguine and linger over the luminaria. Jerry has brought the stars inside with a constellation of more than 340 working chandeliers. The effect is

certainly worth the monthly $5,000 ComEd bill and the occasional head conk to a tall waiter. Make sure you visit the wings in this museum . . . the rest rooms. Bronze plaques, drawings, and old advertisements are mounted above and around the, ah, receptacles.

In warm weather, dine in the outdoor cafe, which is garnished with larger acquisitions: Cast- and wrought-iron pieces, mantels, fountains, entablatures, and more statuary than a potentate's palace. Even the facade of Gulliver's is not left unscathed, or rather, unadorned, as it's plastered with terra-cotta and faience. Like the antiques, the menu is a mix of pastas and pizzas (they make over four hundred nightly), all of it deliverable. But wouldn't you rather dine in? Where else can you ziti right down and gnocchi back some wine while you savor the fettuccine and fixtures that Jerry has rigatonied, all for a few penne?

HALA KAHIKI HAWAIIAN LOUNGE

2834 River Road
River Grove, IL 60171
(708) 456-3222
Map: Suburban West

For a delightfully goofy night out with friends or a romantic evening for two, put on your muumuu and hula dance over to the Hala Kahiki Hawaiian Lounge in River Grove. Rose and Stanley Zuharshke slapped this place together back in the 1960s, not because they're particularly enamored with Hawaiian culture but because they needed to redecorate and didn't have much cash—and what could be cheaper than bamboo and some old coconuts?

They've come a long way since then, and you'll really feel like you've stepped into a Honolulu dive when you belly up to the bar and order one of the eighty-five drinks on the menu, some of which are actually flaming when they arrive at your table (very few burnt lips have been reported). Speaking of the menu, you won't find any food on it, unless you consider pretzels and fortune cookies a two-course meal. But by the time you've sampled such exotic drinks as a Suffering Bastard, or a Missionary's Downfall, you'll forget about the absence of foodstuffs. Don't miss the gift shop, where you can pick up everything you need for your next luau, from grass skirts to tiki torches. Aloha, and pass the pretzels.

ILLINOIS NUT AND FANTASIA CHOCOLATE COMPANY
3745 West Dempster Street
Skokie, IL 60079
(847) 677-5777 or (800) 590-NUTS
www.illinoisnut.com
Map: Suburban North

Your dreams can be made real—all you have to decide is whether you want them in milk, semisweet, or white chocolate. Illinois Nut and Fantasia Chocolate Company creates deliriously decadent confections, including edible baskets and bowls made out of chocolate and filled with a bounty of dried fruits, nuts, and more chocolate. Did we tell you they make chocolate? Their Chocolate Lover's Platter is 16 inches of apricots, oranges, pineapple, and kiwi, English toffee, peppermint patties, and hand-dipped truffles. Quick, call the dentist. For people who don't care for chocolate (philistines), Illinois Nut carries a selection of other sweets: taffy apples, bulk nuts and candy, jumbo muffins, brownies, and cookies. You'll still have to call the dentist, but with many of the items pareve, at least you won't have to call the rabbi. After you've bonded with their bonbons, why not spread some bonhomie by giving gifts to your friends and business associates? This company does custom creations.

You think of an idea—say, your business card or corporate logo or even a model of the stomach for that upcoming gastroenterology convention—bring in the artwork, and they'll make a mold for the chocolate and place each one in its own labeled box. Classy. Memorable, too. They've made chocolate ties, cars, pianos, bottles, coffee mugs, even chocolate dentures. You might want to pick up some of those false teeth. They'll be a funny gift for that dentist you'll be seeing so much of.

JOHN'S ELGIN MARKET EXOTIC MEATS
1620 Gilpen Avenue
South Elgin, IL 60177
(847) 741-6374
www.BBQonwheels.com
Map: Suburban West

Our vegetarian readers may want to skip this segment, since John's specialty is to turn wild game into snack sticks and jerky. Buffalo, bear, elk, moose, caribou, and wild boar can all be found in the exotic display case. We even spotted "gator tail" and "turtle sticks" for sale. In jerky form they all look pretty

much the same, but John claims each meat has its own distinctive taste. Rather than sample the "roadkill" flavor, we took his word for it.

John's great-grandfather opened the market back in 1880, and it wasn't long before its products could be found in truck stops and convenience stores nationwide. The "wild game" moniker is actually a little misleading, since the animals providing John's meats are all farm-raised. (Does that make them "tame game"?) During hunting season John has an interesting side business: deer processing. Hunters bring in their kills so that he can cut them up with his band saw and prepare the meat for their freezer. That's far preferable to bringing a deceased Bambi home to your wife and kids. Vegetarians, you may resume reading . . . *now.*

KENDALL COLLEGE SCHOOL OF CULINARY ARTS

Dining Room
2408 Orrington Avenue
Evanston, IL 60201
(847) 866-1399
www.kendall.edu
Map: Suburban North

Gourmet food at Burger King prices. Hitch your tongue to a truckload of cheap, tasty treats when you dine at the restaurant at Kendall College. At any given lunch or dinner, you could be savoring curry marinated mussels, mushroom strudel, and pan-seared pork tenderloin, all prepared and served by students of the college's School of Culinary Arts. The cooking kids rotate through all the positions of the restaurant, front and back, to gain real-world experience. You'll gain a couple of pounds when you experience the pâtés *en croute* and coq au vin. The cuisine includes classic French and can be had for a handful of francs; the three-course lunch menu is only $16. And the Dining Room is BYOB, so, depending on your budget, you can accompany your meal with a Beaujolais or a Bud. Come on one of their special nights, for example, the Grand Buffet ($20), and you'll be sampling the students' final exams of mousses, galantines, and ballotines. Even if you don't know what you're eating, moan as if in the clutches of epicurean ecstasy. You want the cooks to get A's, don't you? The menu changes seasonally, so check them out on-line and then call for reservations. When we were there, a suburban library association had just finished wolfing down a pistachio-stuffed creation. They said the dish was "Excellent!" (Coming from a bunch of book mavens, we were expecting a comment more like "Prodigiously transcendent!")

LITTLE BUCHAREST RESTAURANT

3001 North Ashland Avenue
Chicago, IL 60657
(773) 929-8640
www.bucharest.com
Map: Chicago North

For a slice of Eastern Europe where the music is loud and the helpings are huge, there's only one place to go in Chicago. Little Bucharest has been in business for over three decades, and that's probably thanks to the home-made food and the charismatic owner, Branko Pradovich. Branko, who bears a passing resemblance to Roman Polanski, lets his wife do the cooking while he works the dining room, keeping everybody in a festive mood. As his hired musicians serenade you, he's liable to gleefully break a glass on the floor and lead his customers in a Romanian song. Then there's the thin plastic tube filled with a mystery liquor that Branko offers up to all takers, placing one end in the recipient's mouth and blowing on the other end until the tube is empty. Ask what it is and Branko will tell you "holy water," but we've heard it tastes like a mixture of antifreeze and cologne.

The menu features entrees like goulash, chicken paprikash, veal paprikash—in fact any dish that ends in -ash is liable to be served up. We recommend the Taste of Romania platter, which includes the four major Romanian food groups: meat, meat, meat, and sauce. If you need any further enticement to visit Little Bucharest, perhaps you'd like to know about the free limousine service. That's right, if you call ahead, Branko will send a limo to your door and deliver you to the restaurant, free of charge. Now that's an even better deal than the free holy water. OK, *way* better.

PERRY'S DELI

180 North Franklin
Chicago, IL 60606
(312) 372-7557
www.perrysdeli.com
Map: Downtown

Try to get something at this place and you might just hear, "Whad'ya want, Bonehead?" No, you're not at home, that's just the owner, Perry, slingin' some attitude with the food. At this deli, the abuse level runs as high as the sandwiches. And the sandwiches are mountainous. (What, you didn't hear me the first time, Forrest Gump?) Perry's is home to the triple-decker sandwich: obscenely extravagant concoctions with unusual combos of meats, cheeses, and bread. The Caveat Emptor has roast and corned beefs, turkey, Muenster, Swiss, and Russian dressing on rye. It's the United Nations of noshes. Adding injury to (Perry's) insult, it's also served with a pickle and slaw. (You don't like a little roughage in your diet, Mr. Tighty Pants?) If you want to read the whole menu, plan on taking a personal day. Better yet, check out the menu on the Web site before you come in, otherwise, if you ask Perry what's on a certain sammy, he's likely to tell you "whale blubber." The ribbing is good-natured and certainly a small price to pay to get your hands around one of this deli's bad boys. By the way, if you can stand Perry's repartee, then we dare you to stomach this: The Peter Panski is a sandwich made with ham, peanut butter, bacon, lettuce, tomato, mayo, and—Sweet Lord, don't make us go on.

PHIL SMIDT'S RESTAURANT

1205 North Calumet Avenue
Hammond, IN 46320
(800) FROG-LEG
www.froglegs.com
Map: Multistate

Phil Smidt's has been dishing up frog legs across the border in Hammond, Indiana, since 1910. Those little critters' gams must be popular, since this place now has seven dining rooms and seats 450 people. If you're wondering why frogs are so big in Hammond, it seems they were once indigenous to the area—until Phil's started sautéing or frying all those legs (they serve around a half million pairs a year). Now the owners have to import most of their frogs from places like Indonesia, but there's one thing that hasn't changed: People still say it tastes like chicken.

Hammond might seem a bit far afield for a dinner date, especially if you don't have a car, but never fear; you can hop on a train called the "Frog Leg Express" (our name) that leaves from Chicago's Union Station and drops you off in front of Phil Smidt's in just twenty minutes' time. Once there, take a gander at the display case near the back entrance that's chock-full of frog paraphernalia. When it's time to order, if you refuse to eat something you dissected in high school, there are plenty of other tasty options on the menu such as the grilled chicken, which tastes a lot

like itself. The leg of frog is the specialty here, though. In fact, they have a guy in the kitchen whose only job is to cross all the frogs' legs. The chef claims it's because the presentation looks sloppy when the legs are splayed, but one customer had another explanation: "The poor frogs are bashful!"

PRAIRIE JOE'S RESTAURANT

1921 Central Street
Evanston, IL 60201
(847) 491-0391
Map: Suburban North

When you were a kid, didn't you love to go up and explore in your Grandma's attic? It was loaded with all those cool knickknacks and bric-a-brac. But she wouldn't let you bring food up there, would she? Prairie Joe's solves that problem by decorating its diner with the detritus of daily life from the last half century. Owner Aydin has blanketed the walls and ceiling with gewgaws. You'll see old cameras, movie projectors, lamps, kitchen gadgets, Grandma (whoops, no Grandma), tin men, and other outmoded objects. Call it a societal autopsy, if you will. Aydin also finds room to display his own paintings. Customers have compared his work to Picasso. Sadly, Picasso's dead and cannot defend himself.

Besides being the curator, Aydin's also the chef. His creations include lots of homemade soups (Potato-Spinach, Hammy-Cheesy-Eggy) and gooey concoctions wrapped in tortillas—the food's as eclectic as his collections. Cheap, too. Become a regular and your picture goes on the wall—either a photo or one painted by the proprietor. Come back in a month and the antiques change. Aydin's wife is delighted by the cafe's décor. Otherwise, all this stuff, she says, "would probably be at home."

RODIZIOS RESTAURANT AT MEYER'S CASTLE

1370 Joliet Street
Dyer, IN 46311
(773) 646-5613 or (219) 865-8452
www.meyerscastle.com
Map: Multistate

This place is pampas. Rodizios restaurant has taken the South American cowboys' chuck wagon off the range and put it into your range, right across the border in Indiana. The gauchos' custom of spit-roasting their meat on skewers over a charcoal fire has been re-created here at this Argentinean and Brazilian steak house. The prix fixe dinner starts off with a palate-preparing potable called a *caipirinha*. Then you're invited to roam their prairie-size tapas (cold veggie, seafood, and meat dishes) and pasta bars. When you're ready for the main course, Rodizios waitstaff will come to your table, flourishing skewers stacked with ribeye, pork tenderloin, chicken, salmon, and trout. The restaurant says its roasted delicacies will "arrive in never ending waves, and keep coming until you push back from the table saying 'enough.'" The place offers a wide selection of South American and Spanish wines and has more martinis than the Rat Pack.

Rodizios is located in Meyer's Castle, one of only seven certified castles in the United States. Built for businessman Joseph Meyer in 1931, the mansion is a three-story, terraced affair of stone, red clay, copper, and oak. Walk around the verdant grounds—which can be reserved for your next shindig—and you'll see the castle's pets: peacocks, swans, and even llamas. Speaking of pets, Rodizios sadly has one house rule concerning its tsunami of a spread: no doggie bags.

SARKIS' CAFÉ

2632 Gross Point Road
Evanston, IL 60201
(847) 328-9703
www.sarkiscafe.com
Map: Suburban North

Walk into Sarkis' Café for the first time and you may mistake it for just another greasy spoon. You will soon be disabused of that notion by the fiercely loyal clientele, many of whom have been coming here since they were tots. Why? Well, the food is delicious enough (the sign outside boasts WORLD'S BEST OMELETTE), but most folks would say it's the charismatic owner that keeps them returning year after year. Sarkis Taj was born and raised in Jerusalem, and when he first came to the States he managed to get work as a dental technician. Eventually, though, he wanted to get out of people's mouths and put food *into* those mouths, so he opened the cafe in 1965. He's been keeping customers in stitches ever since, with a steady stream of affectionate malarkey to rival any nightclub entertainer.

The best time to come is a Saturday or Sunday morning, when the tiny restaurant is overflowing with old regulars, new regulars, and college kids working off their illegal hangovers. When you first enter you'll notice that the walls are covered with snapshots of customers, including one of former president Jimmy Carter. Don't be surprised if Sarkis greets you with a kiss on the cheek, especially if you're a child or a pretty girl. When it's time to order, try the Disaster. It's a beef sausage patty covered with cheese on a bun. (When we asked if the Disaster referred to what it was doing to our arteries, Sarkis exclaimed, "Body needs grease, buddy, just like car!") Then notice how Sarkis never needs the cash register to figure out your bill but does it all in his head—maybe because everything seems to cost $5.00. Whatever you pay for your plate full of food and earful of Sarkis, it'll be a bargain.

SWEDISH BAKERY

5348 North Clark Street
Chicago, IL 60640
(888) 561-8919
www.swedishbakery.com
Map: Chicago North

Would you like to pick up a Swedish Blonde? This cookie's available. All you have to do is walk up and ask for her. Check out her best friend, too, the Marzipan Princess. High maintenance? No. High calories? Well, you don't come to the Swedish Bakery worrying about your waistline. You come to this Andersonville Swede shop for sweets. They have case upon case packed with pastries, pies, tarts, tortes, cream puffs, and cookies. They have so many baked goodies, they should rename their country's capitol "Stockyerholm." There's a pastry for every part of your day: scones for breakfast, filbert sandwiches for lunch, and a cherry-chocolate cake for dessert.

After dinner, throw one of their buttercreme logs on the fire in your tummy. Like their snow, these people lay it on thick. They use a trowel to apply the filling on their layer cakes, and for the marzipan cake they start with a hunk of the stuff the size of a football. We're getting a myocardial burp just thinking about them. Don't forget to taste one—or all—of the coffee cakes, such as the famous, pull-apart Seven Sisters or the Edelweiss cake (which we hear is selling much better now that they changed the name from the original Alewives cake). Brush up on your Swedish by buying the Vort Limpa, Julekaka, and Toska Bitar. What are they? Who knows? All we care to know is when our order will be ready.

TONY SPAVONE'S RISTORANTE

266 West Lake Street
Bloomingdale, IL 60108
(630) 529-3154
www.tonyspavones.com
Map: Suburban West

For most restaurants, the only requirement is that you come hungry. For this one, you also better come with the lyrics to "That's Amore." That's because the host, Tony Spavone, loves singing as much as he loves serving food. He carries a cordless mike, cruises around the restaurant, and croons to his customers. And, like an old dog, he'll turn on you (with the microphone, that is) and the next thing you know, you'll be warbling "When the moon hits your eye" over your plate of pizza pie, to the delight of the other patrons (or, depending on your singing ability, to the detriment of the

clientele). If you have some talent, Mr. T. will even let you give an impromptu concert. This menu of musical variety is fun and infectious. The restaurant regularly erupts into a massive conga line. Spavone's likes to say that you can come here and, after an hour, you're all one big family. They wouldn't say that if they were with our family on Thanksgiving. Like that fall feast, the food here is plentiful. Choose from an assortment of pastas, steaks, and seafood. Try such house specials like Rigatoni ala Vodka or Eight Finger Cavatelli. Ala telli you that their homemade cannoli are *molto "ciao-*able." Come to Spavone's and sing for your supper. Music and Mangiare. Buon Appetito!

WHITE FENCE FARM

11700 Joliet Road
Lemont, IL 60439
(630) 739-1720 or (815) 838-1500
www.whitefencefarm.com,
www.pattywaszak.com
Map: Suburban South

The friendly folks at White Fence Farm definitely aim to please, whether it's their friendly service, their outdoor petting zoo, or their Branson-style live show. The farm bills its specialty the World's Greatest Chicken, and judging by the hordes of people that come through the doors every evening, they just might be right. The original dining room opened in 1920 and seated one hundred people; now they've got twelve dining rooms seating twelve hundred, and current owner Bob Hastert claims

they go through half a million chickens a year. The wait to get a table can sometimes be long, but don't worry: The huge lobby and waiting room provides plenty of diversions for would-be diners. You'll find a car museum (seriously) and several display cases full of collections that have been willed to White Fence Farm by now-deceased patrons, including stuffed dolls, music boxes, hood ornaments, even corn hooks. And outside there's that petting zoo, with forty animals that include a full-grown llama.

But the highlight of any visit to White Fence Farm has got to be the country-and-western show in the back room, a delightfully cheesy lounge act featuring a bundle of entertainment energy named Patty Waszak. Patty plays ten instruments and has about six costume changes during the course of this hour-long extravaganza. She's joined onstage by four other showfolk, who may not possess her versatility but definitely share her knack for pulling the audience's heartstrings, whether it be with a patriotic USO medley or a tribute to *Cats*. So if you're passing through Lemont and spot the white fence, by all means come for the chicken, but stay for the schmaltz!

MORE FOOD & DRINK

CARNICERIA LA CARIDAD
3569 West Fullerton Avenue
Chicago, IL 60647
(773) 342-0410
Map: Chicago West
*Delightful grocery with Hispanic
specialties.*

EDGEBROOK'S BASKIN-ROBBINS
5337 West Devon Avenue
Chicago, IL 60646
(773) 763-9778
Map: Chicago North
*Ron Model creates unusual themed
window displays that change with
the seasons.*

FISH GUY MARKET
4423 North Elston Avenue
Chicago, IL 60630
(773) 283-7400
www.fishguy.com
*Suppliers of exotic fresh fish to the
finest restaurants in town.*

HEALTHY FOODS LITHUANIAN RESTAURANT
3236 South Halsted Street
Chicago, IL 60608
(312) 326-2724
Map: Chicago South
*Heaping portions of homemade
Lithuanian cuisine: your doctor
might dispute the "healthy" claim . . .*

MAXINE'S CARIBBEAN SPICE
1225 East 87th Street
Chicago, IL 60619
(773) 933-4714
Map: Chicago South
*Tasty jerk chicken and music from
the islands.*

MOO AND OINK
7158 South Stony Island Avenue
Chicago, IL 60649
(773) 493-7100
www.moo-oink.com
Map: Chicago South
*Barbecue and soul food grocery with
chitlins to go!*

NUTS ON CLARK
3830 North Clark Street
Chicago, IL 60613
(773) 549-6622
www.nutsonclark.com
Map: Chicago North
*Nuts, candies, and dried fruits
galore.*

RAINBOW CONE
9233 South Western Avenue
Chicago, IL 60620
(773) 238-7075
Map: Chicago South
*Six-flavored ice-cream cone has been
the specialty here since 1926.*

SHOPPING

AN ECLECTIC SELECTION FOR THE SELECTIVE CONSUMER

AMERICAN SCIENCE AND SURPLUS

5316 North Milwaukee Avenue
Chicago, IL 60630
(773) 763-0313
www.sciplus.com
Map: Chicago North

If the chance to poke around junk is music to your ears, then this disco of the discarded will have you dancing in the aisles. For over sixty years, American Science has been selling surplus—medical, mechanical, and many things malformed. They have (are you ready) beakers, glass jars, graduated cylinders, test tubes, vials (forget that costly fertilization, make your own home in vitro kit here), wiper motors, transformers, switches, magnets, rubber wheels (for the budding robot builder), telescopes, gas masks, anatomical charts, flat files, needle files, wind-ups, miles and miles of wire (think mad scientist), plastic frogs, inflatable dogs, trophy tops, plunger bottoms, duct tape, cellophane tape, transparent tape, gaffer's tape, wooden clogs (hurry, they only have 139 left), glass knobs, ivory knobs, and plastic knobs. They have products that have failed (Larva Candy), overstocks (human powered face masks), overruns (Taco Bell Dog Bobbing Head Dolls), misprints ("Weelcome"), and just things malevolent (Iraqi Mine Warning tape). The staff provides descriptions for each item—a double-sided adhesive tape is labeled "Hypocrite Tape: Never trust a two faced tape, they're trouble." And if they don't know what an item is, you can still have it for 50 cents. Think closeouts, clearance, liquidation, fire sale, tag sale, yard sale, garage sale, gray-market merchandise, and you'll be thinking you'll want to visit this house of losers.

AUGUSTINE'S SPIRITUAL GOODS

3114 South Halsted
Chicago, IL 60608
(312) 326-5467
Map: Chicago South

Hoodoo voodoo? They do. Augustine's has the supplies to service practitioners of all the magical arts, including astrology, Santeria, Wicca, and pretty much anything pagan and polytheistic.

To keep your rituals running smoothly, start by choosing something from the selection of oils. They have hundreds of pure, root, and blended oils that will help draw things to you (Bingo Oil) or keep things away (Banishing Oil). They even have oils for when you don't know what you want (Multi-Purpose Oil). They are the Saudi Arabia for oils. They also carry incense, tarot decks, amulets, and waters for your bath or floors (Augustine's Sweet Red Sex Wash). For those who not only don't know what they want but don't know how to do it, the store has a leviathan-size book section.

We visited Augustine's after their invitation to us stated they had a potion to fix sagging TV ratings. Now, you know we don't care one jot about ratings. All we care about is delivering to our viewers thought-provoking pieces. However, purely for research, we picked up the potion (Yellow Dock Root) plus a few other things. Funny, after we left, our ratings did go up, but we also beat a traffic ticket (Law Stay Away Candle), can now control our station manager's mind (Power Mojo Bag) and are all enjoying animalistic lovemaking on the linoleum (*Extra* Sweet Red Sex Wash).

Maybe you should get your mojo moving to Augustine's and check out their voodoo, doll.

BERLAND'S HOUSE OF TOOLS

600 Oak Creek Drive
Lombard, IL 60148
(630) 620-0026 or (800) 339-0026
www.berlandtools.com
Map: Suburban West

A towering Babel of tools. Berland's has everything that a builder or tradesperson or proficient weekend woodworker could desire. Power tools, hand tools, trades tools, any bit, any accessory, even clothing. This palace of product offers tools from 420 vendors, representing over fifty building trades, from iron-

workers and cement finishers to carpenters and electricians. The store carries more than sixty types of circular saws and everything is available for demonstration. Bring in your wood, plug in the tool, and saw, sand, or slice away. Talk with owner Dwight "the Tool Man" Sherman to find out what's on the cutting edge for tools. (It's cordless—

lighter, leaner, and lots of power.) His knowledge of hardware is surpassed only by his passion for it. Just ask his kids, whom we think he named Stanley, Delta, and DeWalt. If you can't get to this temple of torque, tune in to the TV show, *Tool Time,* on channel 62, WJYS. It's a fast-paced pastiche of product demos, dancing girls, parodies, dancing girls,

on-site applications, and dancing girls. *Tool Time* serves its demographic by understanding that there *are* two things guaranteed to capture an audience: power tools and pulchritude.

BRADFORD EXCHANGE

9333 North Milwaukee Avenue
Niles, IL 60714
(800) 323-8078 Exchange Floor
(847) 966-2770 Museum
www.bradex.com
Map: Suburban North

What do Marilyn Monroe, Judy Garland, and King Tut have in common? They've all been commemorated on collectible plates. Find out why people get almost apoplectic over these pretty porcelain platters when you tour the Bradford Exchange's museum, a collector's Valhalla. This company has been manufacturing limited-edition plates for over a hundred years, and it serves up hundreds and hundreds of them here. *The Wizard of Oz,* the Beatles, Snow White, Rhett Butler, Santa— if it's an icon, it's on a plate. Missed spotting Elvis at the 7-Eleven? Well, he's here, on plates celebrating highlights from his movie and music career. But only a young, svelte El is depicted, thank you . . . remember, these are plates, not roasting pans. Are you wondering who gets the itch to collect this kitsch? Stop and read the huge wall of comment cards—decidedly gushy odes to these circular ceramics. The average collector is a middle-aged, married woman. But don't think she's staying home to dust her china, she's trading it. True to its name, you can visit the exchange at Bradford. While the traders aren't exactly screaming "Plate! Plate! Plate!" in the pit, it's a tad more genteel than that, you can observe the tote board listing the latest quotes for the most desirable plates. One of Bradford's first plates, Frozen Window, issued in 1895 for 50 cents, is now trading at over $5,000. Hmmm, $5,000. Maybe Grandma won't notice that bare spot on her dining room wall.

CHICAGO FOOD CORP

Food Market
3333 North Kimball
Chicago, IL
(773) 478-5566
Restaurant Supply
5800 North Pulaski
(773) 478-0007
www.chicagofood.com
Map: Chicago North

As you can tell by its title, this company is an Oriental foods market. If you couldn't tell that from its name, then don't expect to be able to read the labels on the products, either. Unless you're a simultaneous interpreter at the UN, you'll have difficulty decoding the Korean and Chinese packaging. But, don't let that stop you. If you're a cook, this huge store, with a staff to match, sells enough of the familiar—tofu, wasabi—to make it the only Asian food supplier you'll ever need. Indulge your culinary curiosity by experimenting with some of the more exotic ingredients and you'll be inspired to create epicurean feasts fit for Genghis Khan. Or, hopefully, someone friendlier. Chicago Food also has a deep deep-sea department that offers octopus, crabs, clams, and fish-kebabs. To complement the multicourse meals you'll be making, pick out a bottle from the liquor section. Besides plum wine and Asian beers, a best-seller is Jinro, a Korean drink with 24 percent alcohol. ('Couple bottles of that and we'll *all* be reunified.) If you're a gourmand, visit Chicago Food's dining area. It's a casual setup with a couple of tables, and all the food is available to go. Watch as the kitchen crew assemble their sushi, hand-rolling the layers between a bamboo mat. And, if you get run down from too much shopping, tasting, or watching, try Chicago Food's preferred pick-me-up, ginseng drink. A spokesman says, "It invigorates your body. You don't need Viagra." Evidently, it picks up other run-down things, too.

CIGARS AND STRIPES

6715 Ogden Avenue
Berwyn, IL 60402
(708) 484-1043
www.hammerhed.com
Map: Suburban West

Cigars and Stripes in Berwyn is not just a store that sells stogies, it's a sort of club-house for the neighborhood characters or, as owner Ronnie Lottz calls it, "a commune for artists and weirdos." Maybe it's because the matchbooks given out to customers read "WANTED: perverts, bikers, and derelicts." More than likely, though, it has to do with Lottz, who has personality with a capital *P* and is clearly no slouch at drawing attention to himself and his establishment. The 15-foot-long cigarette he has out front, its glowing tip billowing real smoke, certainly provokes curiosity. And on one wall of the tiny store you'll see some pictures of Ronnie in his former life as a pro-wrestling manager for two hulking behemoths named the Moondogs; "Spot" and "Rex" would let Lottz do all the talking since they could only bark.

The store itself has about sixty to seventy types of cigars available, and that's not all that's for sale. There are several kinds of beef jerky and an eye-catching selection of hot sauces, which are arranged on the shelves in order of their potential for damage. The lower shelves hold the mild sauces with names like Candy Ass, a little higher you'll find Rectal Rocket Fuel, and then on the very top is something called Mad Dog Inferno, which Ronnie claims is virtually inedible.

Since our initial visit, Cigars and Stripes has even added a kitchen and makeshift bar to serve patrons. Apparently the jerky with the hot sauce chaser wasn't doing the trick.

As for that cast of characters we mentioned, you'll find them milling around outside the entrance most warm evenings, trading jokes and showing off their cars or motorcycles. When they go inside, it's to jaw with Lottz, hold a hot sauce taste-off, or listen as the tuxedoed crooner who calls himself Gigolo Johnny launches into an impromptu Sinatra tune. Through it all, that giant cigarette keeps on smokin'.

CITY NEWSSTAND

4018 North Cicero Avenue
Chicago, IL 60641
(773) 545-7377
www.citynewsstand.com
Map: Chicago North

City News says, "People who read magazines know stuff that people who don't . . . don't." If you want to be engorged with enlightenment, then visit the store that's overflowing with publications. City News will feed your greed for knowledge with a selection of more than six thousand magazines and newspapers. From *Bazaar* to *Bizarre*, they offer an argosy of ordinary to arcane monthlies, weeklies, dailies, gazettes, sheets, and tabloids. They have so many magazines, you can talk in titles alone: *Nosh* on the *Goldmine* of *Variety* and *Details* to *Shape*, *Spin*, and *Drive* your *Life*, whether you're a *Wired Senior Golfer* into *Nylon* or a

Low Rider, MacAddict Mad about *Montana Trailer Life.* They've got stuff—and *Stuff UK*—you just won't find at your Barnes and Noble. But, unlike B&N, it's not a bookstore, so back off, you hardback freaks. Think what a popular dinner guest you'll become when you spout bons mots gleaned from the *Journal of Polymorphous Perversity.* Go to the Web site to see if City News carries your copy of *Alpacas* or any other magazine. Start filling your mental filing cabinet with frivolous facts by reading the "Things We Learned While Reading" section. For example, "Chocolate is rated one of the 10 most dangerous foods to consume while driving." Betcha didn't know that. We did, of course, because we read *Route 66* magazine. (Why, yes, we can be at your house for a late supper at nine.) If you want to indulge your interests, improve your skills, or just upgrade your bathroom library, come graze in this pasture of publications.

COOPER USED HOTEL FURNITURE

1929 South Halsted Street
Chicago, IL 60608
(312) 226-2299
Map: Downtown

If you've always wanted your home to have the comfort and amenities of a hotel, why not shop at Cooper Used Hotel Furniture right after they've emptied out a Marriott? These folks aren't thieves, they're liquidators; they've got seven floors of used furniture garnered from hotels and resorts that either closed or changed their interior design. You'll find chairs, lamps, beds, end tables, desks, and color TVs at pretty low prices. If they aren't low enough, you're welcome to haggle with the salespeople. And there is other stuff besides furniture, like a whole floor of carpeting and a roomful of that marvelously

generic art you always find in hotel rooms—care for fifty framed prints of the same purple flower?

Cooper has a colorful history that began over a hundred years ago when Louis Cooper plied Chicago's streets with a pushcart. His goods were culled from the trunks and suitcases left in hotels by guests unable to pay their bill. The Coopers eventually made the transition into used hotel furniture and moved their business into a building that once housed an Al Capone still during Prohibition. They've long since filled the place with furnishings you may well recognize from your last business trip. The risk is that if you overdo the bargain hunting at Cooper's, your home might start to feel like the Radisson. But at these prices it might be a risk worth taking.

DISCREET ELECTRONICS

1156 North Dearborn
Chicago, IL 60610
(312) 664-7797
www.spyshopinc.com
Map: Chicago North

Personal surveillance, corporate espionage, high-tech security—if these are your stock-in-trade or you just like to dabble, sneak into Discreet Electronics, alias the Spy Shop. Actually, there's no way to sneak into this place, since owner Mike Pinsker (not an alias) has rigged the premises with numerous surveillance cameras. There's no better establishment in Chicago to find things like phone taps, night-vision goggles, lipstick cameras, or just about any other gizmo used in surveillance or countersurveillance. We liked the umbrella with removable tip that doubles as a directional listening device, and how about the phone that can distort your voice, rendering it unrecognizable to whoever's listening? There are also various espionage manuals for sale (one was entitled *Get Even: The Complete Book of Dirty Tricks*) and several self-defense items: the cayenne pepper spray is definitely not meant for your salad, and the "screamer," which puts out 120 decibels with the flip of a switch, should not be used as a party prank.

The Spy Shop is a very fun place to browse, and if you're CIA, a James Bond buff, or just paranoid, you might even buy something. Just hope that your nosy next-door neighbor doesn't also shop here.

FANTASY HEADQUARTERS COSTUMES

4065 North Milwaukee Avenue
Chicago, IL 60641
(773) 777-0222
www.fantasycostumes.com
Map: Chicago North

Are you afraid to show your private parts? Meaning, is there a part in you that you've been keeping private? Now's the time to unlock your inner Elvis or unzip your hidden Caesar by draping your desires with a costume from Fantasy Headquarters. These merchants of the masquerade have the clothes to create any character, famous or infamous. Whether you pine to be Pocahontas or have a hankering to be Hannibal (Lechter or the

Carthaginian general), they'll have the wardrobe for your wishes. This castle of costumes covers one entire city block and contains over one million items. This is your hall for all, with clothes for all historical periods, in all sizes, and for all ages, infants and up. And, FHQ can fine-tune your theatrical threads by adding wigs, makeup, and embellishments. They'll make sure when you dress up as a captain from *Star Trek*, you go out looking like a Kirk, not a Picard. (*Pssst.* Before reading any further, look over your shoulder. All clear? Good. Now, for those of you who prefer to be invisible rather than illustrious, FHQ is your undercover coverings specialist. Whether you need to commit some skulduggery or if you're just paranoid, the selection of disguises, including masks, hats, and hair, will camouflage your normally staggering good looks and have you blending in like an Osterizer.)

One item that won't go unnoticed at your next soiree is Fantasy Headquarters' take on the traditional party game Pin the Tail on the Donkey. This one is called Pin the Macho on the Man. And, just so you know, the "man" in question is certainly not wearing a disguise. Or anything else.

GREAT PUT ON

7234 West Madison Street
Forest Park, IL 60130
(708) 771-8081
www.thegreatputon.com
Map: Suburban West

The Great Put On is dedicated to the art of taking it off. This store disrobes, or rather, displays, costumes for the professional exotic dancer. It's a strip mine full of gowns, cat suits, corsets, bustiers, and bikinis. It's all flimsy, funky, and fun. But don't kid yourself, this is a serious business. Young dancers can make up to $1,500 a night—that's not just *college* money, that's B.A.-M.A.-Ph.D.-at-Northwestern money—and they don't do it by wearing "stroll down Michigan Avenue" clothes. The apparel ranges from the ooh-la-la to the outré. If it hasn't got marabou, rhinestones, fringe, or chains on it, it's not here. These outfits are designed to allow the ecdysiast to glide and twirl while enhancing her pneumatic assets. Now, don't feel bad if you don't get paid to striptease-to-please-many. If you're more comfortable doing the Lambada instead of a lap dance, the store offers truly memorable club wear. They'll make sure the garment fits with just enough room to stuff a bill—just in case the muse Terpsichore inspires you to dance to please just one.

So, whether you work the pole or whirl a polka, you'll find a sisterhood of slinky, kinky attire that will have you tripping the light fantastic—and trip you might, the shoes they sell are so high, they're Pikes Peakean.

HENRY'S SPORTS AND BAIT SHOP

3130 South Canal Street
Chicago, IL 60616
(312) 225-8538
(312) 225-FISH (fishing report)
www.henrysports.com
Map: Chicago South

Fatheads, shiners, water-dogs, spikes—if you haven't the faintest idea what these are, you don't fish and you've never been to Henry's Sports and Bait Shop. The store has been a fixture on the South Side for more than fifty years, and the always jovial owner Henry Palmisano is the ultimate fisherman's friend. Who else would stay open from 4:00 A.M. to 10:00 P.M. weekdays (he never closes on weekends) and offer you a choice of eight types of minnows, six types of worms, and three types of crawfish, almost all of them still squirming?

There's a menu above the counter just like at McDonald's, but instead of hamburgers, only fish delicacies are listed. Plenty of fishing paraphernalia and instructional aids are also for sale. Henry and his staff keep their clientele constantly entertained, and it's a great place to congregate with fellow fish enthusiasts and trade secrets before you hit the lake. So if you're the type of angler who picks worms off the sidewalk after a heavy rain, take our word for it—you're better off at Henry's.

HOUSE OF MONSTERS

1579 North Milwaukee Avenue,
Gallery #218
Chicago, IL 60622
(773) 292-0980
www.thehouseofmonsters.com
Map: Chicago West

Ophthalmologist Barry Kaufman has turned a lifelong interest in horror and mayhem into his own store. Located on the second floor of Bucktown's Flatiron Building, the House of Monsters is filled to the gills with everything gruesome. The walls drip with vintage horror movie posters, the shelves are choked with monster models and masks, and the bins bubble over with books and record albums of the macabre. There's a plentiful video section, which includes Kaufman's own foray into filmmaking entitled *Red*

Christmas, featuring a machete-wielding Santa Claus. Barry will gladly demonstrate the functions of the battery-operated Mothra or radio-controlled Godzilla to customers, often while singing their theme songs in an eerie falsetto.

The proud owner accumulated his monster goods over a period of twenty-five years, filling his apartment and three rented warehouses. He finally decided to make his stuff available to the public, and fellow monster enthusiasts are glad he did. They flock to the store on weekends, often selling their collectibles to Kaufman or trading theirs for something of his. Not everything on display is for sale, like the lifelike bust of Charles Laughton as Quasimodo (there are only five in existence) or the grotesque mask of Linda Blair from *The Exorcist,* signed by the star herself. The inscription? "You make my head spin."

HOUSE OF WHACKS

3514 North Pulaski Road
Chicago, IL 60641
(773) 725-9132
www.houseofwhacks.com
Map: Chicago West

When *Wild Chicago* first aired our segment on this latex clothing store in 1994, it was, to put it gently, an aberration. Back then, the only time a "normal" person wore latex was if he or she were a doctor wearing gloves. Yet here was a store supplying fetishists with rubber corsets and crotch-zip pants and, yes, latex gloves. (God knows what perverted doctor-patient examination they played with those.) House of Whacks was considered so offbeat, the owner didn't even want to give out the address of the store to our viewers. She said, "If they can't find it, they don't belong there." Well, a lot has happened since then, and Whacks has gone mainstream. How mainstream? Besides having a published address and Web site? They offer plus-size latex clothes—their Whole Lotta Love line. They still carry the old fetish faves of cat suits and two-way zip shorts, but now they also stock contemporary

flared pants, camis, and split tube skirts. The technology behind latex has also improved. Before, your choices in colors were black, black, or black. Now, the House offers items in more than ten colors, including vibrant pink, purple, olive, and transparent—yep, like being wrapped in Scotch tape. They even have—gasp!—a lower-priced line "designed to fit both your butt and your budget." What was once aberrant is now . . . adorable. This is fun clothing. Of course, some things don't change. Whacks still advises latex wearers to keep away from sharp objects and to stay out of the sun. Stay out of the sun? Yeah, right. If you're wearing transparent latex, you wanna be seen.

HOWARD FRUM JEWELERS

5 South Wabash Avenue, Suite 814
Chicago, IL 60603
(312) 332-5999
www.howardfrum.com
Map: Downtown

You may have seen Howard Frum on his cable TV ads hawking his wares with the phrase "Hey, wanna buy a watch?!" Actually you can do much more at Howard Frum Jewelers—you can sell or trade your current watch, get it fixed, or simply sit back and enjoy the floor show. You see, Howard Frum is a one-man force of nature. Whether he's animatedly bargaining with customers over the counter or genially abusing potential buyers over a speakerphone for the amusement of his in-store patrons, Howard is always entertaining.

As for his merchandise, it's all high-grade stuff: He showed us one watch that had just been purchased for $12,750. High prices don't scare away the watch collectors who frequent Frum's; they often just come to kibitz with the owner. If you see a pretty blonde behind the counter, that's Howard's wife. He originally met her when he sold her a ring for her first marriage! It's a true salesman who can sell himself along with the product . . .

I DO BRIDAL CONSIGNMENT

6742 West Belmont Avenue
Chicago, IL 60634
(773) 205-1234
www.idobridalconsignment.com
Map: Chicago West

"Something old, something new, something borrowed, something blue." When you buy a wedding dress here, at least you'll have the first part taken care of. I Do Bridal sells "once worn" bridal garments. Walk down the aisles and you'll find a selection of more than five hundred gowns in all sizes and in all colors from white to off-white to bright white to Betty White. They're priced at 50 percent off retail and generally range between $400 and $600. The range of styles, though, is bigger, wildly bigger. On any given day, the store will stock everything from satin slip dresses that drape like a second skin to full, frothy confections of fabric. Like any resale store, it's hit or miss. You could unearth an elegant Vera Wang design or get tangled in an antebellum Scarlett O'Hara affair that looks suspiciously like the model for the crocheted dress those dolls wear to cover people's spare roll of toilet paper. I Do's offering of bridal attire runs the gamut from virginal to Vegas showgirl. All of the garments have been dry-cleaned, and the shop sells veils and slips, too. Owner Kelly Hamilton started the service when she couldn't find an inexpensive, "gently worn" gown for her own informal wedding. Now, she tells future brides to come here and "save the money for the honeymoon."

If you've already done the marriage thing and you've got a dress to dump, bring it to Kelly on consignment. Might as well make some bread on those bridal threads.

IMPERIAL CLOTHIERS

4560 West Touhy Avenue
Lincolnwood, IL 60640
(847) 676-2020
Map: Suburban North

Right next to the infamous "purple hotel" where mob accountant Alan Dorfman got whacked is a nondescript building that houses Imperial Clothiers. There's nothing nondescript, though, about the owners or the clothing they sell in the outlet store around back. Walk down the endless aisles of suits and sport coats and you will see a wide array of colors and fabrics in styles that range from semiconservative to just this side of pimp wear. Fake leopard skin, plaids, lime greens, Day-Glo oranges—it's no surprise that, when he was still with us, the famously flamboyant local sportscaster Tim Weigel used to shop here.

Imperial sells most of its wares to big-name department stores like Carson's or Nordstrom's, but at the outlet store you skip the middleman, so the price is definitely right. There are tailors on the premises to do alterations, and if you're lucky you'll get waited on by the animated father-and-son owners. Sy and Paul Rosengarten work their customers like a well-honed comedy team; here's an exchange we witnessed:

Paul: You're getting a rash from all the Dacron in that jacket.

Sy: But it looks good with what you're wearing!

Customer: The jacket?

Sy: No, the rash! (Rim shot here.)

INTERNATIONAL BEAD AND NOVELTY COMPANY

111 North Wabash Avenue, No. 714
Chicago, IL 60602
(312) 332-0061
Map: Downtown

The Nazis bought ornamentation for their helmets at this supply company. Actually, the costumers for the Broadway show *The Producers* purchased spangles to embellish the headgear of the dancing German soldiers for the number "Springtime for Hitler." International Bead's owner Ronald Klein says he's not surprised they found what they needed, because his store has "hundreds of thousands of items." IB has been selling decorations for clothing and crafts and supplies for jewelry since 1918. You'll find buttons, rhinestones, sequins, trims, and beads dating back to the early 1900s. The store is a warren of drawers, boxes, and cases that display–or hide—an eclectic selection of festooning finery. If you need a garnish that's gilded, tasseled, or sparkled, it's here, somewhere. "We don't throw anything out," says Ron. What makes "the Bead" really unusual is its customers. Ronald says he often gets people who use his applications for odd purposes. Architects buy the bric-a-brac to dress their models, building engineers fix old parts with the store's metal findings, and a lot of lawyers stop by. One attorney ordered 20,000 beads to demonstrate random probability for a patent trial. Architects, engineers, and lawyers. Sounds like IB could also be a dating paradise—if you don't mind the lawyers.

JAN'S ANTIQUES

225 North Racine Avenue
Chicago, IL 60607
(312) 563-0275
www.jansantiques.net
Map: Chicago West

Don't be fooled by its simple name. This store—18,000 square feet, 2 floors—doesn't just carry vintage tables, lamps, and chairs; it is filled, crammed, crowded, and corked with every architectural item from homes built between the 1800s and 1950. Jan's has windows, wood moldings, newel posts, balusters, stone statuary and ornamentations, iron gates and grates, china, tiles, stained glass, light fixtures, bikes, tubs, tin ceilings and, yes, kitchen sinks. Bathroom sinks, too. And toilets. And medicine cabinets. And all the hardware to go with everything. Ad infinitum. So, if you come looking for a door, be prepared to search through hundreds of them, then hundreds more doorknobs, plates, and hinges. You might need a bloodhound to help you find your way out of here, because the aisles are very narrow and packed Hancock Building high. You can't see over them or around them. At the center of this maze, you'll find the mistress of this massive merchandise. Jan has been working directly with demolishers for years. She'll salvage absolutely any item she thinks will have value to the homeowner, rehabber, or artist. Not only can she identify what any carved, cut, chiseled, or cast item is, she can give you decorating ideas. Plus, she maintains a wish list for your hard-to-find requests. Parking is abundant, just like the store. When you come, bring your tape measure and your truss. Remember, they made things a lot bigger and heavier in the old days.

JAZZ RECORD MART

444 North Wabash Avenue
Chicago, IL 60611
(312) 222-1467
www.jazzmart.com
Map: Chicago North

When asked to describe jazz, Louis Armstrong said, "There are some people that if they don't know, you can't tell them." Well, baby, if you're hip, you already know about the JRM. But, if you're a frigid feline who wants to be a cool cat, then scat on down and pluck the plentiful pickings at the world's largest jazz record store. They got more vinyl than the furniture on your patio, Daddio. They have LPs, CDs, 45s, 78s, cassettes, VHSs, DVDs, paraphernalia, and more, filling 8,500 square—but

they're not square—feet. Their selection of syncopations includes Dixieland, ragtime, bebop, hard bop, big band, and swing. They got your solos, duos, trios, quartets, and quintets. They got spoken word of Lenny Bruce, Jack Kerouac, and Malcolm X—now that's platter chatter. They got powerful performance discs of Parker (Charlie), Prima (Louis), and the Sisters (Pointer). They got your killers (perennial best-sellers like Miles Davis's *Kind of Blue*) and your killed (99-cent "unwanted" LPs). They got miles of aisles with a bevy of bins just blowing out with the bodacious sounds of Art Blakey and

Oscar Peterson. Check out their Web site for upcoming in-store performances and book signings or to receive their newsletter or catalog. If you gotta have that hot wax in your cool hand, Luke, then slide your trombone to the Mart and do some extended-play(ing) around. As Satchmo said, "Here's swinging at you."

JULES 5 & 10

2062 North Milwaukee Avenue
Chicago, IL 60647
(773) 342-7149
Map: Chicago North

A good variety store should be like a circus: a special destination filled with the fantastic alongside the familiar; a carnival for the senses. At Jules 5 & 10 you'll feel that "big top" atmosphere without having to throw up your cotton candy. You get a glimpse of it, tantalizingly, from the outside. The eye is assaulted with racks and racks of ridiculously priced clothing (T-shirts, 99 cents) and the ear is serenaded with the tweets of parakeets (buy the cage and they throw in the bird free). It's all designed to lure you inside. The staples of the variety are here: notions, kitchen utensils, and ceramic curios. You can also pet the puppies in the pet department or purchase goldfish or doves (the latter being sold as a friend or as a food). Smell wondrous aromas in the ethnic apothecary: eucalyptus ointment, garlic hair conditioner, and baby bovine balm (loosey-goosey translated from Pomada La Vaquita). The most popular department? Cockroach and rodent eradication. Jules carries all the heavy artillery for home extermination: spring traps, glue traps, and roach motels. About the rats in the neighborhood, the owner says, "We've had some big ones . . . they look like alley cats." Fortunately, with their weapons-grade supply of antimammal munitions, "we make sure they disappear."

There's not much you can buy for a nickel or a dime anymore—maybe a piece of candy—but there is one remnant left from the olden days: If, like a kid at the circus, you overindulge (with shopping, not eating), they'll hold your purchases with their "Free Lay-A-Way."

JUST FAUCETS

540 South Arthur
Arlington Heights, IL 60005
(847) 255-0421
www.justfaucets.com
Map: Suburban North

Your toilet sees more of you than your mother does. Make it proud of you by keeping it performing with parts from this plumbing supply place. Whether you've got a pesky leaky faucet or a toilet that runs (quick, catch it), you can snip that drip with a part from the colossal inventory. You'll find parts from all manufacturers—Delta, Moen, Kohler—servicing toilets and sinks made from the 1920s on. Cracked commode lid? No problem. This shop has a plethora of porcelain toppers—yes, even in avocado—dating back to when toilets were called "crappers." Afraid to do your own plumbing repairs? Well, hold your water, Just Faucets will walk you through it. The store has instructional models—sort of a toilet-tank teaching aid—and they'll give you a schematic from the dealer's book detailing the parts and installation steps. Then you'll know the difference between a ball cock, nipple, and cock hole cover (something the nuns wouldn't tell you). Customers who return with success stories receive a Certificate of Achievement award. Some people are so overflowing with pride, they've had their certificate framed. It looks nice over the bidet. Don't ever be embarrassed if you suffer from bathroom incontinence. Bring your problem to this plumbing hospital, they're sure to cure your H_2O woe.

MAGAZINE MEMORIES

6006 West Dempster Street
Morton Grove, IL 60053
(847) 470-9444
www.magazinememories.com
Map: Suburban North

Tucked into a Morton Grove strip mall is a remarkable collection of pop culture memorabilia that goes by the inadequate name of Magazine Memories. Sure, there are magazines—over fifty thousand of them going back more than a hundred years—but there are also newspapers dating back to the Civil War, ten thousand posters, and hundreds of stand-ups (those life-size cutouts of your favorite famous people). Owner Bob Katzman began collecting at age three, and he still travels around the country and surfs the Web to find his latest treasures. Amazingly, his entire collection burned up in 1985, and what you see in the store is just what he's accumulated *since then.*

It would take you months to peruse everything on these shelves, but rest assured that if you're looking for something in particular, Bob can help you find it, and if it isn't in stock he'll usually be able to order it for you. If you're like us, you'll feign interest in an old *Atlantic Monthly* and then head for the Adults Only section, where you'll find a comprehensive *Playboy* archive going back to the very first issue. If you're *not* like us, you'll look at them for the articles.

MAISON RUSSE

1720 Ogden Avenue
Lisle, IL 60532
(630) 963-5160 or (800) 778-9404
www.therussianshop.com
Map: Suburban West

Joseph Stalin's a doll—a wooden doll that is—and you'll find him and his politburo pals secretly nesting in Lisle. A sign on the outside of this store reminds you that you are 5,017 miles away from Moscow, but inside you'll find a gulag full of crafts and curios from Russia. They have amber jewelry, Orthodox icons, lacquer boxes, cobalt net porcelain, shirts and shawls, books, borzoi art, and tin wind-up toys. And, they have a Valley of the Dolls. No, these aren't the pul-

chritudinous, pill-popping dolls of neglected Russian writer Jacqueline Susannovich. These are the popular nesting dolls. Called *matryoshka*, or, "mother," these wooden toys pop open to reveal a succession of dolls inside. Their collection includes a set depicting past Soviet premiers and one mother doll that contains thirty progressively smaller dolls—now, that's one fecund female! Maison Russe offers wedding registry and consignments, and the store will even rent their riches for parties. They have samovars, swords, dinnerware, and portraits; everything you'll need to turn your dump into a dacha. Take a troika to the House of Russia for some tchotchkes and treasures. As Nicholas and Alexandra said, you won't be "tsarry."

MAXWELL STREET MARKET

Canal Street between Roosevelt Road and Sixteenth Street
Chicago, IL 60607
Map: Chicago South

If you can't find it on Maxwell Street, you don't need it. *Wild Chicago* producer Harvey Moshman has been bargain hunting at Chicago's oldest outdoor flea market for decades and has acquired everything there from snow tires to a slightly used tuxedo. Sure, it's but a shell of its former self since it moved a few blocks east to Canal Street from the original turn-of-the-century location, but the wonderful assault on the senses remains. Round the corner off of Roosevelt Road on Sunday morning and it's like Brian Urlacher is hitting you at midfield.

For better or worse, booming Hispanic music has replaced most of the blues sound the market was known for, but the smells of fresh cilantro and grilled meats cooking are a welcome addition to a neighborhood once recognized only by the scent of grilled onions and Polish hot dogs. Really, how many of those tube steaks can a person eat and live to tell the tale?

Tools, jewels, watches, socks, hats, books, records, and a million more items are available to those who enjoy bargaining. There are more than four hundred merchants spread across half a mile of Canal Street. If you hanker to haggle, Maxwell Street Market is your Mecca.

MIKE BJORN'S FINE CLOTHING

5614 Sixth Avenue
Kenosha, WI 53140
(262) 652-0648
Map: Multistate

The men's clothing business is not the easiest way to make a buck, but Kenosha's Mike Bjorn can sell you just about anything, and you'll have a lot of fun buying it. They say you've gotta have a gimmick, and the wily Bjorn has several. The official name of his store is Mike Bjorn'$ Fine Clothing and Museum, and it's the *museum* part that seems to lure plenty of curious people across the state line and through the door. There's a lot to take in once you're inside: a zombie in a casket, a life-size Conehead in a Wisconsin football jersey, a giant abominable snowman that doubles as a tie rack—everywhere you look is a feast for the eyes. There's an array of antique musical instruments, blimps, shark's teeth, and model ships (Mike Bjorn's Sea World). A lot of this stuff is hanging from the ceiling, so you're liable to have a stiff neck on your first visit.

As enjoyable as the museum gets, the main entertainment at Bjorn's is definitely the owner. It comes as no surprise that Mike moonlights as half of a music-and-comedy team at the local Holiday Inn. To his customers, he's sort of a self-aware snake oil salesman: He may lay on the charming sales pitch a little too thick, but he knows it and lets you in on the joke. Mike's pride and joy is his tuxedo collection, which lines one wall on mannequins, their heads masked with celebrity faces. It makes ordering your tux easy—"I'd like the Darth Vader, and he'll take the Richard Nixon." Downstairs in the basement is Bjorn's Museum of Tuxedo Wonders, a motley assortment of fashion "don'ts" that Mike sells for $29.95 each (with shoes). Even at that price, these plaid, puke-green, or paisley monstrosities do not leap off the rack, they sort of crawl off the shelf. Yet the always-positive Bjorn calls them "classics."

MILITARY AND POLICE SUPPLY

7351 West Madison Street
Forest Park, IL 60130
(708) 366-9711
www.gistuff.com
Map: Suburban West

For all your mace and flak jacket needs, come to Military and Police Supply in downtown Forest Park. Despite the name, this place is not just for soldiers and cops—civilian enthusiasts are welcome. You will see items for sale here that you just can't find in your average suburban shop, like a thousand-pound bomb (deactivated), a missile launcher (also deactivated), and packages of MRE (meals ready to eat) from the Gulf War. Come to think of it, the merchandise definitely leans toward the military rather than the police, and some of it is not for the faint of heart; like an olive-colored banner, for instance, with the words "Kill a Commy for Mommy" emblazoned on it. We admired the alarm clock that blows reveille when it goes off, but we can't imagine anyone but the most gung ho private wanting to hear that for more than one morning.

Owner Rick Boyce is an army veteran who clearly has a deep appreciation for the instruments of war and crime fighting. He'll gladly fit you out in a new police-issue bulletproof vest, or he'll play, if requested, one of the "Running Cadence" tapes that are for sale: "I don't know but I've been told / MRE's are rarely sold!" Sound off, one-two . . .

O'FIELD'S HEMP STORE

1547 North Wells Street
Chicago, IL 60610
www.ofields.com
Map: Chicago North

When you see the word *hemp*, is the first thing that comes to mind "getting high"? Wrong, try "getting dressed." This boutique offers clothes and paraphernalia made with the fiber derived from hemp. The only high you'll get is seeing what versatile products are made from this plant. Hempen fabric is surprisingly supple and, for you activists, totally sustainable. This store carries an abundant crop of freshly harvested boxer shorts, bras, slumber wear, T-shirts, and pants, all of it rather comfortable

looking and some of it as loosely structured as a badly rolled joint. Don't worry, you won't get busted owning this stuff. It's quite legal to wear clothing made from hemp, just still quite naughty to grow it. So, you can proudly purchase these products in broad daylight instead of skulking around searching for some dealer on a dark street corner. Don't be a dope and miss seeing the whimsical caps with slogans like "Hemp Wanted" and "Do Not Smoke This Hat." You'll have a narcotic effect on others when you perform your ablutions with hemp-based shampoos, soaps, and oils. If you're interested in an alternative fiber, check out hemp. You never really enjoyed wearing petroleum-based fabrics, anyway, though we're sure you looked slick. After donning these duds, at least you won't break out in uncontrollable giggles and get a munchie attack.

PAUL C. LEATHER

2418 West North Avenue
Chicago, IL 60647
(773) 278-6780
www.paulcleather.com
Map: Chicago West

If political parties bore you, then join the party of pleasure on North Avenue. Mr. C will satisfy your sartorial desires with made-to-order leather lingerie: underwear, fetish wear, bondage wear. If leather puts you in a lather, then have a custom outfit created by this carnal couturier. Choose from chaps, masks, and corsets, all shapes, all sizes, in traditional or patent leather (for Sundays). Paul says his garments are "crafted by people who share your passion for fantasy and fetish." *We* say, we're thinkin' gift list. Anyhoo, the construction is meticulous and made for "strenuous" wear. The corsets are all steel boned and designed for women and men. The styles are as fetching as their names: the Patricia, the Francis, the Mindy (oops, now how'd this writer's name get in there?). Paul recommends you order your holiday outfit early—nothing like a voluptuous Veterans Day. After picking out some tanned attire, how about something for your home? Bondage equipment. Designed by an architect of agony—or ecstasy if you prefer—is the suspension swing. It's a saddle on springs that allows the legs to be, well, you can figure it out. Come to this Eden of erotica and just like Adam and Eve, your innocence will be lost when you take a bite of the seductive items proffered by this seller of the sensual.

POLICE AUCTION

2800 South Western Avenue
Chicago, IL 60608
(312) 746-6777
or (312) 746-7657
Map: Chicago South

"But, Officer, I only left my garage door open for a second!"

"I know, ma'am, but that's all it takes for a bad guy to steal your bike."

If you've ever had your ride ripped off or anything else filched, then now's the time to get something similar to it back—cheap—at auction. The Chicago Police Department hosts sales of stolen, abandoned, or unclaimed items from its evidence-recovery property section. Bikes, books, jewelry, memorabilia, and electronics are all offered for sale by our conscientious constabulary on the third or fourth Saturday of the month. You probably won't find your stolen stuff here, but you'll find everything else. The swag has included a food disposal, toolboxes, chain saws, umbrellas, and a wheelchair. Yes, someone stole a wheelchair. Concerning the poachers of our personal items, a police spokesman said "anything that they can get a few bucks for . . . they'll steal it." You'll find plenty

of steals here to replace an item kidnapped from your collection, to buy for parts, or to resell on eBay. Terms for the auction are cash and take it away, preferably in your own, not "borrowed," car.

And about that wheelchair? We'd like to think that it was abandoned rather than stolen. And that the person it belonged to was healed through medicine or a laying on of hands and was so deliriously happy, he just got up and walked away. At least, that's what we prefer to think whenever we see our Uncle Walter wheeling around in his slightly used $10 chair.

QUIMBY'S BOOKSTORE

1854 West North Avenue
Chicago, IL 60622
(773) 342-0910
www.quimbys.com
Map: Chicago West

From the arcane to the profane, this store has every periodical you could possibly pine for—as long as you confine your pining to the truly "odd" in periodicals. Quimby's inventory is decidedly *not* mainstream. They have sections devoted to mayhem (*Charles Manson*), conspiracy theory (*Spy TV*), and Japanese adult comics (*Slut Girl*). Go fish for all things fetish (*Fetish Realm*), cross-dressing (*Lady Like*), or just generally erotic (*Exotique*). Nope, nothing so prosaic as *Playboy* here. Quimby's extends its alter-

native streak by selling several self-published magazines: *Giant Robot* (everything Asian), *Horizontal Action* (naked women and punk rock), and *Polka Scene 'Zine* (guess). The store also carries numerous local 'zine authors whose titles you probably won't find on the U. of C.'s reading list (*Cop Porn*). If you have an idea for an opus (*My World?*), print it and staple it and they'll take it on consignment. Then you might be invited to join one of their book-reading and signing events. Otherwise, if you're looking to fill a void in your personal library with something other booksellers have been lax to stack (breasts, butts, tattoos, transvestites, chicks, comics and prose, both purple and profound,

to name a few), come to Quimby's. Shopping here, as the owner says, is "like finding a severed ear in a field."

SEEN ON SCREEN

Stratford Square
Bloomingdale, IL 60108
(630) 295-8758
www.ontelevision.com
Map: Suburban North

Admit it, you've ordered one of those products from late-night TV. Like the one that will guarantee you a HEAD OF HAIR IN A CAN or make you THINNER AND SLIMMER TODAY. But then there's always the postal purgatory as you wait days to receive that life-altering item. Well, clap off—*clap, clap*—your Clapper and head over to Seen on Screen. S.O.S. is the store that sells merchandise AS SEEN ON TV. Now you too can GET FIT QWIK when you workout with Thighs of Steel or the ExerFlex Ball. After you've had a ball getting fit, imagine a SEXIER YOU IN SECONDS when you go from a B to a D cup with the Wonder Shaper bra inserts, or try on Hairagami, which, we think, folds your hair into the shape of a crane. Have MEALS IN MINUTES with the indispensable aid of Egg Ware ("Presto! Perfect Eggs") or Salsa Magic! (which is more like Salsa Menial! as it's a manual food processor). Of course you'll find the ubiquitous Ginsu knives and Ronco products and old standards like the Singing Bass Wall Plaque and Gas Blasters, a phonic flatulence toy. (Maybe that one's not so standard.) THEY MAKE GREAT GIFTS! Think of Fluffy with the

Lift 'n Sift Litter Box or how's about giving Dad a tee in the toilet with Potty Putter—Complete With Do Not Disturb Sign. Now, *that's* disturbing. THERE'S SOMETHING 4 EVERYONE! Go to the Web site to find a store near you and become YOUNGER AND WRINKLE-FREE but only if you act NOW, NOW, NOW.

SHAKE, RATTLE AND READ

4812 North Broadway
Chicago, IL 60640
(773) 334-5311
Map: Chicago North

Owner Ric Addy says his place has "a rock and roll attitude mixed with a literary attitude." He's got the last fifty years of pop culture in books, records, magazines, and memorabilia pinned up, crammed in, and stacked up at his store. The top-selling used books—with prices starting at $3.00—include early lesbian lit (which is more popular than seeing an old lesbian lit) and the mass-marketed, midcentury detective novels like *Lie Down Killer* ("She clawed his handsome face to mark him a killer"). The cover art alone on these noirish novels is becoming collectible. Shake, Rattle also carries an extensive supply of music magazines. If you make a trip here, bring your unwanted printed matter to sell or trade. If Ric says "no" to your "gold," then dump 'em outside in the "free" bin provided. Among the store's rarer items, they have almost every *Playboy* since 1958 ("The articles are great," Ric says) and old, underground newspapers. The latter are remnants from Ric's hippie-commune-living days in San Francisco. He moved here after the scene in "Haight-Ashbury went to hell." Speaking of underground, ask him to tell you about the network of tunnels beneath his store. Once used to transport coal, the subterranean passageways served a different purpose for Al Capone and his pal "Machine Gun" Jack McGurn. Ric says when McGurn's club was raided, "they'd lock the booze in there, count the money, play cards." Evidently, they drank the booze down there, too. There's a whole wall of urinals. Our guess is they didn't expect Mrs. Capone to make a pit stop and play some pinochle.

SOMETHING OLD, SOMETHING NEW

1056 West Belmont Avenue
Chicago, IL 60657
(800) 441-4900
Map: Chicago North

We've all known people who refuse to throw anything away. Something Old, Something New is a store that has used that philosophy for fun and profit. It's dedicated to the proposition that all used or damaged merchandise can be recycled— or in this case resold for as little as 25 cents. Most of said merchandise happens to be clothes, though the store does have things like used books and diaper seconds (we were warned that "they leak a little"), as well as secondhand ice-cream machines from McDonald's. The garments are split into two sections. One consists of seconds and irregulars, and the other is optimistically named Vintage, which in this case is a fancy way of saying "used."

When you walk by Something Old, you can't help but be curious about what you see through the windows. The bright lighting and long, straight aisles of merchandise bring to mind a supermarket for clothing, and then you spot a sign that says SAVE UP TO 99%! Now that's a discount. Inside you'll find pants, shirts, suits, dresses, over-coats, and even underwear, though the owners admit that used undies don't exactly leap off the rack. The staff here is not above putting labels or price tags over the flaws in the irregular garments, anything to move them out the door. Their motivation is a basement piled to the ceiling with boxes and bags of goods waiting to come upstairs. When you factor in the store's "buyback" policy (bring anything back in any condition and get 50 cents) the chances are slim that the basement floor will ever be seen again—especially if those leaking diapers don't start selling.

STANTON HOBBY SHOP

4718 North Milwaukee Avenue
Chicago, IL 60630
(773) 283-6446
www.stantonhobby.com
Map: Chicago West

"Idle hands are the devil's play-ground." Kick Satan off the swing when you get your hands busy with a new—or old—hobby from Stanton's. The shop carries all the crafts you remember as a kid, including Monogram brand model kits. The kits are a compact way to indulge your creativity, and you'll probably build them better than when you were a child (you won't be so preoccupied with the smell of the glue). Owner Joe Stanton says a lot of the older hobby kits are back in vogue and selling, espe-cially the Paint by Number sets and jigsaw puzzles. If you're looking for a phys-ical rather than a mental hobby, go fly a kite. Stanton's has several kits for kites and wind socks or the supplies you'll need to build them from scratch. And the shop sells bridge-building kits, architectural tools, and radio-controlled cars, boats, planes, and tanks.

If you see the track setup in the store, you'll know Stanton's has a connec-tion to the Scouts. Besides offering Boy and Girl Scout uniforms and badges, they "do the derby." Cub Scouts come here for their pinewood derby kits and to take their projects out for a test run. Joe says the track is for the kids, but he finds the dads are just as excited. And dollhouse enthusiasts will find a home here. This hobby haven has all the mechanicals necessary to replicate a real house, from electric and plumbing to miniature hardware and food. An employee told us that "some people even have sound effects of toilets flushing." Satan is going nowhere *near* those people.

STONER CONNECTION
www.stonerconnection.com

These guys jumped bail. Or, rather, they jumped and bailed out of operating a brick-and-mortar store. Here are the facts. When *Wild Chicago* first visited Stoner's Custom Shoppe, which specialized in Chicago Police and Fire Department novelty merchandise, it was located on Milwaukee Avenue. Whenever we needed another pair of panties emblazoned with the Fire Department's logo, we knew where to find our supplier. Then, when we went to do the follow-up for this book, we found the gang had taken a walk. We thought they'd gone underground, but, after a little detective work, we apprehended them on the Web.

Though operating under an alias (now known as the Stoner Connection), they still carry the usual suspects from the store: unique gift items that law enforcement or fire department enthusiasts will find arresting. They have replica badges, clothing, jewelry, baseball caps and mugs (coffee, not shots), most with the CPD or CFD logos. Stake out their T-shirts with slogans like "Homicide: Our Day Begins When Yours Ends" and "Chicago Police: Our Bars Never Close," certainly apparel that will elevate you above plainclothes. How about flashing an "Our Bite Is Worse Than Our Bark" shirt while you patrol with Fido in his distinctive CPD black-and-white checkerboard-patterned leash and collar? It's nice to know you can make the collar on Stoner's copper collection via the Internet. No more flat-footing it to a store. Case closed.

STRICTLY MEN

13 River Oaks Drive
Calumet City, IL 60409
(708) 868-1088
Map: Suburban South

If you like guys blowing smoke up your ash, then this cigar emporium is the place for you. Strictly Men carries an exhaustive line of Macanudos, plus Partagas, Padrones, and other hard-to-find cigars. There's also a treasury of tobaccos, pipes, and smoking accessories. After shopping, don't be in a hurry to leave with your leaves; Strictly Men encourages you to stick around, spark your big butt, and bust your gums with the regulars. This store evokes an earlier era when the cultured class retired after dinner for some conversation over stogies. If politics is your passion, you'll get some lively debates here, especially if you don't lean far enough to the Right. Strictly Men has plenty of La-Z-Boys (the chairs, not necessarily the men), and the shop even boasts a library, which has more Oliver North than Ogden Nash. It's a very clubby atmosphere with people bringing in food or having it delivered and spending the day complimenting each other's ash.

For you men out there, you know nothing beats having a perfecto in your pocket to give you confidence with the ladies.

You'll find some ladies in the back of the store, trimming hair in the "men's only" barbershop. "A Gentlemen's Cut with a Lady's Touch" is how they phrase it. When we asked a stylist why she cuts only men's hair, she replied, "They're a lot less grief and better tippers."

TEN THOUSAND VILLAGES

719 Main Street
Evanston, IL 60202
(847) 733-8258
www.tenthousandvillages.org
Map: Suburban North

How would you like to be a Medici? Lorenzo de' Medici and his Florentine family were famous for their patronage of artists. When you purchase a craft from this Evanston store, you'll be the benefactor to one of over 250 artisans who would otherwise be unemployed. Your support, the store says, guarantees a living wage for the artist and his or her family. And you have a global village of handicrafts to choose from. They carry baskets from Vietnam, jewelry from Kenya, instruments—that even the most musically challenged can play—from Burkina Faso and Cameroon, and cloth, wooden, and clay dolls from all over. You'll be aiding not only artists in developing countries but also some in our own backyard. When you pick up homemade soaps and dried foods here, you'll be assisting Chicago women trying to move off welfare. Travel to the Web site to take a virtual tour of the Villages' good-intentioned goodies and—not to sound too Sally Struthers about this, but—to read stories about the artisans themselves, such as the Andes flute makers or the Haitian metal sculptors. Patronize the artists by purchasing their output and you might earn a nickname like Lorenzo the Magnificent did. 'Course, in your case, it would be Mike the Marvelous or Tim the Terrific. And, one day, the crafts-people you support could become the next Michelangelo or Botticelli. Volunteer to work in the store if you really want to fly with this patronage thing, though, to be honest, we can't imagine Larry de' Medici getting his hands soiled prepping paints for Michelangelo.

TEXTILE DISCOUNT OUTLET

2121 West Twenty-first Street
Chicago, IL 60608
(773) 847-0572
www.megafabrics.com
Map: Chicago West

Unhappy with the fabric of your life? Only interested in material things? Then bolt on over to the world's largest retail textile outlet. This fortress of fabric is 75,000 square feet filled with flannels, worsteds, brocades, and cottons. There's a surfeit of sensuous silks and gossamery chiffons, plus buttons, zippers, and ribbons. You'll woof (and warp) over the upholstery and drapery fabrics, too. The kaleidoscope of cloth changes constantly; Textile Discount Outlet receives more than 100,000 new yards a month. OK, so some of the fabric looks like casino carpeting—so garishly colored that Liberace would blush—but that's more than made up for by the outlet's deep discounting. How deep? Fabric that

was originally $90 a yard sells for $6.50. Now *that's* "Davy Jones's locker" pricing.

Do we hear wedding bells? Make your own gown from their mountains of matri-monial material and lace. You'll save so much, you'll be serving truffles, not tacos, at the reception. Looking for that perfect leopard print to complement your sofa?

Bring in a swatch, and they'll match it and give you a quote. Here's one quote: "Our first, second and last rule is to make the customer happy." You'll be giddy with TDO's unfathomably extensive selection of fabrics and finery. Pack a lunch when you go—it takes time to shop stockpiles of stuff—if only to have the crumbs to leave a trail. Legend has it all they found of a customer who got lost in the outlet's vault of velvets was the skeleton.

TRANSFORMATIONS

146 North Oak Park Avenue
Oak Park, IL 60301
(708) 383 8338
www.transformationsbyrori.com
Map: Suburban West

Now here's a store that really lives up to its name! Transformations in downtown Oak Park caters to men who enjoy dressing up as women, otherwise known as transvestites or cross-dressers. We're not talking about transsexuals, who have had an actual sex change; these folks would rather just *pretend* to be women, usually in secret, since many of them are married with children and have employers who would not understand their predilection. Transformations offers all the accoutrements necessary to achieve femininity, from a full array of fine clothing (check out the Too Hot to Trot rack) to an ample supply of silicone breasts and padded fanny panties. But owner Rori Scheffler doesn't stop there. She also provides beauty clinics in the back of the store, where customers get helpful tips on hair and makeup. And for those who are firmly in touch with their womanly side but still walk and talk like a truck driver, Rori conducts workshops in the basement on feminine movement and speech. Men, you might be surprised at how different it

is to get into a car with a dress on, and if you think all that's needed to sound like a woman is a good falsetto, you've been watching too much Monty Python.

It should be noted that Transformations is patronized by real women, too. After all, the jewelry, wigs, and feathered boas for sale are equally appropriate for their fashion needs. But Rori's main clientele is clearly the cross-dressing crowd, for whom this store is a veritable godsend. It's even somewhat of a social hub, since Rori and son Soto (sometimes known as Lisa) host an occasional party, like their "Brides and Bridesmaids" dress-up bash.

So if you're a would-be girl in need of a makeover, hightail it over to Transformations and start stocking up. And don't forget the cross-dressers' best friend—beard cover!

U-PULL-IT AUTO PARTS

14101 South Leavitt
Blue Island, IL 60406
(708) 385-5597
www.areliableautoparts.com
Map: Suburban South

Are you missing the bumper to your Blazer? Is your Mustang's muffler malfunctioning? Then pull into this self-service salvage yard. When it comes to parts, you need it, you see it, you pull it. There are acres of used autos and trucks, foreign and domestic, just waiting for you to denude. The yard estimates a savings of between 50 percent and 75 percent off dealership and other stores' prices when customers peel the parts themselves. Find a headlight ($1.00), hood ($40.00), horn ($2.00), hubcap ($4.00) or hinge ($2.00) . . . and that's just the *H*'s. There are hundreds of thousands of parts for you to plunder. Come with your work clothes and tools, they'll supply the washtub for your cleanup. If you've got big muscles but a tiny wallet, then you'll want to attend the Pull-A-Thon. Several times a year, U Pull It hosts a sale where you can buy all the parts you want for one low price. The catch is you have to carry them for a distance of 20 feet without letting them touch, roll, or drag on the ground. Over fifteen hundred people come to watch or participate in these marathons. If picking or lugging parts isn't your pleasure, then how about searching for some riches? Dig around the debris that people leave behind in their rides. There could be untracked treasure tucked away in the trunk or glove compartment. Because really, think about it—when was the last time you looked at what's under your seat?

YESTERDAY STORE

1143 West Addison Street
Chicago, IL 60613
(773) 248-8087
Map: Chicago North

Tom Boyle will buy, sell, or trade just about anything that comes from the past. He has crammed millions of items into his tiny store, making Yesterday a true pack rat's paradise. There are drawers brimming with old magazines, glass cases filled with baseball cards and campaign buttons, shelves overflowing with movie stills and comic books—he has even taken to hanging stuff from the ceiling. Boyle's main interests are history, sports, and movies, and the result is that his collection of collectibles is amazingly eclectic—and voluminous. He laments that for every bag of memorabilia he sells, a bigger bag comes in.

If you've ever gone to a Cubs game, you've probably seen Yesterday, a small yellow building a few blocks away from Wrigley on Addison. It has been in business for over a quarter of a century, and we have a feeling some of the merchandise has been there for at least that long. But occasionally you'll stumble across something that will bring back a childhood memory or spark your interest in a piece of the past. For that reason alone the store is a great place to browse and buy. Please buy, otherwise Tom Boyle may soon have to run his business from the sidewalk.

MORE SHOPPING

ALCALA'S WESTERN WEAR
1733 West Chicago Avenue
Chicago, IL 60622
(312) 226-0152
www.alcalas.com
Map: Chicago West
Chicago's largest retailer of Western shirts and hats.

ARCHITECTURAL ARTIFACTS
4325 North Ravenswood Avenue
Chicago, IL 60613
(773) 348-0622
www.architecturalartifacts.com
Map: Chicago North
"Objects of desire, pieces of a lost world, the unusual and the aesthetic," so they say.

ASH'S MAGIC SHOP
4955 North Western Avenue
Chicago, IL 60625
(773) 271-4030
Map: Chicago North
Mr. Ash demonstrates the tricks before you buy them.

COOK BROTHERS WHOLESALE
240 North Ashland Avenue
Chicago, IL 60607
(312) 421-3400
Map: Chicago West
Knicknacks and other goods sold wholesale to the public.

ROSENBLUM'S WORLD OF JUDAICA

2906 West Devon Avenue
Chicago, IL 60659
(773) 262-1700
www.alljudaica.com
Map: Chicago North
All things Jewish, including rabbi trading cards and yarmulkes with logos of Chicago sports teams.

SALVAGE ONE

1840 West Hubbard Street
Chicago, IL 60622
(312) 733-0098
www.salvageone.com
Map: Chicago West
Warehouse of "architectural reclamation, singular antiques and curiosities."

SPORTS EXCHANGE

4159 North Western Avenue
Chicago, IL 60618
(772) 583-7283
Map: Chicago North
Used sporting equipment bought and sold.

STARS OUR DESTINATION

705 Main Street
Evanston, IL 60202
(847) 570-5925
Map: Suburban North
Headquarters for the best selection of sci-fi literature in town.

UNCLE FUN TOYS AND NOSTALGIA

1338 West Belmont Avenue
Chicago, IL 60657
(773) 477-8223
www.unclefunchicago.com
Map: Chicago West
The top stop for odd trinkets, joke gifts, and stocking stuffers.

SERVICES

HOW CAN WE
HELP YOU?

ANCHOR BOARD-UP AND GLASS

3100 West St. Charles Road
Bellwood, IL 60104
(800) 400-0002
Map: Suburban West

In a way, these folks are sort of an ambulance service for buildings. When fire, vandalism, or natural disaster strikes, Anchor Board-Up will race to the premises to secure it from further intrusion, often getting there before the fire trucks and police cars. Once they've gotten the harried home or business owner to sign on the dotted line, they start placing sheets of plywood where there once were windows and doors. All this, of course, assumes that Anchor gets to the site before its competitors. The board-up business, you see, is a relatively dog-eat-dog affair, and all the dogs have police scanners. If two show up simultaneously, a bidding war ensues, which would be quite entertaining if the customer had not just suffered a catastrophe.

Anchor tries to get an edge by having eight trucks cruising the city twenty-four hours a day, waiting for calamities to occur. Not all jobs originate on the police scanner; people with gaping holes to fill often call direct, and it turns out that the phone book is another board-up battlefield. They all want to be first in the yellow pages, so when Anchor found out that Buzy Bee had changed its name to A Buzy Bee, Anchor promptly started a companion business: A-Apple Board Up. Aaaattaboy!

AVON MAN
ROBERT FRANKLIN

(847) 869-0469

Quick, who's your Avon representative? Yeah, you probably have a better chance of naming your state representative. Robert "Success" Franklin is about to change that. He wants to be your Avon Ladies Man. And ladies, what a man he is. He describes himself as "Mr. Clean without the earring." In a flip on the role traditionally held by women, this loopily cheerful fellow sells lotions and bath oils to the cracked and stinky masses. In a further attempt to separate himself from the usual pack of pretty peddlers, he'll deliver anywhere, anytime. His motto is "You Ring, We Bring," and you'll sing knowing you can get your fix of Skin So Soft lotion whenever and wherever you

are. He draws a crowd when he drives his minivan-mall into the neighborhood; it's like an ice-cream truck for adults. His license plate says it all: U R AVON. "It's too egotistical to say I AM AVON," Robert says, it's all about you, you soon-to-be-more-beautiful thing, you. (He didn't get that middle name for nothing.) If you are, like some of us, naturally sweet-smelling and impossibly fetching, then you might want to purchase something from one of the other lines he carries in his warehouse-on-wheels: Fuller brushes, Tupperware, Stanley mops, Watkins dry goods, and Amway. Bob would probably offer more, but he's run out of room for signage on his auto-bazaar. Hey, did you hear the one about the traveling salesman who—Um, never mind.

BARBIE DOCTOR
MIKE SCHMIDT
(773) 384-1215

There's a price on Barbie's head. And her body. And the box she came in. A pristine-condition Barbie doll can fetch up to $10,000. Unless you were forward-thinking—or totally anal—and never decanted her from her original packaging, chances are your Barbie has been bandied about like a shuttlecock. If she's looking more rag than doll, bring her to Mike Schmidt, the Barbie Doctor, and his sanitarium for synthetic dolls. Mike can repair your Mattel marvel and restore her to her unnatural perfection. He has a family practice, so you can bring Skipper, Ken, and Midge in, too. Herr Doktor is a hair doctor. Bad-hair days are Barbie's most common problem, and he can detangle, defrizz, and reweave her coiffure. And, since Mattel stopped offering parts, he can locate and replace missing limbs—like the one that got blown off after her date with G.I. Joe. Plus, he can treat her most bizarre ail-

ments; green ear, a skin cancer that develops from her earrings; and vinyl tears, a fatal flaw in her DNA that causes her head to become separated from her neck. Kind of beats a bad-hair day, huh? He'll only see your dolly by appointment, but it's worth it just to see his waiting room. On display are some of the two thousand dolls in his personal collection, many whose outfits he changes seasonally. Whether you want to hand down the plastic princess to your child or plan to push Barbie into prostitution by selling her to the highest bidder on eBay, there's help, so hang on—which is probably what your Barbie's head is doing right now.

BIG HAIR

2012 West Roscoe Street
Chicago, IL 60618
(773) 348-0440
Map: Chicago North

There are two reasons why this salon has managed to thrive in its commercially competitive neighborhood. First, because they do big hair. The stylists here create coiffures that are going to get you noticed, or at least cause some unease among the general population. Color is a specialty. You could say they're blind to color. The palette pros at BH will streak, tint, shade, highlight, dye, even variegate your locks with almost any color, from sienna to sapphire. They also do BIG hair—big as in "big as a house." They can mousse your mop and mound it so massively high, you'll look like you just left the court of Louis XV and Madame de Pompadour. Their reputation for styling the 1950s pompadour is so good, they list several Elvis impersonators among their clientele. BH owner Patricia Miller was so fond of her own piled-high pouf in the 1980s—she once teased her tresses up 1 foot—that she named the salon after it. Second, little price. All of these tonsorial theatrics are relatively inexpensive. As of this review, haircuts can be had for $10. Sure, you *could* go to one of those chain bang-cutters for about the same price, but would you be sitting a chair away from Mr. Blue Suede Shoes? So, there you go. Big Hair. Little price. And, if we can add a third reason: open Sundays.

BRONZEVILLE'S 1ST BED AND BREAKFAST CLUB

3911 South Martin Luther King Drive
Chicago, IL 60653
(773) 373-8081
www.bronzevillesbb.com
Map: Chicago South

The only time you want a *2nd* or *3rd* next to your name is when you're a national bank. Otherwise, who remembers you? Can you remember a bronze medalist in skiing? See? While there is a *bronze* in this establishment's title and it does indeed deserve a medal for its services and appointments, there's nothing third place about it. Not only is this the Bronzeville area's First B&B Club, but it's also Chicago's first one to be owned

and operated by African Americans. The "city within a city" of Bronzeville has long been a hub for African American entrepreneurs, and this posh palace is yet another example. The owners have turned an old crack house into a center for slumber, dining, entertainment, and rejuvenation. The rooms are furnished in mahogany and cherry woods and feature fireplaces and Jacuzzis. After spending the night on down-filled pillows and comforters, you can down a full breakfast of crepes, eggs, waffles, pancakes, and more. There's also a butler on board twenty-two hours a day (he's got to sleep sometime) to turn down your bed, draw your bath, and bring breakfast to your door. Whether you're an overnight guest or not, you can enjoy the gourmet soul food and Caribbean cuisine in the dining room or get a cut, manicure, and massage at the day spa and salon.

Maybe Bronzeville's 1st should change the *B&B* from *Bed and Breakfast* to *Beautiful and Bountiful.*

CLINICAL PERFORMANCE CENTER

University of Illinois at Chicago
(312) 996-2989
www.uic-cpc.com
Map: Chicago West

We found a place where it pays to be sick—actually, to pretend you're sick—and if you don't mind the backless gowns and the occasional "Full Monty," it's a pretty good gig. The Clinical Performance Center hires actors to portray patients for medical students, who are sent here to improve their diagnostic skills and bedside manner. The actors are required to study up on the case they'll be mimicking and may receive a little training on their intended disease, but at least there are no lines to learn, only symptoms to fake. Once they're in the examination room itching, coughing, or groaning, the "clinical performance artist" is playing to an audience of one, who takes his or her (imaginary) medical history and sometimes performs a physical. All encounters are videotaped for the students' use, but the actor is encouraged not to play to the camera, even if the West Nile or schizophrenia act is going really well.

For future physicians, the center provides a safe environment in which to learn their trade; there is no danger of misdiagnosing a *really* sick patient and causing the person to flatline. For the actors, they do have to put up with some poking and prodding (as well as some *un*gratuitous nudity), and they won't hear any applause, but there is the satisfaction of knowing that they're helping to train better doctors. That, and a pretty nice paycheck.

CUSTOM MEDICAL STOCK PHOTO

3660 West Irving Park Road
Chicago, IL 60618
(773) 267-3100
www.cmsp.com
Map: Chicago North

There's not much of an upside to a bad skin rash or a large bunion, but we know a place where you can make money from conditions such as these. Custom Medical Stock Photo is the largest clearinghouse of medical and scientific images in the world. The business collects photos and illustrations of medical conditions and things of interest to science, then licenses or sells them to medical journals, major magazines, even the Super Bowl telecast. Owners Mike and Henry say they have a quarter million pictures on file, and judging by the sampling we saw, a lot of them can be a tad gruesome. Ever seen an X ray of a seven-toed foot? Or a cranium with the brain exposed? Not pretty. *Warning:* Don't chew your own hair unless you wouldn't mind seeing a picture of a hair ball in the shape of your stomach.

Where do they get this stuff? Well, they have a long list of regular suppliers, but they also will occasionally run an ad in the *Reader* soliciting people with an abnormality, syndrome, or unusual disease. If these folks have a good-quality photo of their condition, great, otherwise they're invited to model for CMSP in its state-of-the-art photography studio. If you need a "before" picture prior to a surgery, you're also welcome to come down, but *you* have to pay *them* for that service. Mike and Henry are not averse to using themselves or their family to get a good picture. A baby tooth of Mike's daughter is on file, as is a rather intrusive look at Henry's wife giving birth to their first child. Still, they thrive on outside submissions, so if you've just been involved in an industrial accident, go straight to Custom Medical Stock Photo for some cold hard cash. Okay, maybe a quick detour to the emergency room first . . .

ELMO'S TOMBSTONES WHILE-U-WAIT

6023 South State Street
Chicago, IL 60621
(773) 643-0200
Map: Chicago South

You shouldn't have to wait an eternity for a tombstone, since you'll have to spend an eternity *under* the darn thing. Maybe that's why Elmo's is doing such a lively business. The artisans here promise to produce your tombstone "while you wait," though few people are in that much of a hurry. The process involves blocks of granite, rubber stencils, a sandblaster, and some black paint, and it takes about 2½ hours for each stone. The folks at Elmo's can give you the standard design with the cross, praying hands, and roses, or they can customize, perhaps incorporating a picture of the deceased into the layout. They want their customers satisfied, even if they're 6 feet under.

The slogan here is "Before You Go, Call Elmo," but the fact is that the place is run by a guy named José. Elmo passed on a few years ago (bet he gave himself a great deal on a tombstone!), and José never bothered to change the signage. In the backyard is where the finished stones are held for delivery, as well as the duds with flaws that render them unusable. José told us about one that was supposed to read IN GOD'S CARE but came out IN DOG'S CARE. Guess that one is headed for the pet cemetery . . .

FOUR SEASONS AMUSEMENTS

109 South Bloomingdale Road
Bloomingdale, IL 60108
(630) 893-3456
www.fourseasonsamusements.com
Map: Suburban West

For a good time, and a potentially violent and stomach-turning time, call Wally at Four Seasons Amusements! The irrepressible Wally Nekyha, who is fond of calling his business "Wally World," is the purveyor of just about anything that stands a chance of amusing you. You've probably seen some of Four Seasons' wares at street fairs, block parties, and the like. Wally can rent you a merry-go-round, a "strongman" hammer and bell, or a Wall of Velcro. Perhaps you and your friends or business partners or neighbors need to vent some pent-up aggression. What better than those really big sumo suits or those oversize boxing gloves to do the trick? If you lean more toward the nausea-inducing activities, there's the Human Gyroscope, the Barrel of Fun (put five people inside and start spinning), or an inflatable hollow wheel that rolls the hapless fun seeker across any terrain. Wally's pride and joy is the Toilet Dunk Tank—hit the target and a toilet empties water onto whomever's in the cage. Nekyha told us, "For an extra charge, we use dirty water!"

If this brand of hijinks doesn't appeal to you, Wally World might still get you to part with some of your hard-earned cash with his Autograph Department or the Fifties and Sixties Collectibles section. The signatures of big stars like Marlon Brando, Marilyn Monroe, Babe Ruth, and Al Capone grace the walls, and Wally can also offer you Beatles bedsheets or some rare "Shindig" cologne. Most of the customers, though, come for the amusements—and then have to go elsewhere for bandages and motion-sickness pills.

HAROLD WASHINGTON LIBRARY

Information Hotline
400 South State Street
Chicago, IL 60605
(312) 747-4300, ext. 7
www.chipublib.org
Map: Downtown

You're missing the last dwarf. You can only name six of the seven, it's 4:55 P.M., and a beer hangs in the balance. Who are you going to call? Why, the library's info hotline, that's who. The Information Center at the Harold Washington Library is staffed by reference librarians just hankering to hit the books to provide quick answers to your questions concerning almost all subject matter. (Question: What is Lady Macbeth's first name?) Now, you're probably thinking you could get the same results to any query by hopping on-line. Well, that's fine if the answer will settle a bar bet. (Q: What does *M&M* in M&M candies stand for?) But what if you need to know the answer to the question "Is the song 'Amazing Grace' under copyright protection?" for that big presentation at work? Perhaps a juicy promotion hinges on the correct answer. Are you going to trust the Net? The library researchers live by a golden rule— they will always quote an answer from a *printed* source. Even if it's a simple question with an answer they know (Q: What's the longest river in the world?), they'll check the books. And, since it's the main library, they've got a gazillion of them to check. So, whether it's helping with your child's homework or nailing that last detail for the job, give them a call. Then you'll be the smarty-pants. But, be warned. There is one question they won't answer. Know what it is?

Answers:

(1) Doc, Happy, Bashful, Sleepy, Dopey, Sneezy, and Grumpy; (2) Lady Bruoch Macbeth; (3) Mars and Murrie; (4) Nope, "Amazing Grace" is in the public domain; (5) The Nile in Egypt; (6) Lottery numbers.

HAROLD WASHINGTON LIBRARY LISTENING/VIEWING CENTER (LVC)
400 South State Street,
Eighth Floor
Chicago, IL 60605
(312) 747-4850
www.chipublib.org
Map: Downtown

If you think the library is only for musty tomes and hushed, reverent tones, then you should fox-trot up to the eighth floor at the Harold Washington Library and explore its music resources. The library's exhaustive collections of sound recordings and videotapes are available, free, for your relaxation or research in the LVC. Listen to over 150,000 music recordings, spoken words, and interviews covering all aspects, from folk to funk. Particular strengths lie in jazz, blues, and gospel with 400 hours of Dick Buckley's *Archives of Recorded Jazz*, the *Chicago Blues Archives*, and 100 *Jubilee Showcase* programs. Indulge your serendipity and you could be aurally excited by Stan Freberg (humor), Jussi Björling (Swedish tenor), or Robert Mitchum (calypso—yes, Bob does calypso).

If you sing calypso, or anything else, don't waste it in the shower. Grab your towel and your "tra-la-la" and practice at the library. It has six practice rooms that also come equipped with a piano and a video monitor for instructional tapes. Who knows, tuning your talent here might help you turn your "do-re-me" into dough. And you'll have a clever anecdote about "how it all started" when you're being interviewed for that cover story in *Rolling Stone*.

HEALER SHAYNA BRACHA
(847) 520-8012
www.shaynabracha.com

Shayna Bracha is a shaman-in-training (and a wizard in a previous life) who claims that she can heal what ails you while teaching you to paint. This elflike and irrepressible mother of one calls herself "a healer and energy worker—I'm here to bring light and color into your life!" She found her career during a long bout with chronic fatigue syndrome and fibromyalgia, when her husband and child urged her to take up painting. Bracha says the more she painted, the better she felt, though it took a shaman from Peru to complete the cure. Determined to heal others the same way she had been healed, by combining art with shamanism, she soon started seeing patients by appointment at her home.

Her treatment begins with a "cleaning," first with sound (Shayna directs a high-pitched "Ooooo!" at the ailing customer), then with a crystal (which she waves around the patient's body). Once cleaned, it's time to start painting under the nurturing guidance of this shaman-to-be and wizard-that-was. If the ill art student is not crazy about his or her own artwork, Shayna reassures the person that it's the process of creation that does the healing, not the final result.

Bracha's own process of creation seems to have gotten a little out of hand. Not only has she amassed hundreds of canvases (which are for sale but aren't selling fast), she's also turned her brush on her own house; the garage, porch, kitchen walls, several doors, and the picnic table all bear her riotous strokes of color. When you see the bizarre nature of some of her painting, you'll realize that Shayna's art is as alternative as her medical treatment. Be advised that neither one is covered by your HMO.

HOSTELLING INTERNATIONAL
J. Ira and Nicki Harris Family Hostel
24 East Congress Parkway
Chicago, IL 60605
(312) 360-0300
www.hichicago.org
Map: Downtown

If you think paying $24 a night for a nice room in the heart of the Loop is too good to be true, you'd be right. But if you're lucky enough to have a zip code other than "606—" then, my friend, you are very much in luck, for that means you are entitled to be a guest at Youth Hostel of Chicago.

Hostelling International opened the place in 2000 as an affordable option for international and out-of-town visitors, who are welcome to stay here for up to fourteen days. Forget about the "rustic" hostels that you've been to elsewhere: This is a veritable hosteling Taj Mahal with state-of-the-art kitchen facilities, keycard security system, and a communications room with a bank of Internet kiosks to help keep up with e-mail on the road. There are even two restaurants available to guests, and we can attest that the Mexican one was pretty good.

The typical room has six beds, lockers for valuables, and a private bathroom (try finding *those* in a European hostel!). The spacious lobby rivals that of any $100-a-night hotel, with the added amenity of a Ping-Pong table in the corner. And no hotel can offer you the opportunity to befriend people from all over the world. Ultimately, it's the international camaraderie, not the great price, that makes hostels in general, and this one in particular, such a great deal. As for us 606ers, guess we'll just have to move out of town . . .

HOUSE MOVERS
Lykowski Construction, Inc.
(574) 291-8858

Thomas Wolfe wrote *You Can't Go Home Again.* So, don't. Bring the whole home with you. If you need to move but hate giving up that showplace of a house, consider placing it on show when you hire these structural engineers to move it. From extracting your house from its present dwelling all the way to plopping it down at its new location, this group makes being driven out of house and home fast and effi-

cient. Using beams, jacks, and hydraulic dollies, Lykowski will cradle your casa as it moves oh so slowly down the street.

Upon arrival at your destination, the crew will push it onto the lot using brute strength (OK, using a front-end loader) and jack it back up so it can accept a new foundation. They'll even organize an army of civil servants for the job. Several police officers are needed to block intersections and direct traffic around your "mobile" home (talk about yer outdoor plumbing) and they'll call in the SS—Streets and Sanitation—to drop the streetlight wires to accommodate the overhead. You'll supply the party as you watch old and new neighbors setting up lawn chairs to watch the progress of this very moving experience. Prices for this project start at around $20,000. But if you absolutely adore your abode and you've considered today's housing market, this might be the best move you ever make.

INTERNATIONAL COMPUTER RECYCLING

1824 West Thirty-fifth Avenue
Gary, IN 46408
(219) 887-7000
Map: Multistate

It is perhaps the largest computer graveyard in the nation, with over 5 million pounds of discarded equipment in its possession. The folks at International Computer Recycling receive material from all over the world, which they then weigh, stack, and eventually dissect into parts that can be distributed to the proper recycling locations. If you've ever wondered what to do with that old computer once you've either replaced or broken it, this is your most earth-friendly, guilt-free option. You see, before businesses like this, all those monitors, cables, keyboards, and motherboards were going into landfills; now they can be piled

haphazardly in ICR's huge warehouses to await an afterlife in some other piece of machinery.

Don't think for a second that this place is going to resell your Apple or IBM to other users for a profit. They can't for the same reason you couldn't: In this fast-paced world of computer hardware, 99 percent of these e-contraptions are obsolete. But don't feel sorry for owner Michael Rushakoff—when you deal with the kind of volume that he does, you're still going to make a pretty good buck recycling. That's why he's willing to make house calls for particularly big donations to his inventory. Businesses that close their doors or upgrade their computer sys-

tems can have ICR pull up to their loading dock and collect their unwanted equipment. Once back at home base, there are many ways to take the junk apart, and a lot of them involve abusing it severely with hammers and other tools of destruction. If you've had a rocky relationship with your personal computer, rest assured that when you bring or ship it here it will receive its just desserts.

MITT MENDER KENNY GAND

120 Willow Road
Rochester, IL 62563
(217) 498-7812
www.ballglove.com

So your baseball glove is coming apart at the seams, but you can't bear the thought of throwing it out. There is a man whose mission it is to mend your mitt. His name is Kenny Gand, and he calls himself the Mitt Mender. Actually, he was going to call himself the Glove Doctor, but his Uncle Mike talked him into his current title. He's turned a room of his house into a leather workshop where he labors to bring damaged gloves back to their former glory. Simply ship your ailing beauty to Kenny and he'll fix it, usually for around $20.00 (plus $5.00 for return shipping). He promises a turnaround time of no more than a couple of days, since he understands that most folks don't have a backup mitt. As someone who's played baseball since he was age seven, Gand can empathize with players who have sentimental attachments to their "gamer"—that glove they've always relied on when the chips are down and the game's on the line.

In addition to repairing mitts, Kenny also makes them from scratch. Using an old (unmotorized) sewing machine, he constructs each leather beauty by hand, proudly stitching in the autograph *MM* when he's done. Then he takes a piece of wood that looks like the leg of a chair and pounds the crap out of his new creation in order to break it in for its future owner. When we asked why someone should buy from him rather than a sporting-goods store, Kenny brusquely answered, "A lot of heart, sweat, and wrist aches went into making these gloves." We don't doubt it, Ken, now just put down that wooden chair leg!

MURCO RECYCLING

(708) 352-4111
www.murco.net

Have you ever walked into somebody's house, seen an appliance you liked, and just torn it out of the wall? Well, that's exactly what happens at a "demolition auction" as practiced by the friendly folks at Murco Recycling. Say someone has bought a property and doesn't want the house that sits on it. These people make plans to demolish said house, but before they do, they call Murco to sell off and disperse all used building materials, and by that we mean *all:* doors, windows, carpeting, flooring, tubs, toilets, appliances, even landscaping. That way nothing goes to waste (or to landfills), the owner makes some money, Murco makes some money, and some lucky buyers get some incredible deals.

The auctions get started at about 8:00 A.M., when the front door opens and the customers flood into the house to see what's available. There are usually three auctioneers on the premises, and they communicate with each other by walkie-talkies. ("Tell anybody who wants daylilies to get their butts back here!") Once the bidders make a successful purchase, they must be able to rip it out of the wall, floor, or garden, load it into their car or truck, and haul it off the premises by 5:00 P.M. that day. The sight of a small

mob descending on a home with sledgehammers and crowbars and then thoroughly gutting the joint can raise alarm bells; the day we attended, the local police showed up at about midday, but it didn't seem to faze the Murco people in the least. When we joked that they might get arrested, one auctioneer said, "Not before we sell these cops some landscaping."

NADEAU'S ICE SCULPTURES
7623 West Roosevelt Road
Forest Park, IL 60130
(708) 366-3333
www.nadeauice.com
Map: Suburban West

Some art takes years to create, but at Nadeau's Ice Sculptures they don't really have the luxury of time; their raw material tends to melt in a matter of hours, so it's chop-chop and then back into the freezer to await delivery. Nadeau's cranks out about sixty frozen beauties a week for parties and special events around Chicago, and they come in all shapes and sizes. Need an ice Christmas tree with lights frozen inside? How about a sculpture of a man doing some ice fishing—in ice? You name it and these folks can probably sculpt it. They once were asked to encase a cryogenically frozen fur coat in a block of ice. The customer then placed it on his fiancée's front lawn, handed her an ice pick, and said "Happy Birthday!"

The first step in Nadeau's process is to force the air out of the future ice block so it comes out crystal clear and not pure white. Then, following a design the client has either drawn for them or described, the Nadeau's artisans etch an outline on the block, rev up the chain saw, and start cutting. For detail work it's a chisel that does the trick. Nadeau's will deliver the finished product to its intended banquet hall so that it can begin dripping for delighted onlookers. Don't tell Mr. Nadeau this, but it seems like a lot of effort for something that's just going to end up as a puddle.

NATE'S LEATHER

2950 West Sixty-third Street
Chicago, IL 60629
(773) 925-1973
www.natesleather.com
Map: Chicago South

The Chicago Police have been staking out Nate's for years. Not because this store is into nefarious dealings—no, cops run here for their hides. Nate's makes the official leather jackets, and other clothes, worn by our city's police force. For decades the shop has been servicing the CPD with its tooled tools of the trade. In addition to jackets, police officers can buy leather vests, fanny packs, and belly holsters—all with plenty of room to conceal their snubbie (i.e., a place to place a peace officer's piece). For the discerning female officer, they offer a purse with a side pocket to house her heater, sort of like Prada for police. They also make a nifty nylon cover for bulletproof vests; it

keeps the cops cool in their Kevlar, plus it repels ketchup and doughnut stains. Doing a takedown on the bad guys can put some wear and tear on that tactical gear, and since Mom can't slide those suckers under her Singer, the cops bring their clothes to Nate's for repair and rehab. They'll reinforce a seam or switch Velcro closures for the more sturdy zipper. Retired police officers, get off the patio and paddy wagon it over here with your old CPD jacket. Nate's does a brisk business buying and trading these Johnny Law leathers. For you civilians looking for civvies, the store does custom work: chaps, pants, skirts, "you name it, we make it." How good is Nate's? They made matching chaps and jacket for a 650 pound—that's size 70—motorcycle rider. We'll bet that's one happy hog.

PEDDLING PURVEYOR HERB PERRY

North Avenue between Central
Avenue and Austin Boulevard
Chicago, IL 60639
Map: Chicago West

Herb Perry can sell you a plethora of products from the five huge shopping carts he trails off the back of his bicycle. You'll find him on North Ave between Central Avenue and Austin, the Peddling Purveyor of the West Side. His most prevalent merchandise seems to be underwear and baseball caps, but he also offers a wide variety of household items. Herb's customers are mostly people who happen to be driving by, and he has plenty of regulars. When we last spoke with him, he even had plans to add another cart that would serve as a mobile hot-dog stand.

It all started over a decade ago when Perry found himself walking the street without a place to live. He began soliciting handouts and discarded goods from local stores that he would then sell to passersby from a shopping cart. Soon he was purchasing more desirable merchandise from wholesalers and expanding his business to five carts and a bike. His entrepreneurship has since earned him a year-round gig and a roof over his head; his driving, on the other hand, has earned him a reputation as a daredevil. Herb has a habit of weaving through traffic with his minicaravan, often passing within inches of startled motorists' bumpers. He claims he's never been involved in an accident, and we hope he never is. A five-cart pile-up would not be a pretty sight.

PEDICABS

North Side, centered around
Oz Park and Lincoln Avenue,
Chicago
Map: Chicago North

If taking a wild ride in the open air appeals to you, we know of a merry band of peddlers who may have just what you're looking for. You've seen them waiting outside Wrigley Field on game day or lurking on the outskirts of a street fair, sitting atop their bicycles with the two-seat chariots on the back. A good pedicab driver must have the strong legs of a Lance Armstrong and the personality of a carnival barker, and the ones here in Chicago all seem to meet those requirements. They're certainly not afraid to harangue passersby about the advantages of pedicab travel, and as for leg strength, we overheard one pedicaber claim to have ferried two 400-pound sisters around town. Bet he wished he had charged by weight!

It's usually not much more than $5.00 per mile to hop on one of these Chinese-made contraptions, and if you ask us, that's a bargain. Not only is it a pleasant ride under the sun or stars (or canopy if it rains), but there's also the invariably entertaining patter from the driver, who's often supporting an acting career with this job. If the patter stops, it probably means your driver's out of breath—and that you or your date needs a diet!

 ## BEHIND THE SCENES

One of the grizzled veterans of pedicabbing is an actor named Ron Dean, who you may well recognize from screens both big and small. He's had featured roles in a slew of movies shot in Chicago, including *Breakfast Club*, *The Fugitive*, *Chain Reaction*, and *Code of Silence*. On TV, he's been a semiregular guest star on such series as *Early Edition*, *Angel Street*, and *Crime Story*, and has made two appearances on *Frazier* as Martin Crane's cop friend Frank. Come to think of it, Dean almost always plays a police officer. *NYPD Blue*, however, cast him as "Concerned Father." Go figure.

RAINBOW MOTEL

7050 West Archer Avenue
Chicago, IL 60638
(773) 229-0707 or (773) 586-7269
www.rainbowmotel1.qpg.com
Map: Chicago South

If your idea of a vacation is going to the islands but you only ever get as far as Blue Island or Stony Island, then a Hawaiian island is the place for you. The "Hawaiian" is one of the fantasy suites at the Rainbow Motel. For four hours or overnight, you and your little "love pineapple" can vacation by relaxing on a bed as big as Don Ho, listen to the surflike sounds gurgling from the whirlpool, and soak up the painted vista of Diamond Head. When we visited the Hawaiian—without our pineapple—owner William Talbert said about the suite, "It's the Cadillac of what you're getting." If the Hawaiian seems too "sunny" for your taste, the Rainbow offers more destinations than a travel agent. Other choices include the Little Vegas, the Space Walk, and the Valentine. For more whimsical lovers, there's the Out To Lunch, with its bed dressed to resemble a BLT. The Rainbow doesn't have room service, but then, if you're renting it only for four hours, food is probably not a priority. William said of his motel dedicated to love and romance, "The women love it. That's number one. And if you can please the lady, you can please anybody." Take a moment to underline that. Mr. Talbert has since moved on—he's living in the "Retirement Suite"—and new owner Amy Ratliff has fantasies of her own. She now offers guests a complimentary rose—when available—and plans to build a boutique selling lingerie, just in case you come not wearing any. Who is the ideal Rainbow customer? Amy says, "Regular people who want to get away from the kids."

SAUSAGE MAN JOE PERL

Deli Direct
(773) 255-6327 Sausage Hotline
(847) 520-1020 shop
(800) 321-DELI toll-free number
www.delidirect.com

He's a vendor of viands, a jobber of jerky, a monger of meats. He's Joe Perl, a traveling sausage salesman. Each night this Willy Loman of liverwurst will drive out to several bars peddling his Polish. To entice customers to buy his beef, he'll bring in a hundred-pound smorgasbord of sausages, cheeses, hot sauces, and horseradishes for sampling. Taste the liver, beer, or Cajun sausage or try a hot sauce so fiery that you'll burn your lips just picking up the bottle. Even the names of the sauces are incendiary: Ultimate Burn and Raging Red Rectum. Joe urges people to try everything, but don't overindulge or you'll be likely to hear the reprimand, "You get a sample, not supper!" When you're ready to purchase, just step outside to his refrigerated truck and get your fix of kielbasa, salami, lobster tails, steaks, and deer jerky. This merchant of venison must be pleasing his pork-loving patrons, because they'll chant "Sausage Man, Sausage Man" when they see him drive up. He even has groupies following him from bar to bar to get a hold of his meat. His motto is "Have

Sausage/Will Travel," and he does, wienering his way through twelve bars each night, selling over four hundred pounds of sausage alone. If you've got to get your hands on some hard salami and miss seeing Joe, call his twenty-four hour sausage hotline and he'll bring his best wurst, and everything else, to a barstool near you.

SINGING CAB DRIVER RAY ST. RAY
(312) 905-3634

We met a singer-songwriter who's found the perfect day job for trying out his music. Well, maybe not perfect, but he's guaranteed a captive audience! Ray St. Ray calls himself the Singing Cab Driver, and lets you know it the minute you enter his cab. He claims that after his first couple of months as a cabbie he realized that he hated the radio, so he started writing and singing his own songs at work. When we met him in 1995 he was up to seventy-one songs, and who knows how many he's got by now? Passengers are asked to choose among four categories: Love, Sex, Social Significance, or Other. He then serenades them with one of his ditties, which all show a strong Talking Heads influence (he even sounds a little like David Byrne). Don't expect any instrumentation—Ray refers to his brand of entertainment as "the ultimate unplugged experience."

St. Ray has sought other outlets for his music, starting several bands over the years and even performing a one-man cabaret show called "The Singing Cab Driver Show." But he's received the most accolades with the cab as his venue, actually getting named 1995 Taxicab Driver of the Year by the International Taxicab and Livery Association. Sure, there's always the occasional fare that begs for silence, but most people seem to appreciate his act. As Ray St. Ray told us, "It's pretty difficult to get a cab driver that speaks English, let alone sings!"

SMELL AND TASTE RESEARCH CENTER
845 North Michigan Avenue,
Suite 990 West
Chicago, IL 60610
(312) 938-1047
www.smellandtaste.org
Map: Chicago North

If your sense of smell isn't up to snuff or you've got a bad taste in your mouth, you'll need to stop by the Smell and Taste Research and Treatment Center on the ninth floor of Water Tower Place. There Dr. Alan Hirsch is ever vigilant in sniffing out the cause for problems of the nose and tongue. He has also made some important discoveries related to these two senses. For instance, his tests revealed that a certain smell could improve the speed of learning by 17 percent, another could increase slot machine usage significantly, yet another could reduce appetite (liver and onions does it for us). Hirsch has also experimented with how odors affect sexual arousal. By measuring

the penile and vaginal blood flow of volunteers as they were subjected to various smells, he found out that the aromas of pumpkin pie and lavender turn men on, while cucumber and Good-n-Plenty do it for the ladies. This information could be used to treat patients with sexual disorders—or as a fun conversation starter at parties!

The center is one of only three places in the country exclusively engaged in the field of smell and taste. Wander through its halls and you're liable to see any number of strange looking contraptions being used in strange tests and treatments. In one room we came upon a machine that looked like the "orgasmatron" from the movie *Sleeper*. It turned out to be a module employed to assess the degree of claustrophobia in the presence of different odors. Wonder if the employees ever sneak into it with pumpkin pie and a box of Good-n-Plenty?

SPACETIME TANKS FLOTATION CENTER

2526 North Lincoln Avenue
Chicago, IL 60614
(773) 472-2700
www.spacetimetanks.com
Map: Chicago North

So you say you're cashed in and stressed out, lacking mental clarity and craving relaxation? The SpaceTime Tanks Flotation Center has been catering to your ilk since 1982, making it probably the oldest such establishment in the country. The tanks themselves contain a dense solution of Epsom-salt water that, when you're floating in it, gives you the illusion of being weightless (it's only 10 inches deep, so nonswimmers need not worry). The idea is to combine this weightless feeling with the removal of all external stimuli—no light, no clothes, no nothing—to achieve an altered state of mind and body. In case that doesn't work, this place also offers massage therapy and something called the Light and Sound Machine, which we were told is like electronic LSD.

All in all, it's the perfect place to unwind after a trying week in the workaday world. If you start to have second thoughts about whether altered states and technoshamanism are really the answer, you might just want to take a glance at the SpaceTime staff. They are all *really* relaxed, so if it works for them, chances are it can work for you.

STEREO EXCHANGE

4743 North Western Avenue
Chicago, IL 60626
(773) 784-0004
www.turntablerepair.com
Map: Chicago North

Is your Pioneer pooped out? Your Phillips got a floppy arm? Then take that troubled turntable to the technicians at Stereo Exchange. They repair home, auto, and motorcycle audio equipment. Buy, sell, and install it, too. Customers say that "they're like doctors for electronics."

And indeed they are. Like an internist, they'll diagnose the problem and then, like a proctologist, they'll dig deep into the bowels of your equipment to fix it. After washing their hands, they'll present you with your restored turntable, ready to take on 33s and 45s. These "direct drive" doctors can also perform surgery on receivers, tube stereos, and old phonographs. They'll mend your Marantz and fix a broken Bose. And, when it comes time to pay the bill, unlike regular physicians, these guys will take a trade, and even that's negotiable. These audiologists once took in trade a couple of iguanas. When asked about this liberal lizard policy, they said it all depends on "what you want and what you got." If you've got an RCA that's DOA, go to Stereo Exchange. But check the Web site first. Just like medical doctors, office hours vary. By the way, if you have skilled hands, the Exchange is always looking for someone to join the practice.

TATTOO REMOVAL

The Advanced Laser Center
1900 East Golf Road, Suite 1101
Schaumburg, IL 60173
(847) 619-1680
www.theadvancedlasercenter.com
Map: Suburban West

If you get a tattoo that you later have second thoughts about, you no longer have to grin and bear it. Just go to a place like the Advanced Laser Center and have the slate wiped clean, with no mess and minimal pain. The certified technicians at ALC are equipped with something called a Q-Switch Ruby Laser specifically designed to remove tattoos without scarring. The average removal for a professional tattoo takes four to eight treatments, each one lasting just several minutes. It's not that different than going to the dentist, except they make you wear goggles for eye protection. Plus, removing a tattoo turns out to be much less painful than removing a cavity—one patient likened the pulse of the laser to the snap of a rubber band.

There are numerous reasons why people end up patronizing this particular business. Sometimes the wearer has outgrown his or her tattoo or gets a job where it would be frowned upon. Gang members who are parting ways with their gang come here to remove the obsolete insignia. More often than not, though, the client's unwanted tattoo involves the name of an ex-lover. (Wonder how long it took Angelina to get "Billy Bob" off her flesh?) The removal procedure can get a little tricky if the work to be done is on a tush or a ta-ta. When we asked about the strangest location that ALC has ever had to remove a tattoo from, they told us of a man with the Tasmanian Devil cartoon character adorning his inner thighs, the hands seemingly supporting the fellow's genitals. Now that's one place you do *not* want a rubber band snapping.

TYPEWRITER REPAIR

Independence Business Machines
1623 West Montrose Avenue
Chicago, IL 60613
(773) 248-5548
Map: Chicago North

Do you like manual stimulation? Then grab your Royal and get it cleaned and oiled at one of the last service shops in Chicago. Now some of you might be thinking that on the time line of communication, typewriters are as archaic as cuneiform. While a wealth of authors will swear by their Smith Coronas, did you know that these "qwerty" cuties are the only things that work with those preprinted forms favored by health-care and government workers? (And you know how quick *they* are to change—the Grand Canyon changed faster.) And, unlike the planned obsolescence of computers, typewriters are built to last a hundred years. Steve Kazmier

has been repairing the wrongs done to 'writers since 1956. He'll overhaul your Olivetti, or other brand, in no time—usually three days. He also carries several vintage typewriters, including a 1930 Royal used by Ernest Hemingway. We now know why Hemingway's style of writing is considered macho and tough. It wasn't his attitude, it was his typewriter. It's brutal punching those keys. If you think you might be the type to type your great American tome on a typewriter, Mr. Kazmier sells newer manuals. Just think, no more batteries or backing up to worry about. Typewriters don't need no stinkin' batteries and you get a hard copy every time. We evin braut r Royel in fer Steev 2 fix and now that quick brown fox is jumping over that damn lazy dog again. Ding!

WE FIX BIKES

Curt Evans
(847) 828-6825
wefixbikes@aol.com

Is your Schwinn not schwingin'? Your Huffy a little puffy? Your Lemond a lemon? Don't take your bike to the repairman, have the repairman come to you. We Fix Bikes is a traveling cycle clinic that services your broken bicycle right on the sidewalk. WFB can tune up brakes and gears, fix flats, and generally just straighten things out, on the spot. Air and oil are free, but if it takes a tool to treat your bike, you've got to take your wallet out. This portable pedal hospital is a bicycle itself (a four-wheeler) piled impossibly high with tools, spare parts, and tires—all it needs is Granny and Jethro waving on top. The bike carries three hundred pounds of gear, and

riding it is like, as driver Curt Evans said, "pedaling a motorcycle." But you'll be glad this Florence Nightin-Cannondale comes fully equipped, because you never know when you'll encounter a wounded wheel, deranged derailleur, or spooked sprocket. The bike "ambulance" can be found wherever cyclists congregate, like college campuses, or you can make an appointment via phone or e-mail. WFB will have your bike tamed and trained so you can go ahead and take on mountains or just the usual urban assault.

MORE SERVICES

AD AIRLINES
888 SKY WRITE
www.adairlines.com
Can fly your message over large gatherings, like Wrigley Field or the lakefront.

AURA-HALO BALANCING HAIRCUTS
Aslana Bebar
(847) 602-0590
www.theblissbody.com
Aslana will cut your coif and retune your aura in the same visit.

DREAD STARCHILD WEAVING AND BEAUTY SALON
1703 East Fifty-fifth Street
Chicago, IL 60615
(773) 955-2700
Map: Chicago South
This Hyde Park salon specializes in dreads for an elegant new look.

HAND WRITING ANALYST LOTTIE LEE MASON
510 West Belmont Avenue
Chicago, IL 60657
(773) 296-9889
Lottie Lee sees the real you through your handwriting sample.

SKYVIEW PHOTOGRAPHY
(847) 949-6805
www.blimpographer.com/ilusa
Aerial photos taken from a minia-ture blimp by remote control.

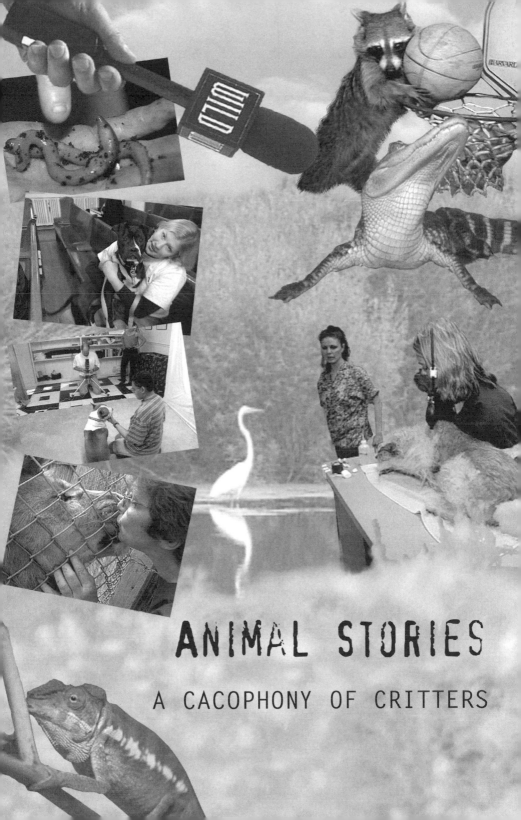

ANIMAL STORIES

A CACOPHONY OF CRITTERS

A DOG'S LIFE

2274 North Clybourn
Chicago, IL 60614
(773) 281-5577
www.adogslifechicago.com
Map: Chicago North

It's doggy day care, camp K-9, and for you dog owners who feel guilty about leaving your pet home alone or at a kennel, it's the answer to your prayers. At A Dog's Life, Amy Robinson and her staff give each dog lots of tender loving care. Just drop your pooch off before work and rest assured that by the time you come back that evening, he or she will have had plenty of exercise and, more importantly, some serious socialization with other dogs. If you're going out of town, A Dog's Life does take extended-stay guests, and though it may cost a little more than a kennel, it's a whole lot more fun for your dog.

Amy makes sure to break up her charges into compatible groups before they're let loose into the yard, so that a rowdy black lab doesn't run roughshod over a teacup poodle. Meanwhile, you can spend the day without worrying that Rover is destroying your house, since he's busy destroying Amy's. We heard only one "complaint" from clients—when they show up to retrieve their dogs, the happy campers aren't always so enthusiastic to see them.

AMAZING ANIMALS BY SAMANTHA

3555 North Milwaukee Avenue
Chicago, IL 60641
(773) 549-EEKS (3357) or
(800) 903-EEKS (3357)
www.amazinganimals.biz
Map: Chicago North

Don't let the bubonic plague fool you. Rats are not all bad; in fact, according to "Rat Lady" Samantha Martin, they make good pets and great performers. Her first business was called Rat Company and Friends, a touring show that featured "the acro-rats" doing stunts like jumping through hoops and balancing on the high wire.

Since then, Samantha has branched out to other species, so she changed the business's name to Amazing Animals by Samantha.

What's really amazing is how she keeps over two hundred creatures under one roof, meaning her home. She's divided her residence into the predator room and the prey

room; now if one of the acrorats isn't cutting it, she can feed it to the snake, which provides good incentive to her puny performers—nail that landing or you're reptile chum!

Step through Sam's front door and you might be greeted by a ring-tailed lemur, a skunk, or an African jungle cat. Some of these animals are clearly more talented than others. There's a raccoon that plays basketball and a prairie dog that bowls strikes, while all the alligator can do is make an appearance (but that gets your attention!). Besides the live shows she does for parties and special events, Martin hires her charges out for movies, TV shows, and the occasional documentary (anybody see *Rats among Us?*). Her Madagascar hissing cock-roaches have appeared in several horror flicks—as Samantha cheerfully states, "They're great for eye sockets!"

ANIMAL 911

3735 West Dempster Street
Skokie, IL 60076
(847) 673-9110
www.animal911ltd.com
Map: Suburban North

It's midnight and your pet pooch, Elmer, has developed a case of doggy diarrhea. Where are you going to get help for your hound at that hour? When life gets messy (like Elmer), you need to know where there's a veterinarian on call overnight. Animal 911 is an emergency clinic that's open when other clinics are closed. The vets here will take a look at your leaky Elmer, or other creature in crisis, anytime between 5:00 P.M. and 8:00 A.M. weekdays, plus they're open weekends and major holidays. They handle canines, felines, birds, reptiles, and many exotic pets. They've treated everything from a miniature pony that ate too many Frango mints to a cross-dressing cockatoo. That the bird wore a dress wasn't the problem; he was a circus performer. No, the problem was when the monkey decided to bite off one of his legs. The clinic was able to stabilize him

and now he's back doing his act in, we'll assume, a pirate costume.

Pets, like people, don't always take ill at the most convenient times. So, it's comforting to know that there's an animal ER open at odd hours that can help your sick Siamese or ailing Airedale or an Elmer with an anal volcano.

CHICAGO BIRDERS

Montrose Point
on Lake Michigan
(312) 409-9678
www.chicagobirder.org
Map: Chicago North

The early bird catches . . . not a lot of sleep. Not if you want to spot some speckled sparrows with this fellowship of fine feathered bird-watchers. On Saturdays and Sundays, this posse of peepers gets up at dawn's crack to try to catch some of Chicago's migratory birds. Our city is very friendly, avianwise, as it's only the second city to sign the International Migratory Bird Treaty. Montrose Point makes a good viewing area because of the thicket of trees, known as the Magic Hedge, that offers the curlews, crows, and Kirtland's warblers a place to rest and catch up on their birdie gossip. Over three hundred species have been recorded here (including swamp sparrow, hermit thrush, and groove-billed ani), and chances are someone in this group can do their birdcall. These weekend watchers, like birds, are very social, often as noisy, and they even mate. One couple paired up after meeting at these ornithological outings. Heads up—female birders are the minority in this flock. To join them, you'll need patience (for spotting), protective clothing (ticks are a fowl thing), and to know how to pish (making sounds to flush out the birds). If you choose to leave your warm nest to catch the early-bird special at the Point, you'll be offered a buffet of tasty Audubon-bons.

CHICAGO HERPETOLOGICAL SOCIETY

2430 North Cannon Drive
Chicago, IL 60614
(773) 281-1800
www.chicagoherp.org
Map: Chicago North

This is a support group for people who've caught the bug. We're not talking about herpes, the inflammatory skin disease, but rather herpetology. This is the branch of zoology that focuses on reptiles and amphibians. Interestingly though, both herpes and herpetology are based on the same Latin word for "to creep." The Chicago Herpetological Society is a group of enthusiasts who've turned their "herp" hobby into a habit. They meet monthly to promote their goals of "education, conservation, and the advancement of herpetology." Hit one of their meetings and you'll be met with everything that slides, slithers, hisses, and snaps. They bring frogs the size of toasters and pythons longer than history. They feature speakers who are nationally recognized herpetologists—though we can't imagine anyone recognizing a herpetologist unless they were another herpetologist—conduct workshops, and take field trips. The society has over a thousand two-legged members and they travel to herp happenings like ReptileFest and to zoos, where they get behind-the-cages tours. Check out the Web site for upcoming events, adoption info, and to take a peek at the centerfold . . . the Herp of the Month. Find out, too, when they schedule their annual Show and Tell. Members bring their Nile monitors and African leopard tortoises together for a casual petting zoo. At the event we attended, they even had catering. Willard's Rodent Ranch brought a tempting buffet of mice so the reptiles could, well, you know how the food chain works.

D & D WORMERY
348 Hillside Drive
Roselle, IL 60172
(630) 529-4832
Map: Suburban West

Don Braun is a former biology teacher who stopped dissecting worms and started growing and selling them. He runs D & D Wormery out of his garage, which is crawling with ten types of fish bait. There are wax worms, red worms, night crawlers, and also an assortment of minnows. He even has "medium" leeches available, and if they're medium, you don't want to run into the large. The only types of bait actually raised on the premises are the red worms; everything else Don purchases from wholesalers. He keeps his red

worms, also called bloodworms, in a stack of drawers filled with organic peat that he dusts with worm chow. In their dark, square world of dirt, these darn things reproduce at a feverish rate, doubling their population every sixty days. It helps that they're hermaphrodites (possessing both sex organs), so that when they mate they simply exchange sperm cells. They also have five hearts, which we suppose makes it a lot easier to fall in love with their fellow worms.

Once his little breeders are grown and his other bait purchased, Braun sets about packaging his goods and distributing them to his vending machines. He started with just one machine back in 1980 but has since expanded to eighteen spread across the Chicagoland area. His worm, minnow, and leech empire has earned him a tidy profit and an amusing nickname: "Master Baiter."

LAKE CALUMET

West of Torrence Avenue and
122nd Street
Chicago, IL 60633
(773) 646-4773, Calumet
Ecological Park Association
www.lincolnnet.net/cepa
Map: Chicago South

Viewed from the Bishop Ford Expressway, the Lake Calumet region isn't much to look at. The lake itself has been mostly filled in, rendering it sort of a glorified puddle, and it's surrounded by the belching smokestacks and steaming slag pits of big-time industry. But get out of your car and walk down into this quagmire, and you'll discover a wetlands teeming with rare wildlife, Chicago's own version of the Everglades. There's the occasional coyote (really), but what you really want to look for are the many species of birds that nest here, several of them endangered. Belted kingfishers, white egrets, and black crowned night herons all can be found in the skies above Lake Calumet. On one visit we even got to see a baby black crowned night heron attempt its first flight—which looked an awful lot like falling out of a tree to our uninformed eyes.

If you do venture into this wilderness, be prepared for a lot of mosquitoes and wear sturdy, waterproof boots. Oh, and always remember that if that misguided proposal for a Lake Calumet airport had gone through, you'd be walking through a baggage claim area instead of the most unlikely wildlife refuge in America.

LEE WATSON'S REPTILE SWAP

Crosswinds Farm
110 West Schaumburg Road
Streamwood, IL 60107
(630) 837-4005
www.reptileswap.com
Map: Suburban West

At Lee Watson's Reptile Swap, you can buy, sell, or trade just about anything slithery, slimy, or sluggish. Herpetological hobbyists come to this gathering on the first Saturday and third Sunday of every month to either add to their lizard or snake collection or upgrade to a better model. The selection on display at the swap is gargantuan—you're liable to see Carolina box turtles at one table and red-faced bearded dragons at another, while a Burmese python stares at you from a nearby cage. We liked the red-eyed tree frogs, one of which

leaped onto our camera lens and wouldn't let go. We also met an alligator whose owner had named him Security. Pretty darn good security, we imagine.

If you're wondering how so many people could consider snakes and lizards as pets, especially the ones that can kill you with one bite, consider this: They don't have fur, which means they don't shed on your furniture or trigger your allergies! If these uncuddly creatures still don't appeal to you, there are other things besides reptiles on sale. How about some Madagascar hissing roaches or a nice pet scorpion?

A warning: Don't get too attached to the cute little mice and fuzzy little chicks for sale. Here at Lee Watson's swap, they'll soon be reptile food.

PET BLESSING

St. Paul's Church by the Lake
7100 North Ashland Avenue
Chicago, IL 60626
(773) 764-6514
www.stpaulsbylake.org
Map: Chicago North

If you're hoping your pet will eventually be able to join you in the Kingdom of Heaven, there's a church that's willing to bless him or her no matter what denomination or species. St. Paul's Church by the Lake holds its Pet Blessing once a year, always right around St. Francis Day.

Francis of Assisi, of course, was the patron saint of all living creatures and sort of a religious Dr. Dolittle: Not only could he speak to animals, he once negotiated a deal with a wolf to stop terrorizing

a town. Really.

We didn't see any wolves at St. Paul's, but we did see dogs of many breeds, as well as cats, bunnies, birds, even fish. The service began appropriately with the hymn "All Creatures Great and Small," followed by a prayer that was greeted with many hallelujahs in the form of barks, meows, and tweets. Then the parishioners and their pets lined up in the center aisle and took their turn before Father Heschle. The father dutifully asked each pet's name and proceeded with the blessing, which always ended with a splash of holy water onto fur or feathers. Sometimes it was hard to keep a straight face when words like "Let your blessing be upon Tecate FitzTiger" were intoned, but it was clear that for some of the pet owners, this was a very solemn occasion. Many stayed for the reception, where cookies and doggy treats shared a table. All the owners looked relieved that there had been no "accidents" in the pews, and as for the pets, well, we sensed a certain spiritual enlightenment. Either that or they were happy about the snacks.

PORTAGE PARK ANIMAL HOSPITAL

5419 West Irving Park
Chicago, IL 60641
(773) 725-0260
www.portagepark.com
Map: Chicago West

She had been told she needed a mastectomy. She took the news well, being as stouthearted as she was bodied. Now, on the operating table, her doctor was making the first incision, confident in the knowledge that the patient was a survivor. She's a fighter and, fortunately, not a biter. She'll recover healthier, and, the best part, with a lot less chest hair. Yes, this guinea pig will pull through.

If you've got a mammal with a malfunctioning mammary or other distressed domesticated animal, then check into the Portage Park Animal Hospital. It's the Mayo Clinic for marsupials, reptiles, rodents, birds, canines, and felines. They offer the same cutting-edge diagnostic and therapeutic medical treatments for the tamed beast as you'll find at a hospital for humans— for example, laser surgery, ultrasound, blood and urine analysis, EKGs, dental care, gerontology, and acupuncture. You can have your lizard tested for metabolic bone disease or get the plaque removed from your Pomeranian. Plus, PPAH has "tele-medicine." Doctors can get their paws (or claws) on information about your pet's particular problem by networking globally with specialists over the Internet. So, if your Chihuahua is not feeling so wow-ah, they can consult with someone in Mexico or Japan or wherever. Y'know, in one respect, this hospital might even be superior to the hospitals that handle people. When it comes to the much maligned topic of hospital food, at least here all the patients think of it as "treats."

SERPENT SAFARI

Gurnee Mills Mall
6170 Grand Avenue
Gurnee, IL 60031
(847) 855-8800
www.serpentsafari.com
Map: Suburban North

Sundays at 4:00 P.M. That's when you'll want to be at this reptile zoo. Because that's when they feed the baby. Baby is a 400-pound, 27-foot-long Burmese python. And Baby has a big appetite. This snake can snarf down seven whole chickens in one sitting. Baby bites, constricts, then swallows them whole . . . and never burps a bone. If Baby is still stuffed from last week's snack, don't worry, there are always plenty of other slithery, slimy things to watch during the zoo's hand-feeding time. "America's Finest Reptile Zoo," as Serpent Safari bills itself, is located in the outlet mall in Gurnee. After a hectic day of pillaging and plundering, stop in, slow down, and observe these creeping creatures. The zoo gives guided tours—you wouldn't want to be alone, would you?—of their snakes, lizards, turtles, and alligators. You'll find the snakes are real charmers when you hold a python, boa, or other reptile in the petting section. The zoo suggests you hold your child's next birthday party here. And, while it's certainly a novel idea—compare that to hiring a clown—it might just inspire the budding herpetologist in your family or validate a kid who looks like Boris Karloff.

Owner Lou Daddano has always liked reptiles. In fact, he's kept some of them in the basement of his home. His wife told us, "Lou puts them on leashes, walks them around the front yard, and you'd be surprised at the number of cars that stop." No, we wouldn't. And, again, we apologize for calling 911 on you.

SUTTON DOG PHOTOGRAPHY

3417 Church Street
Skokie, IL 60203
www.suttonstudios.com
Map: Suburban North

Picture this phone conversation: "Hello, Josette? It's Bobbi . . . Good, thanks, and you? . . . Oh, I'll bet the park was lovely this time of year. Anyway, I'm calling to tell you I just came from my sitting with David. . . . Yes, darling, *the* David Sutton just shot my portrait. . . . Oh, I *know* I'm one lucky dog. His work is in all the top magazines, *Canine Images, Pet Life, Best Friends* . . . The shoot? It was marvelous! He had water for me—bottled, of course—and the most delicious petit fours . . . all right, yes, they were *biscuits.* Oh, and Jo, I think David was flirting with me. . . . *Because* he was making the most interesting noises, trying to get my attention. Well, I gave him what he wanted; this old me still has some new tricks in her. David made me feel like a puppy again. I swear, with his lighting and everything, the man made me look five years younger, which, for us, is more like thirty-five! Speaking of old, did you see Holly? . . .

Yes, her master took her fur coat away. She didn't get a haircut, she got a shearing! . . . Oh, I *know* I'm a bitch. But, thanks to David, at least I'm a beautiful bitch! . . . *My* master? Of course she was at the shoot, she's got me on a short leash, y'know? She wanted to get in the photo, too! I had to put my paw down. This portrait was just of me. I'll let her hang it

in her office. Let her have the permanent record of my glorious self. Who knows, it might even be worth money someday. Anyway, I'm just hoping David adds me to his on-line gallery . . . You haven't gone? Oh, darling, you must see it. What that man docs with fur is fabulous! . . . Why, yes, David still does his 'charity' work—he shoots cats, too."

VAHLE'S BIRD AND PET SHOP

4710 North Damen Avenue
Chicago, IL 60625
(773) 271-1623
Map: Chicago North

He's the perfect mate. He's attractive, has a beautiful voice and always greets you with the words "Hello, Pretty. Hello, Pretty. Hello, Pretty." All right, he does have a bit of a parroting problem, but, really, that's not a problem because he's a parrot. Vahle's has been supplying Chicagoans with terrific—and talkative—pets for five generations. The shop carries buckets of birds: canaries, parakeets, macaws, cockatiels, and exotic finches. Stepping into the store is an experience in itself. It's all bright, feathered flashes of outrageous color and a cacophony of calls. Audubon himself would suffer sensory overload. The birds are so noisy, you can hear their tweets from the street. Jard and Barbara Vahle breed and hand-raise many of the birds and know everything ornithological. Asked what he lines his cages with, Jard replied, "A silica sand base with 30 to 32 percent flint oyster shell and magnesium grit." Gee, we were thinking either the *Trib* or the *Times*. "Nope, none of them," he says, "because the ink will get on the feathers and rob the ability to breathe." *That* kind of bird-poop-scoop is why you come to Vahle's. And when it comes to supplies for your songbird, think of them as the Whole Foods for fowl. Vahle's hand-mixes its seed using ingredients like safflower, flax, rape, and red millet. Sweet treats for your parakeet. If you've never owned a bird before, *you're* in for a treat. They offer companionship and unconditional love, and they live a lot longer than Rover. Plus, you get the best guarantee from Jard: "The bird will be perfect or I will replace it. Period." Pick up one of the talkaholic African Grey parrots and you can teach your new companion to mimic the perfect partner: "Glad you're home, glad you're home!"

VALHALLA PET CEMETERY

3415 North Winnebago Road
Winnebago, IL 61088
(815) 335-7207
Map: Multistate

Is your pet nearing the end of his days? Has it got one foot, or three, in the grave? Before that sad day arrives, you should think about where its earthly remains will rest. When the backyard or toilet is not a fitting enough farewell for your furry, feathered, or finned friend, then perhaps you'll consider handing over your pet's eternal needs to Valhalla. Named for the Norse hall that housed the souls of slain heroes, they will inter your terrier, tabby, hamster, or horse (Sam K, who galloped off this globe, 1963). Your beloved companion will find comfort and company here, in this large memorial park. One can almost see the ghosts of cavorting canines taking a celestial whiz on one of the many trees that dot the cemetery (Hansie, who bit off more than he could chew, 1997). Many mournful owners have surrounded their pet's final pad with decorative touches: lifelike

statues, plaster fireplugs, and even tiny fences (as if little Trixie will have anything but a fat chance of getting out of *this* yard). On the day of your pet's burial, take advantage of Valhalla's viewing room, where you and your family can gather to say good-bye and recall the decedent's endless endearing hijinks (Bootsie, happily there are no hair balls in heaven, 1989). Plan now for the day when Kitty learns there's no "tenth life" or when Bowser finally catches his tail. R.I.P.

VALLEY OF THE KINGS SANCTUARY AND RETREAT

W7593 Townhall Road
Sharon, WI 53585-9728
(262) 736-9386
www.votk.org
Map: Multistate

Valley of the Kings is a sanctuary and retreat for big animals that have been abandoned or abused, and if you become a sponsoring member, you'll get to come very close to some beautiful and potentially dangerous creatures. Sixty-two big cats roam the premises including lions, tigers, jaguars, pumas, and even a liger (half lion, half tiger). We also spotted bears, a bull, two goats, and a mule, kept in a separate area from the cats to avoid demonstrating the food chain.

Many of the Valley's residents were originally purchased by extremely naive people who thought that a baby tiger—or other soon-to-be-big carnivorous animal—could be raised as a pet. Frequently what happens is that they don't feed them properly, they physically abuse them when the animal doesn't behave like a dog, and then they frantically get rid of them before they are big enough to eat the kids. If the animal is lucky enough to be sent to Valley of the Kings, it will be pampered for the rest of its life. Owners Jill and Jim make sure their guests are well fed (they go through fifteen hundred pounds of food a day) and have plenty of room to roam on their expansive property. Members are invited to feed the animals right through the fence; usually it's raw chicken for the big cats, while the bears seem to like Twizzlers.

Regular visitors often bond with certain residents and can pet them with no fear (of losing an arm). And if you're really lucky, Jill will show you one of the hair balls the size of softballs she's collected from the lion's den.

So the next time your children see *The Lion King* and beg you for a pet Simba, talk them out of it and take them to Valley of the Kings—it's closer than going to Vegas for Siegfried and Roy. But be sure to call ahead for hours and admission procedure. Your kids would bite your head off if you take them out there when it isn't open.

MORE ANIMAL STORIES

ANIMAL KINGDOM
2980 North Milwaukee Avenue
Chicago, IL 60618
(773) 227-4444
www.animalkingdominc.com
Map: Chicago West
Menagerie that's been on Milwaukee Avenue for more than a half century.

DOGGIE BEACH
Lake Michigan south of Addison
Map: Chicago North
Romping ground for socially well-adjusted pooches.

LIVING SEA AQUARIUM
811 West Devon Avenue
Park Ridge, IL 60068
(847) 698-7258
www.livingseaaquarium.com
Map: Suburban North
Feed the sharks, pet "Splash" the ray, and touch all kinds of aquatic life.

OLD TOWN AQUARIUM
1538 North Wells Street
Chicago, IL 60610
(312) 642-8763
www.oldtownaquarium.com
Map: Chicago North
Abundant supply of rare and beautiful tropical fish.

SCRUB YOUR PUP
2935 North Clark Street
Chicago, IL 60657
(773) 348-6218
Map: Chicago North
Self-service dog wash.

DAY TRIPPIN'

EXPEDITIONS
TO THE WILDS
BEYOND

CHEESE FAVORITES

Baumgartner's
Cheese Store and Tavern
1023 16th Avenue
Monroe, WI 53566
(608) 325-6157
Map: Multistate

Chalet Cheese Co-op
N4858 Highway N
Monroe, WI 53566
(608) 325-4343
Map: Multistate

No trip to Wisconsin is complete without ingesting a large portion of smelly cheese, and there's no better town to do just that than Monroe. It's home to the only producer of Limburger cheese in the country, the Chalet Cheese Co-op, and also where you'll find the Best Cheese Sandwich in the World at Baumgartner's Cheese Store and Tavern. The two favorite items on the menu here are the cheese and salami sandwich on rye, which costs $3.95, and the $2.75 Limburger and onion sandwich on rye, which comes with a free breath mint.

Baumgartner's has been around since the 1930s, when the sandwiches were a dime and the beer was a nickel. Over the years they have developed some strange customs here, like playing Jaas, an old Swiss card game whose rules we would need another book to explain. If you see the cash hanging from the ceiling above the bar, that started a long time ago when traveling salesmen passing through town would give the bartender dollars to hold for them until their return. Where better to keep this money safely out of reach than the ceiling, so the barkeep would fold a coin and a tack into the bill and toss it upwards. The tradition continues today, though you may spot some fifty- and hundred-dollar bills up there. That'll buy a whole lot of cheese sandwiches!

COZY DOG DRIVE-IN

2935 South Sixth Street
Springfield, IL 62703
(217) 525-1992
www.cozydogdrivein.com

Among the many historic sites of Springfield, Illinois, you don't want to miss the Cozy Dog Drive-In, a roadside eatery that originated the popular corn dog. Ed Waldmeier created the batter-covered wiener on a stick back in 1945 and christened it the Crusty Cur. His wife thought that name wasn't all that appetizing and rechristened it the Cozy Dog, coming up with the logo of two corn dogs gettin' cozy. When Ed passed away, his younger son, Buzz, took over the place because, he told us, "I was divorced, unemployed, and drunk, so I needed something to do." He must have eventually sobered up, since he was soon fixing up the secret batter recipe from memory—it seems the list of special ingredients was locked away in a vault for so long that they became too faded to read. Buzz might have kicked one bad habit, but he

eventually gave in to another: divorcing his wife and leaving town. It's his second ex-wife, Sue, who now runs the business.

The Drive-In is located right on old Route 66, which is one reason why part of the restaurant contains a Route 66 collection, complete with pictures, maps, and memorabilia. The other reason is Buzz's older brother, Bob, who frequently spends months traveling up and down the famous road in a van filled with tchotchkes from his trips. Many of the amazingly detailed pen-and-ink maps that you'll see on the walls are Bob's doing.

The delicious deep-fried frankfurters, the Route 66 collection, and the colorful Waldmeier family are all reasons why people come from miles around to this vintage restaurant. They're certainly not coming for their health. As Buzz once declared with characteristic bluntness, "A Cozy Dog a day keeps your doctor in the hay."

DINNER TRAIN

East Troy Electric Railroad
2002 Church Street
East Troy, WI 53120
(262) 642-3263
www.easttroyrr.org
Map: Multistate

No, this isn't about a miniature feast going 'round and 'round some guy's Lionel set in his basement. These are full-size steel suites with real sweets on board. If you're a train buff who likes buffets, then cross the state line and ride the only all-electric dinner train in the United States. From Memorial Day through September, the two car cortege clickety-clacks its way past bucolic scenery while serving you a sumptuous meal. The menus are taken from famous train lines like the 20th Century Limited and the Super Chief, with entrees of prime rib and beef tenderloin. There's nothing like the sway of a train and the swell thought of someone else doing the cooking. The Art Deco cars have been refurbished with mahogany paneling and a bar (go ahead and drink, you're not conducting). While sipping your sherry and gazing out the window, try to spot LeRoy, the railroad's flagman. He drives up and down the line manually stopping vehicular traffic (plebeians) at crossings. The staff is made up of

volunteers (read: train nuts), who welcome
your questions concerning the equipment
and history of the trackage. The train can
also be chartered for special events—here's
your chance to play Artemis Gordon on your
own trolley folly. At the end of the line, visit
the 1910 depot that now houses a museum
and gift shop. (Yea, a wooden "choo-choo"

whistle!) Take the East Troy tummy-train to enjoy some local color, cuisine, and
gamboling wildlife. Just don't forget to wear elastic-waistband pants.

DR. EVERMOR

Route 12
North Freedom, WI 53951
www.drevermor.org

Just south of Baraboo, Wisconsin, along
Route 12 behind Delaney's Surplus, is
the Land of Dr. Evermor, where you will find
many strange and wonderful things. Blessed
with creative hands and a wild imagination,
Tom Every (alias Dr. Evermor) is a builder of
contraptions and a purveyor of whimsy. As such, he has filled a large plot of
Wisconsin land with metal sculptures that defy description. Where some might go
to a salvage yard and see piles of scrap metal, the good doctor sees inspiration.
From castaway machine parts, discarded fire extinguishers, old elevator cages,
even a decontamination chamber from the Apollo Space Mission, he welds
together delightful works of art that range in size from one square foot to a small
city block. Some of the sculptures are recognizable as birds, cats, or bugs. Others,
like Dr. Evermor's Celestial Listening Ears, demand a little more interpretation.

Once Every finishes a piece, his wife Eleanor paints it, and then son Troy
gives it a name; the one called *Brainless* had a screw-off top that revealed a very
empty head. Some of Evermor's creations are quite functional—there's *The
Epicurean,* a giant barbecue grill with huge manual bellows to stoke the flames,
and a round Mr. Potato Head–like sculpture that doubles as a cooler. More often
than not, though, the purpose of an Evermor piece is a figment of the doctor's fer-
tile imagination. About the mammoth *Dr. Evermor's Force* this present-day H. G.
Wells said, "With it, we believe we can perpetuate ourselves back into the heavens
on a magnetic lightning force beam inside a glass ball inside a copper egg."

Every doesn't charge admission to wander into his 2-acre outdoor studio.
The sculptures go for as little as $25 to as much as $700. If you visit, feel free to

bring along that old carburetor you've been meaning to get rid of—it might be just what the doctor ordered.

GOOD'S FURNITURE

200-220 North Main Street
Kewanee, IL 61443
(309) 852-5656
www.goodsfurniture.com
Map: Multistate

Kewanee, Illinois, is known as the Hog Capital of the World, but it could just as easily be called the Furniture Mecca of the Midwest. That's because it's home to Good's Furniture, a mammoth megastore that comprises practically half of the downtown area. We're not exaggerating: Good's takes up a whole block of Kewanee's main street *on both sides*, with a "skyway" that connects the two three-story sections. Its size is not the only factor that makes this place so unique. What other furniture store do you know of where you can have lunch, get a haircut, buy an outfit, and spend the night on the premises? That's right—in its effort to bring people through the door and make them spend the *whole day and night,* Good's offers a rathskeller, an ice cream parlor, a hair salon, a clothing and accessories shop, and yes, a bed-and-breakfast, where the doors open right onto the showroom floor!

Good old Good's has been in business for more than 105 years, but most of the expansion occurred over the last 25. A big reason for all the recent success is the relentlessly cheerful commercial spokesperson Mary Good, the wife of the owner. In TV ads that blanket mid-America, Mary touts all the wonderful qualities of Good's furniture, and it seems to have struck a chord with consumers. They come by the busload from miles around to sample the "Good" life and possibly meet Mary herself. Or maybe it's the vintage plane that hangs above the atrium that draws customers, or the fountain and artificial pool with a water wheel and real fish. Could a *full-service car wash* be far behind?!

MAX NORDEEN'S WHEELS MUSEUM

6400 North 400 Avenue
Alpha, IL 61413
(309) 334-2589
Map: Multistate

If you ever find yourself in Woodhull, Illinois, consider yourself lucky, because you're just 2 miles down the road from the Wheels Museum and a gentleman who is truly one of a kind. Max Nordeen is a tall, no-nonsense farmer in his sixties whose hobby of collecting simply got out of hand. As a result, he converted a horse stable on his farm into a showcase for his many collectibles. Max serves as the museum's tour guide (as well as curator, ticket taker, bookkeeper, and janitor), and judging by the speed with which he delivers his spiel, you can tell that (a) he's given the tour many times before and (b) he's a licensed auctioneer on the side. Despite the museum's name and the giant white wheel out front, Max has much more than wheels to show you. Sure, he's got a truly magnificent collection of vintage automobiles in mint condition as well as eighty-one—count em, eighty-one—pedal cars.

But before you ever get to the car showroom, you're confronted with an eclectic and voluminous display of mementos and oddities that will flat out boggle your mind. Where else can you find an original death notice for John Deere, a thousand-year-old petrified leech, and the world's tiniest grandfather clock, all under the same roof? Ripley's, eat your heart out! Peruse the tokens and tickets from the 1893 World's Fair, ogle at the signed daguerreotype of Buffalo Bill, recoil at

the Nazi Germany memorabilia that includes a baby picture of Hitler, and then snicker at the extensive array of "nudey" material—risqué medallions from Paris, France, a fan used by Fan Dancer Sally Rand, and an "exotic" photo of Wyatt Earp's third wife. With all this vying for your attention, feel free to skip the spark plug collection. Max will understand.

MICHIGAN CITY RIFLE CLUB
WILDWOOD WRANGLERS
Cowboy Action Shootout
7625 West U.S. Route 20
Michigan City, IN 46360
(219) 872-7957
www.kempfgunshop.com
Map: Multistate

Never mind why Michigan City is in Indiana, what's that "ping! ping!" sound you sometimes hear when you pass through town? Why it's (take a deep breath) the Michigan City Rifle Club Wildwood Wranglers Cowboy Action Shootout! Maybe you're like a lot of the folks who attend these semi-regular competitions in frontier marksmanship; as a kid you'd watch Westerns with

Roy Rogers, Hopalong Cassidy, or the Lone Ranger, then run outside and play "fast-draw" with your friends. If so, you can't blame these wranglers for making their childhood fantasies somewhat real by dressing in Western garb and firing their gun at varmints and rustlers. Actually they're just metal targets *shaped* like varmints and

rustlers, thus that pinging sound.

The Wildwood Wranglers hold their shootouts on the fourth Sunday of every month (year-round) and they're open to anyone over the age of 12 with a single-action firearm. At the typical shootout, the cowboys and girls take part in about ten events that sternly test their speed and accuracy with pistol and rifle. Usually, there's some sort of Wild West angle to each challenge: in one event the shooter shouts "Pour me another drink!" while lifting a series of mugs that hide playing cards; once a card is revealed, he or she fires at the target shaped as the corresponding suit (spade, diamond, you get the idea). The faster your time, the better your result, with five seconds added on for each miss (lack of ping).

If you choose to join up with this jovial group of sharpshooters, you'll need to give yourself an alias, such as "Tombstone Tom," "Sassy Sue," or "Dirty Deeds." Sounds like Ol' Hopalong would've fit right in.

MUSEUM OF FUNERAL CUSTOMS

1440 Monument Avenue
Springfield, IL 62702
(217) 544-3480
www.funeralmuseum.org

It's the state's only traveling funeral museum, and it may soon be resting in peace at a town near you. Undertaker Virgil Davis and his wife began collecting funeral artifacts and antiques back in the 1950s, and they gladly contributed their macabre treasures to the Illinois Funeral Directors Association for public display. The association has a stationary exhibit at the Oak Ridge Cemetery in Springfield, but it's the mobile museum that caught our fancy. A veritable "tomb trailer," the traveling exhibit is a mere 35 feet long, but boy, do they pack a lot into those 35 feet. Virgil himself is usually in residence, and he's happy to walk you through or just stand and point. There are items from the Lincoln and Kennedy burials, children's caskets from the 1900s flu epidemic, and an ice casket used before embalming came into vogue. Dead body on ice? That's not so nice, since it only stayed "fresh" for a matter of days.

There is a lot to take in at the Museum of Funeral Customs, but don't linger too long. Soon they'll be hitching it up to a truck and towing it to the next lucky town.

MUSTARD MUSEUM

100 West Main Street
Mount Horeb, WI 53572
(800) 438-6878
www.mustardweb.com
Map: Multistate

How many of you out there absolutely adore mustard? Okay, you seven people, this entry's for you. If the condiment known as mustard makes you go condimental, then take off that straightjacket and head straight to this museum. It's in Mount Horeb, which is like the Mount Sinai for this zesty seasoning—about as far, too. Once you make the pilgrimage, you will be delivered upon the museum's ten jars of the commanding condiment. All right, they do have more than ten, they actually have about four thousand jars. (Boy, we knew you seven people would catch that, you're sharp, sharp as . . . mustard.) The MM has mustards from all over the world and mustards made with everything under the sun—cherries, champagne, maple syrup, garlic, curry. And the best part? While you're learning bits of mustard trivia (mustard plasters were used to treat rheumatism), you can be tasting them, too. There's a store inside offering samples of several mustards. Taste the stuff till your tummy's content or until your tongue falls off. No kidding—some of the horseradish mustards have quite a kick. They'll punch your mouth into the next room. Now, for the kids: they'll love learning about their hot dog's favorite friend and relish the chance to eat a gallon of mustard. Y'know, this might even top the time you took them to the Brussels Sprout Museum. How about spreading the "yellow love" by getting some gifts? Buy a mustard multipack and they'll put your name on the label. Just think, the recipients of that gift will think of you every time they open the refrigerator door. For years and years and years to come.

OLD JAIL MUSEUM

225 North Washington Street
Crawfordsville, IL 47933
(765) 362-5222
www.crawfordsville.org/jail

If you're an old jail buff (and frankly, who isn't?) you'll find one in Crawfordsville, Indiana, that'll make your head spin. The Old Jail Museum houses the last functioning rotary jail in the world, which earned it a spot in the National Register of Historic Places. The prison was built in 1882 and resembles a giant gerbil's exercise wheel that's been placed on its side and mounted on a hollow metal shaft. It was designed to turn 365 degrees in either direction and could be revolved with a crank; they say that in the jail's well-oiled heyday, a little girl could turn the crank with just one hand. There was a single opening that was the only way in or out of the cell "block" and a catwalk that circled the maximum of thirty-two convicts who resided inside. When a prisoner was to be released, the contraption would rotate until his cell was lined up with the entrance/exit, allowing him to walk out, presumably with visions of rectangles dancing in his head.

The main advantage of the rotary jail system was the low maintenance: It required only one guard on duty! The inmates, however, hated it with a passion. Unable to see or fraternize with their neighbors, the cons might as well have been in solitary confinement. The jail was taken out of service in 1973, mostly because the townspeople found it blatantly inhumane. In its ninety-one years there had been only one escape, an industrious inmate who had burrowed through a vent behind his toilet, then down the shaft to freedom. They found him quaffing drinks at a nearby rectangular bar.

RAVEN'S GRIN INN
411 North Carroll Street
Mt. Carroll, IL 61053
(815) 244-4746
www.hauntedravensgrin.com
Map: Multistate

Any trip to Mount Carroll, Illinois (you're probably planning one now), would be terrifyingly incomplete without a stop at the infamous Raven's Grin Inn. Jim Warfield has turned most of his stately three-story home into a haunted house that operates year-round, not just on Halloween, and he takes great pleasure in toying mercilessly with his victim-customers. Jim is a one-man scaring committee, taking your tickets, serving as tour guide, and occasionally ducking out of sight only to reappear out of nowhere in a gruesome mask.

Warfield claims he's been putting together haunted installations since he was eight years old (in his parents' basement), and you'll believe it when you see the ghoulish makeover he's given his circa-1870 domicile, both inside and out. You could even say the Raven's Grin doubles as a sort of homemade amusement park, with trapdoors and a steep slide that sends you from the top floor to the basement dungeon in seconds flat. And if he can't frighten the bejesus out of you, Warfield is determined to at least amuse you, with lame prop gags and an obviously prescripted patter delivered like a borscht belt comedian. Oh, the horror!

SPINNING TOP MUSEUM

533 Milwaukee Avenue
Burlington, WI 53105
(262) 763-3946
Map: Multistate

More than a museum, this is an exploratorium dedicated to the dervishing device. There are so many on display here—the Top 40 plus 1,960 other swirling, whirling, and rotating toys—it'll make your head spin. There are tops made of wood, cardboard, and tin that create optical illusions or moving pictures or go topsy-turvy when spun. And it's all hands-on. Most of the items in this topiary you can take out for a spin. Curator Judith Schulz is the top banana here. She can teach you top secrets—so you can topple your opponent—and discourse on any top topic. She was the spinster (top

trainer) to Mary Steenburgen and Kieran Culkin for the film *My Summer Story.* Off the top of her head—which most always sports a top hat—she says her favorite gyrating gimcrack is from Malaysia, where spinning is a national sport. They use an 11-foot rope to twirl a huge top—it looks like a curling stone—that'll spin for up to seven hours. Besides those in the museum, Judith has collected three thousand more of these conical curios. (She keeps those in her top drawer at home.) You must call in advance for reservations as she schedules a two-hour presentation for groups. After hearing her spiel, you'll want to take a spin into the gift shop. We guarantee you won't go home topless.

34 DRIVE-IN

Old Route 34
Earlville, IL 60518
(815) 246-9700
www.rt34drivein.com
Map: Multistate

For those of us with fond memories of watching a movie from the comfort of our own car, there's a place that's keeping that experience alive and well, from April through October. But before you can "drive-in," you'll have to drive out—way out. The 34 Drive-in is about 80 miles west of Chicago, near a little town called Earlville, Illinois. Its location has allowed it to survive while many situated nearer to the city have fallen by the wayside; it's hard to fight rising property values and the encroachment of bright lights. Set amid the cornfields and beanfields of rural Illinois, the 34 is in no immediate danger of urban sprawl. It does have to contend with the railroad trains that pass very nearby,

but owner Ron Magnoni Jr. assured us that they rarely run at night, and if they do you can still see the picture, even if you can't hear a darn thing.

The 34 Drive-in opened to the public back in 1954 and boasts a 60-by-90-foot screen and three hundred car speakers. Magnoni has been running the place since 1987—and we do mean running, all over the property. First he sells tickets from the little outbuilding near the road, then he hightails it to the projection booth to start the picture. At the end of the night, he's tramping around the grounds with a flashlight waking up the sleepers. Filmgoing under the stars can be truly sublime, and at Ron's establishment it'll only cost you six bucks for a double feature (half that for children). If the picture gets tedious, you can always retire to the restaurant for a corn dog and a soft drink. Try the Green River soda. It tastes really . . . green.

TWO-STORY OUTHOUSE
1022 Front Street
Gays, IL 61928

If you sneeze, you miss it, but tiny Gays, Illinois, has a piece of architecture that's put it on the map to stay. It's a two-story outhouse, possibly the first one of its kind in the United States. It was originally semiattached to the town's general store, which had

guest accommodations upstairs; the unique design of the outhouse allowed boarders to use an open walkway for direct access to the toilet on the second floor without having to schlepp downstairs. The general store was torn down years ago, leaving the outhouse with no inhouse, we guess you could say.

Each story of the outhouse has two holes, one for "his" and one for "hers" (see if you can figure out which is which). For those of you who are appalled that anyone would take the lower level with the awareness of what's happening above them, rest easy. The upper floor is offset by a foot or so, allowing the matter in question to tinkle or plop behind a fake wall. This gem of engineering has been maintained by the Goodwin family of Gays for three generations, going on four. They're glad to give a short (really short) guided tour if asked— no admission fee! By the way, the outhouse has an address, 1022 Front Street, and actually receives some mail. Appropriately, it's mostly catalogs.

WATSON'S WILD WEST MUSEUM

W4865 Potter Road
Elkhorn, WI 53121
(262) 723-7505
www.watsonwildwestmuseum.com
Map: Multistate

Doug Watson's lifelong dream was to have his own Wild West museum, and though Elkhorn, Wisconsin, isn't that far west, the museum that Doug has created is pretty darn wild. He's been accumulating his extensive collection of frontier artifacts for more than thirty-five years, mostly from junkyards, swap meets, and garage sales. Originally he had hoped to locate the museum in Tombstone, Arizona, but on a visit to Elkhorn he saw a barn that was slated for demolition and decided it was ideal for his purposes. He's decked the place out with swinging saloon doors, stained wood walls, and old-timey kerosene lamps. And if you come by horse, there's a hitching post right out front under the sign that says HOWDY, PARDNER!

The first thing you'll notice is the quantity that goes along with the quality. There must be fifty pouches of various brands of chewing tobacco on display, several shelves of frontier footwear, and a whole wall of just coffee tins. Everything's authentic, mostly dating back to the late 1800s and early 1900s. Check out the glass cases full of six-shooters and rifles with names like Winchester, Remington, and Colt. Watson, dressed in full Western attire, is almost always on the premises serving as tour guide and archivist. He delights in describing life in the Old West, using his museum as a giant visual aid.

Watson's Wild West Museum illuminates a fascinating slice of Americana, so get along, little doggies, and head up to Elkhorn pronto. Doug will be much obliged.

MORE DAY TRIPPIN'

BEER NUTS FACTORY AND OUTLET STORE
103 North Robinson
Bloomington, IL 61701
(309) 827-8580 or (800) BEER-NUT
www.beernuts.com
Map: Multistate
Home of the popular barroom snack.

EAA AIRVENTURE
EAA Aviation Center
3000 Poberezny Road
Oshkosh, WI 54902
(920) 426-4800
www.airventure.org
Map: Multistate
The site for the international annual experimental aircraft association fly-in.

GREAT WISCONSIN CHEESE FESTIVAL
Little Chute, WI 54140
(920) 788-7390
www.vil.little-chute.wi.us/
calendar_events/cheesefest.html
Map: Multistate
Celebrating all things cheese up north across the cheddar curtain.

PUNKIN CHUNKIN' CONTEST
Morton Chamber of Commerce
415 West Jefferson
Morton, IL 61550
(888) 765-6588
www.pumpkincapital.com
Map: Multistate
Pumpkins fired from cannons for distance and accuracy.

MAPS

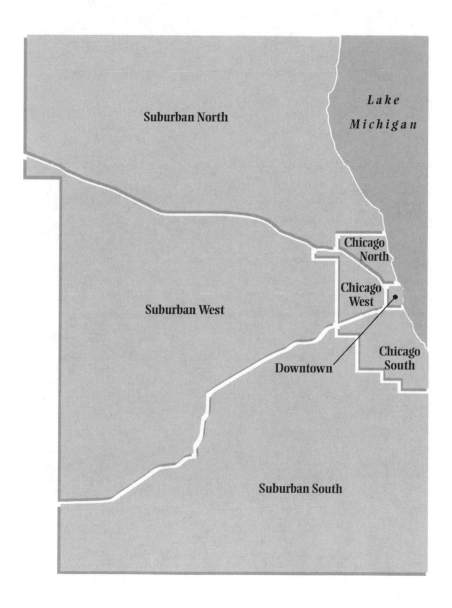

downtown

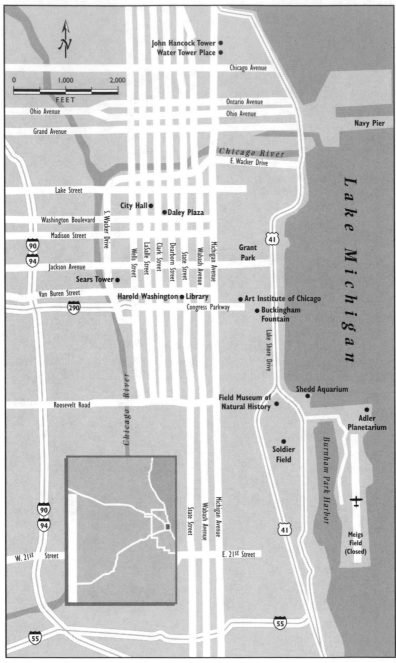

John Hancock Tower ●
Water Tower Place ●

Chicago Avenue

0   1,000   2,000

FEET

Ohio Avenue

Ontario Avenue
Ohio Avenue

Grand Avenue

Navy Pier

Chicago River
E. Wacker Drive

Lake Street

City Hall ●   ● Daley Plaza

Washington Boulevard

S. Wacker Drive

Madison Street

90
94

Grant
Park

41

Jackson Avenue

Wells Street
LaSalle Street
Clark Street
Dearborn Street
State Street
Wabash Avenue
Michigan Avenue

Sears Tower ●

Van Buren Street

290

Harold Washington ● Library

Congress Parkway

● Art Institute of Chicago
● Buckingham
   Fountain

Lake Shore Drive

Lake Michigan

Chicago River

Roosevelt Road

Field Museum of
Natural History ●

Shedd Aquarium
●

● Adler
  Planetarium

Burnham Park Harbor

● Soldier
  Field

90
94

Michigan Avenue
Wabash Avenue
State Street

Meigs
Field
(Closed)

W. 21st Street

41

E. 21st Street

55

55

DOWNTOWN ATTRACTIONS

Auditorium Theatre, 143

Berghoff Restaurant, 153

Cal's Liquors, 170

Chapel in the Sky, 144

Cooper Used Hotel
Furniture, 190

Critical Mass, 61

Federal Reserve Bank, 125

Fencing 2000, 48

Field Museum
Catacombs, 125

Fireman's Muster, 22

Harlan J. Berk Galleries, 128

Harold Washington
Library, 225

Harold Washington Library
Listening/Viewing Center
(LVC), 226

Hostelling International, 227

Hot House, 101

Howard Frum Jewelers, 195

Illinois Institute of Art, 56

International Bead and
Novelty Company, 197

National Vietnam Veterans
Art Museum, 133

Notre Dame Shrine, 140

Perry's Deli, 176

Unshackled, 151

William Harris Lee
Violins, 163

Water Riders, 138

CHICAGO NORTH ATTRACTIONS

A La Turka Restaurant, 169

Adventurer's Club, 3

Amazing Animals by Samantha, 245

American Science and Surplus, 185

Architectural Artifacts, 215

Ash's Magic Shop, 215

Ball Hawks, 15

Barney's Popcorn, 169

Big C Jamboree, 83

Big Hair, 221

Biograph Theater, 153

Center for UFO Studies (CUFOS), 55

Chaim Pinkhasik, 111

Chicago Birders, 247

Chicago Food Corp, 188

Chicago Herpetological Society, 247

Chi-Town Squares, 60

City Newsstand, 189

Cooking and Hospitality Institute of Chicago, 47

Custom Medical Stock Photo, 223

Degerberg Martial Arts Academy, 47

Discreet Electronics, 191

Doggie Beach, 256

Dog's Life, A, 245

Dream Hotline, 48

Edgebrook's Baskin-Robbins, 182

Ellis, Ken, 105

Fantasy Headquarters Costumes, 191

Feitiço Gallery, 107

Free Associates Theatre Company, 86

Garrett Hypnosis and Wellness Center, 49

Green Mill Poetry Slam, 101

Gulliver's Restaurant, 171

Harvey Finklestein's Institute of Whimsical, Fantastical, and Marvelous Puppet Masterage, 87

Hemingway's Apartment, 130

Hotel Intercontinental Chicago Pool, 147

Howl at the Moon, 87

Independence Business Machines, 239

International Museum of Surgical Science, 130

J. Fred MacDonald Film Archives, 140

Jazz Record Mart, 199

Jo-Jo's Closet, 108

Jules 5 & 10, 199

Little Bucharest Restaurant, 175

Magic Incorporated, 89

Merz Apothecary, 149

Miss Continental USA Competition, 29

Mud Bug Club, 29

NaKupuna Ukulele Club, 70

Neo-Futurists, 93

Nuts on Clark, 182

O'Field's Hemp Store, 204

Old Town Aquarium, 256

Pedicabs, 233

Pet Blessing, 250

Pug Crawl, 72

Puppet Parlor, 95

Redmoon Theater, 96

Rosehill Cemetery and Mausoleum, 150

Rosenblum's World of Judaica, 216

Scrub Your Pup, 256

Shake, Rattle and Read, 208

Shortest Butt, Biggest Ash Contest, 35

Siebel Institute of Technology, 54

Smell and Taste Research Center, 236

Something Old, Something New, 208

Southport Lanes, 151

Spacetime Tanks Flotation Center, 237

Special Music by Special People, 56

Sports Exchange, 216

Stereo Exchange, 238

Steve Wolf, 115

Swedish Bakery, 179

Think Small by Rosebud Dollhouses, 76

Trapeze Classes, 56

Turtle Races, 38

Vahle's Bird and Pet Shop, 253

Vienna Beef Factory and Store, 165

Weeds, 99

Yesterday Store, 214

chicago west

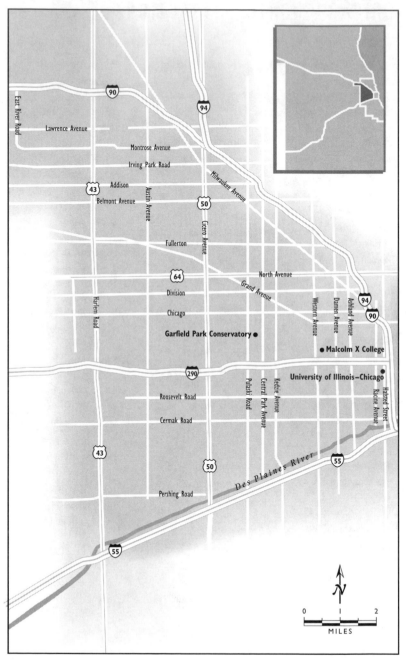

CHICAGO WEST ATTRACTIONS

Alcala's Western Wear, 215

Animal Kingdom, 256

Antique Fabricare Museum, 121

Carniceria La Caridad, 182

Chicago Paintball Factory, 41

Chic-A-Go-Go, 84

Chicagoland Canoe Base, 4

Clinical Performance Center, 222

Cook Brothers Wholesale, 215

Division Street Russian-Turkish Bathhouse, 146

Fannie May Factory Store, 164

House of Monsters, 194

House of Whacks, 195

I Do Bridal Consignment, 196

Jan's Antiques, 198

Leo's Dancewear Factory Outlet Store, 164

Margie's Candies, 148

Mexican Rodeo, 91

Morning Polka Party for Seniors, 92

Museum of Holography, 140

National Italian-American Sports Hall of Fame, 140

Northwest Turners Bingo, 79

Oxxford Clothes, 161

Patio Theater, 149

Paul C. Leather, 205

Peace Museum, 140

Peddling Purveyor Herb Perry, 233

Portage Park Animal Hospital, 251

Quimby's Bookstore, 206

Salvage One, 216

Single Gourmet, 73

Stanton Hobby Shop, 209

Stewarts Private Blend Coffee, 162

Textile Discount Outlet, 212

Uncle Fun Toys and Nostalgia, 216

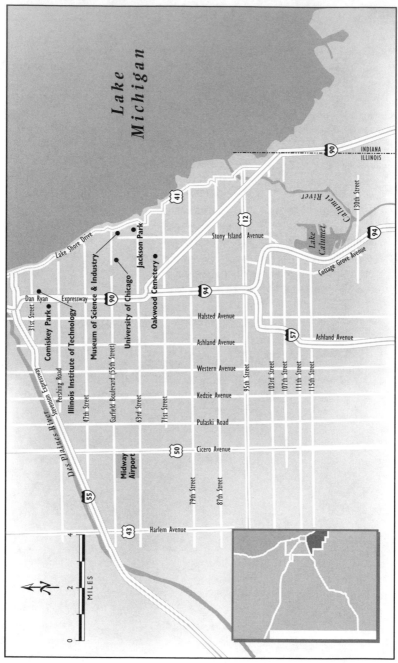

Lake Michigan

INDIANA
ILLINOIS

90

130th Street

Calumet River

41

12

Stony Island Avenue

Lake Calumet

94

Lake Shore Drive

Cottage Grove Avenue

Jackson Park

Dan Ryan   Expressway

31st Street

Comiskey Park

Illinois Institute of Technology

Museum of Science & Industry

University of Chicago

Oakwood Cemetery

90

94

Halsted Avenue

57   Ashland Avenue

Ashland Avenue

Pershing Road

Western Avenue

95th Street

103rd Street

107th Street

111th Street

115th Street

Stevenson Expressway

47th Street

Garfield Boulevard (55th Street)

63rd Street

71st Street

Kedzie Avenue

Pulaski Road

Des Plaines River

Cicero Avenue

50

Midway Airport

79th Street

87th Street

55

43   Harlem Avenue

4

MILES

2

N

0

CHICAGO SOUTH ATTRACTIONS

Advertising Flag Company, 157

American Law Labels, 157

Augustine's Spiritual Goods, 185

Baby Doll Polka Club, 83

Balzekas Museum of Lithuanian Culture, 139

Bronzeville's 1st Bed and Breakfast Club, 221

Cal-Sag Poker Run, 18

Checkerboard Lounge, 100

Chicago Fire Academy, 55

Dread Starchild Weaving and Beauty Salon, 241

Dulce Landia, 171

Elmo's Tombstones While-U-Wait, 224

Filbert's Soda, 159

Fronczak's Hardware, 147

Geoffrey Mac, 117

Gisele Perreault, 117

Healthy Foods Lithuanian Restaurant, 182

Henry's Sports and Bait Shop, 193

Lake Calumet, 249

Maxine's Caribbean Spice, 182

Maxwell Street Market, 202

McGarry's Boxing, 51

Midwest Cricket Conference, 27

Moo and Oink, 182

Nate's Leather, 232

Optimo Hats, 161

Police Auction, 205

Polka Music Hall of Fame and Museum, 135

Rainbow Cone, 182

Rainbow Motel, 234

Ricobene's Classic Car Museum, 136

South Shore Drill Team, 98

Society for Creative Anachronism, 73

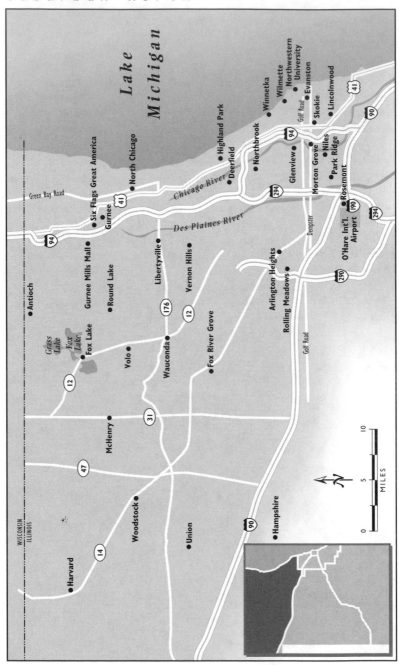

Lake Michigan

Chicago River

Des Plaines River

Green Bay Road

Golf Road

Dempster

WISCONSIN
ILLINOIS

Antioch

Six Flags Great America
Gurnee
Gurnee Mills Mall
Round Lake

North Chicago

Highland Park
Deerfield
Northbrook

Winnetka
Wilmette
Northwestern University
Evanston
Golf Road
Skokie
Lincolnwood

Glenview
Morton Grove
Niles
Park Ridge
Rosemont

O'Hare Int'l. Airport

Libertyville
Vernon Hills

Arlington Heights
Rolling Meadows

Grass Lake
Fox Lake
Fox Lake

Volo
Wauconda
Fox River Grove

McHenry

Woodstock
Union

Harvard

Hampshire

MILES

0   5   10

N

SUBURBAN NORTH ATTRACTIONS

Actors Gymnasium
(Evanston), 45

Air Time Pole Vault Club, The
(Park Ridge), 52

Animal 911 (Skokie), 246

Aquatic Art Team
(Northbrook), 15

Bicycle Racing
(Northbrook), 17

Blarney Island Boat Races
(Antioch), 18

Bradford Exchange
(Niles), 187

Chester Gould Museum
(Woodstock), 123

Chicago Curling Club
(Northbrook), 19

Chicago Rush (Rosemont), 20

Civil War Reenactment
(Glenview), 61

Cufflink Collector Eugene
Klompas (Vernon Hills), 139

Curt Teich Postcard Archives
(Wauconda), 124

Dale Sinderson (Harvard), 113

Dave's Down to Earth
Rock Shop and the
Prehistoric Life Museum
(Evanston), 139

Dearborn Observatory
(Evanston), 145

Disc Golf (Libertyville), 41

Elmer's Watersports
(Evanston), 7

50's House (Rolling
Meadows), 126

Great Lakes Naval Training
Center (Great Lakes), 56

Hartung Museum
(Glenview), 129

Illinois Nut and Fantasia
Chocolate Company
(Skokie), 173

Imperial Clothiers
(Lincolnwood), 197

Impressive Casket
(Gurnee), 160

Just Faucets (Arlington
Heights), 200

Kendall College School
of Culinary Arts
(Evanston), 174

Light Opera Works
(Evanston), 101

Living Sea Aquarium (Park
Ridge), 256

Magazine Memories (Morton
Grove), 201

Minnow Eating (Fox Lake), 28

Museum of Anesthesiology
(Park Ridge), 132

Norge Ski Club (Fox River
Grove), 31

Northern Illinois Police
Crime Laboratory (Highland
Park), 134

Novelty Golf and Batting
Cages (Lincolnwood), 41

Paintball Blitz (Gurnee), 42

Prairie Joe's Restaurant
(Evanston), 177

Raceworld Slot Car Raceway
(McHenry), 33

Riverbend Benders Watercross
(Round Lake), 33

Sarkis' Café (Evanston), 178

Scholl Feet First Museum
(North Chicago), 137

Seen on Screen
(Bloomingdale), 207

Serpent Safari (Gurnee), 252

Sky Soaring Gliders
(Hampshire), 9

St. Luke's Bottle Band (Park
Ridge), 99

Stars Our Destination
(Evanston), 216

Sutton Dog Photography
(Skokie), 252

Ten Thousand Villages
(Evanston), 211

Toby Jug Museum
(Evanston), 140

Valley View Model Railroad
(Union), 76

Volo Auto Museum
(Volo), 138

Windy City Balloon Port (Fox
River Grove), 10

Yasukunai Bonsai Garden
(Morton Grove), 78

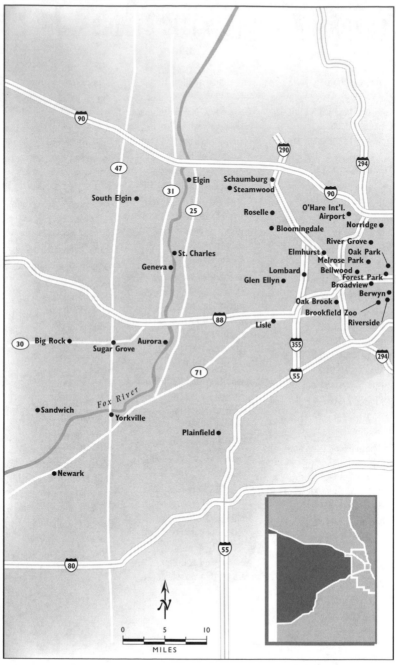

SUBURBAN WEST ATTRACTIONS

A&M Airsports (Newark), 3

African American Heritage Museum and Black Veterans Archives (Aurora), 114

Air Classics Museum of Aviation (Sugar Grove), 121

Anchor Board-Up and Glass (Bellwood), 219

Berland's House of Tools (Lombard), 186

Cigars and Stripes (Berwyn), 188

D & D Wormery (Roselle), 248

Ferrara Pan Candy Company (Forest Park), 159

Fitzgerald's (Berwyn), 101

Four Seasons Amusements (Bloomingdale), 224

Glisson Archery (Plainfield), 22

Great Cardboard Boat Regatta (Glen Ellyn), 23

Great Lakes Model Horse Congress (Bolingbrook), 63

Great Put On (Forest Park), 192

Hala Kahiki Hawaiian Lounge (River Grove), 172

Highland Games (Oak Brook), 25

John's Elgin Market Exotic Meats (South Elgin), 173

Kane County Cougars (Geneva), 27

Lee Watson's Reptile Swap (Streamwood), 249

Maison Russe (Lisle), 201

Maurice Lennell Cookys Company and Outlet Store (Norridge), 164

Mike Englehardt/Poultry Personalities (Yorkville), 106

Military and Police Supply (Forest Park), 203

Model A Ford Club Manifold Cooking (Salt Creek), 67

Mountain Builder John Van Barriger (Big Rock), 68

Nadeau's Ice Sculptures (Forest Park), 231

National Woodie Club Log Jam (Crystal Lake), 71

Nightmares, Inc. (Melrose Park), 165

Polo (Oak Brook), 32

Replogle Globes (Broadview), 165

Rolle Bolle (St. Charles), 34

Squirrel Lover's Club (Elmhurst), 74

The Advanced Laser Center (Schaumburg), 238

Tony Spavone's Ristorante (Bloomingdale), 180

Transformations (Oak Park), 213

Wheaton Community Radio Amateurs (Wheaton), 77

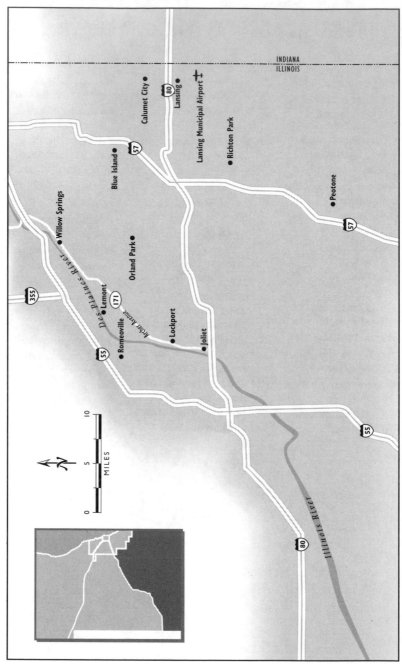

SUBURBAN SOUTH ATTRACTIONS

Beat the Nun (Lemont), 16

Cavallone's West Pizzeria
(Willow Springs), 144

Cookie Jar Museum
(Lemont), 123

Old Chicago Golf Shop
(Richton Park), 135

Pacific Tall Ships
(Lemont), 110

Popular Rotorcraft Association
(Lansing), 5

Powered Parachute Flying
Club (Peotone), 6

Skydive Illinois (Morris), 11

Strictly Men (Calumet
City), 211

Test and Tune (Joliet), 37

U-Pull-It Auto Parts (Blue
Island), 214

White Fence Farm
(Lemont), 181

Willowbrook Ballroom
(Willow Springs), 152

Will-U-Canoe (Romeoville), 9

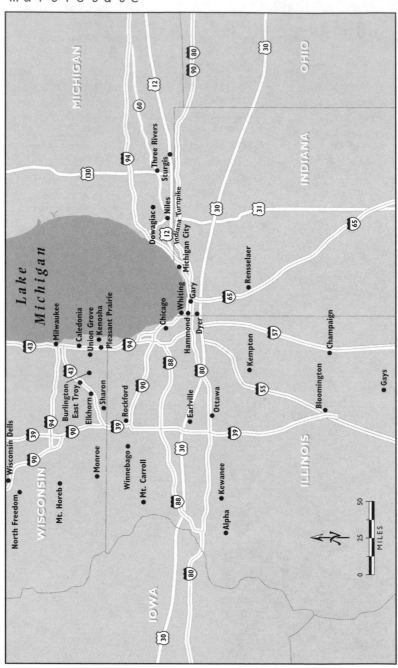

MULTISTATE ATTRACTIONS

ILLINOIS

Adventures Unlimited Press (Kempton), 45

Beer Nuts Factory and Outlet Store (Bloomington), 270

Belt Sander Drag Racing (Sandwich), 41

Good's Furniture (Kewanee), 262

Max Nordeen's Wheels Museum (Alpha), 262

Punkin Chunkin' Contest (Morton), 270

Raven's Grin Inn (Mt. Carroll), 266

Skydive Chicago (Ottawa), 8

34 Drive-In (Earlville), 267

Valhalla Pet Cemetery (Winnebago), 254

INDIANA

International Computer Recycling (Gary), 229

John Dillinger Museum (Hammond), 131

Lake Michigan Winery (Whiting), 164

Michigan City Rifle Club Wildwood Wranglers (Michigan City), 263

Phil Smidt's Restaurant (Hammond), 176

Pierogi Fest (Whiting), 94

Rodizios Restaurant at Meyer's Castle (Dyer), 178

MICHIGAN

International Cherry Pit Spitting Competition (Eau Claire), 26

WISCONSIN

Baumgartner's Cheese Store and Tavern (Monroe), 259

Chalet Cheese Co-op (Monroe), 259

Dinner Train (East Troy), 260

EAA Airventure (Oshkosh), 270

Great Lakes Dragaway (Union Grove), 24

Great Wisconsin Cheese Festival (Little Chute), 270

Kenosha Military Museum (Pleasant Prairie), 132

Mike Bjorn's Fine Clothing (Kenosha), 203

Mustard Museum (Mount Horeb), 265

Night Golf (Caledonia), 30

Raven Sky Hang-Gliding (Whitewater), 6

Spinning Top Museum (Burlington), 267

Valley of the Kings Sanctuary and Retreat (Sharon), 255

Watson's Wild West Museum (Elkhorn), 269

Wilmot Mountain (Wilmot), 11

INDEX

A

A Dog's Life, 245
A La Turka
  Restaurant, 169
AC Rock, 100
Actors Gymnasium, 45
Ad Airlines, 241
Advanced Laser
  Center, 238
Adventurers' Club, 3
Adventures Unlimited
  Press, 45
Advertising Flag
  Company, 157
African American
  Heritage Museum, 114
Air Classics Museum of
  Aviation, 121
Air Time Pole Vault
  Camp, 52
Alcala's Western
  Wear, 215
Amazing Animals by
  Samantha, 245
American Law
  Labels, 157
American Science and
  Surplus, 185
Anchor Board-Up and
  Glass, 219
A&M Airsports, 3
Animal Kingdom, 256
Animal 911, 246
Antique Fabricare
  Museum, 121
Aquarium Bar and
  Grill, 28
Aquatic Art Team, 15

Architectural
  Artifacts, 215
Arena Football, 20
Ash's Magic Shop, 215
Auditorium Theatre, 143
Augustine Spiritual
  Goods, 185
Aura-Halo Balancing
  Haircuts, 241
Aussie Rules Football, 21
Avon Man Robert
  Franklin, 219
Award Collector Jeffrey
  Schramek, 122

B

Baby Doll Polka Club, 83
Ball Hawks, 15
Balzekas Museum of
  Lithuanian
  Culture, 139
Barbie Doctor Mike
  Schmidt, 220
Barney's Popcorn, 169
Baumgartner's Cheese
  Store and
  Tavern, 259
Beat the Nun, 16
Beer Nuts Factory and
  Outlet Store, 270
Belt Sander Drag
  Racing, 41
Berghoff Restaurant, 153
Berland's House of
  Tools, 186
Bicycle Racing, 17
Big C Jamboree, 83
Big Hair, 221

Bill O'Connell's Skyliners
  Big Band, 100
Binns-Calvey, Geoff, 105
Biograph Theater, 153
Blarney Island Boat
  Races, 18
Blues Musician Jimmy
  Burns, 84
Bopology, 100
Bracha, Shayna, 226
Bradford Exchange, 187
Bronzeville's 1st Bed and
  Breakfast Club, 221
Burns, Jimmy, 84

C

Cal-Sag Poker Run, 18
Cal's Liquors, 170
Carniceria La
  Caridad, 182
Carroll, Patty, 116
Carter, Chris, 90
Cavallone's West
  Pizzeria, 144
Center for UFO Studies
  (CUFOS), 55
Chalet Cheese Co-op, 259
Chapel in the Sky, 144
Checkerboard
  Lounge, 100
Chester Gould
  Museum, 123
Chi-Town Squares, 60
Chicago Area Lace
  Guild, 59
Chicago Area Sea
  Kayaking Association
  (CASKA), 5

Chicago Birders, 247

Chicago Curling Club, 19

Chicago Fire Academy, 55

Chicago Food Corp, 188

Chic–A–Go-Go, 84

Chicago Hash House
   Harriers, 20

Chicago Herpetological
   Society, 247

Chicago Laughter Club, 46

Chicago Paintball
   Factory, 41

Chicago Rush, 20

Chicago Scooter
   Rallies, 79

Chicago Sun Club, 59

Chicago Swans, 21

Chicagoland Canoe
   Base, 4

Chicago Temple, 144

Cigar Smoking
   Competition, 35

Cigars and Stripes, 188

Circus Boy Bobby
   Hunt, 100

City Newsstand, 189

Civil War Reenactment, 61

Cleaning Ladys, 100

Clinical Performance
   Center, 222

Cook Brothers
   Wholesale, 215

Cookie Jar Museum, 123

Cooking and Hospitality
   Institute of Chicago, 47

Cooper Used Hotel
   Furniture, 190

Cowboy Action
   Shooting, 263

Cozy Dog Drive-In, 259

Critical Mass, 61

Crowe, Richard, 128

Cufflink Collector Eugene
   Klompas, 139

Curt Teich Postcard
   Archives, 124

Custom Medical Stock
   Photo, 223

D

D & D Wormery, 248

Dave's Down to Earth Rock
   Shop and Prehistoric
   Life Museum, 139

Deaf Elvis, 101

Dearborn
   Observatory, 145

Degerberg Martial Arts
   Academy, 47

Dinner Train, 260

Disc Golf, 41

Discovery Dive
   Charters, 7

Discreet Electronics, 191

Division Street
   Russian-Turkish
   Bathhouse, 146

Doggie Beach, 256

Dr. Evermor, 261

Dread Starchild Weaving
   and Beauty Salon, 241

Dream Hotline, 48

Dulce Landia, 171

E

EAA Airventure, 270

East Troy Electric
   Railroad, 260

Eddie Korosa and the
   Boys from Illinois, 101

Edgebrook's Baskin-
   Robbins, 182

Elmo's Tombstones While-
   U-Wait, 224

Ellis, Ken, 105

Elmer's Watersports, 7

Englehardt, Mike, 106

F

Famous Brothers
   Hysterical
   Bluegrass, 101

Fannie May Factory
   Store, 164

Fantasy Headquarters
   Costumes, 191

Federal Reserve
   Bank, 125

Fencing 2000, 48

Ferrara Pan Candy
   Company, 159

Feitiço Gallery, 107

Field Museum
   Catacombs, 125

50's House, 126

Filbert's Soda, 159

Filmmaker David "The
   Rock" Nelson, 85

Fireman's Muster, 22

Fish Guy Market, 182

Fisher, David, 53

FitzGerald's, 101

Four Charms, 101

Four Seasons
   Amusements, 224

Frank P. Burla Antique
   Pipe and Tobacciana
   Museum, 127

Franklin, Robert, 219

Free Associates Theatre
   Company, 86

Fronczak's Hardware, 147

Fruh, Ed, 116

G

Gand, Kenny, 230

Garrett Hypnosis and
   Wellness Center, 49

Gas Mask Collector Bart Wilkus, 139

Ghost Hunter Richard Crowe, 128

G.I. Joe Collectors Club, 62

Gigolo Johnny, 101

Glisson Archery, 22

Golf Night, 30

Good's Furniture, 262

Great Cardboard Boat Regatta, 23

Great Lakes Dragaway, 24

Great Lakes Model Horse Congress, 63

Great Lakes Naval Training Center, 56

Great Put On, 192

Great Wisconsin Cheese Festival, 270

Green E, The Environmental Elvis, 101

Green Mill Poetry Slam, 101

Gulliver's Restaurant, 171

Gyrocopters, 79

H

Hala Kahiki Hawaiian Lounge, 172

Hand Writing Analyst Lottie Lee Mason, 241

Hang-gliding, 6

Harlan J. Berk Galleries, 128

Harold Washington Library Information Hotline, 225

Harold Washington Library Listening/ Viewing Center (LVC), 226

Hartung Museum, 129

Harvey Finklestein's Institute of Whimsical, Fantastical, and Marvelous Puppet Masterage, 87

Healer Shayna Bracha, 226

Healthy Foods Lithuanian Restaurant, 182

Hemingway's Apartment, 130

Henry's Sports and Bait Shop, 193

Hernandez De Luna, Michael, 108

Highland Games, 25

Hilden, Katherine, 116

Hollywood on Lake Michigan, 153

Hostelling International, 227

Hot House, 101

Hotel Intercontinental Chicago Pool, 147

House Demolition Auctions, 230

House Movers, 228

House of Monsters, 194

House of Whacks, 195

Hovercrafting, 79

Howard Frum Jewelers, 195

Howl at the Moon, 87

Hunt, Bobby, 100

I

I Do Bridal Consignment, 196

Illinois Nut and Fantasia Chocolate Company, 173

Illinois Arm Wrestling, 25

Illinois Institute of Art, 56

Illinois Mycological Association, 69

Imperial Clothiers, 197

Impressive Casket, 160

Independence Business Machines, 239

Inkin' Lincoln Tattoo Jamboree, 64

International Bead and Novelty Company, 197

International Cherry Pit Spitting Competition, 26

International Computer Recycling, 229

International Museum of Surgical Science, 130

International Tarot Society, 79

Inventor Ben Skora and His Robot AROK, 65

J

J. Fred MacDonald Film Archives, 140

Jade's Dungeon, 50

Jan's Antiques, 198

Jazz Record Mart, 199

John Dillinger Museum, 131

John's Elgin Market Exotic Meats, 173

Jo-Jo's Closet, 108

Jules 5 & 10, 199

Just Faucets, 200

K

Kane County Cougars, 27

Kendall College, School of Culinary Arts 174

Kenosha Military Museum, 132

Klompas, Eugene, 139

Koerner, Roy, 116

Klingon Armada International, 65

Kusy, Wayne, 109

L

Lake Calumet, 249

Lake Michigan Winery, 164

Lanaholics, 66

LaSalle Bank Chicago Marathon, 11

Leaping Lesbians, 79

Lee Watson's Reptile Swap, 249

Leo's Dancewear and Factory Outlet Store, 164

Light Opera Works, 101

Lightning and Thunder, 88

Lima Lima Flight Team, 89

Little Bucharest Restaurant, 175

Living Sea Aquarium, 256

Lykowski Construction, Inc., 228

M

Mac, Geoffrey, 117

Magazine Memories, 201

Magic Incorporated, 89

Maison Russe, 201

Margie's Candies, 148

Martin, Greg, 117

Marvin Tate's D-Settlement, 90

Mason, Lottie Lee, 241

Mass Ensemble, 101

Maurice Lennel Cookys Company and Outlet Store, 164

Max Nordeen's Wheels Museum, 262

Maxine's Caribbean Spice, 182

Maxwell Street Klezmer Band, 102

Maxwell Street Market, 202

McCarthy, Gretchen, 110

McCurdy, Pat, 97

McGarry's Boxing, 51

Mentalist Chris Carter, 90

Merz Apothecary, 149

Mexican Rodeo, 91

Michigan City Rifle Club Wildwood Wranglers Cowboy Action Shootout, 263

Microcar and Minicar Club, 79

Midwest Cricket Conference, 27

Midwest Model T Ford Club, 66

Mike Bjorn'$ Fine Clothing, 203

Military and Police Supply, 203

Minnow Eating, 28

Minor League Baseball, 27

Miss Continental USA Competition, 29

Mitt Mender Kenny Gand, 230

Model A Ford Club Manifold Cooking, 67

Mojo and the Bayou Gypsies, 102

Moo and Oink, 182

Morning Polka Party for Seniors, 92

Mountain Builder John Van Barriger, 68

Mud Bug Club, 29

Murco Recycling, 230

Museum of Anesthesiology, 132

Museum of Funeral Customs, 264

Museum of Holography, 140

Mushroom Hunters, 69

Mustard Museum, 265

N

Nadeau's Ice Sculptures, 231

NaKupuna Ukulele Club, 70

Nate's Leather, 232

National Italian-American Sports Hall of Fame, 140

National Vietnam Veterans Art Museum, 133

National Woodie Club, 71

Nelson, David "The Rock," 85

Neo-Futurists, 93

New Duncan Imperials, 94

New Tradition Chorus, 102

Night Golf, 30

Nightmares, Inc., 165

Norge Ski Club, 31

Northern Illinois Police Crime Laboratory, 134

North Shore Rugby Club, 31

Northwest Turners Bingo, 79

Notre Dame Shrine, 140

Novelty Golf and Batting Cages, 41

Nude Recreation, 59
Nuts on Clark, 182

O

O'Field's Hemp Store, 204
Old Chicago Golf
  Shop, 135
Old Jail Museum, 265
Old Town Aquarium, 256
Optimo Hats, 161
Oxxford Clothes, 161

P

Pacific Tall Ships, 110
Paintball Blitz, 42
Paramount Tall Club, 72
Patio Theater, 149
Paul C. Leather, 205
Peace Museum, 140
Peddling Purveyor Herb
  Perry, 233
Pedicabs, 233
Perl, Joe, 235
Perrault, Gisele, 117
Perry, Herb, 233
Perry's Deli, 176
Pet Blessing, 250
Phil Smidt's
  Restaurant, 176
Pierogi Fest, 94
Pinkhasik, Chaim, 111
Playboy Advisor, 51
Pole Vaulting Camp, 52
Police Auction, 205
Polka Music Hall of Fame
  and Museum, 135
Polkaholics, 102
Polo, 32
Popular Rotorcraft
  Association, 5
Portage Park Animal
  Hospital, 251
Poultry Personalities, 106

Powered Parachute Flying
  Club, 6
Prairie Joe's
  Restaurant, 177
Psychotronic Film
  Society, 80
Pug Crawl, 72
Punkin Chunkin'
  Contest, 270
Puppet Parlor, 95

Q

Quimby's Bookstore, 206

R

Raceworld Slot Car
  Raceway, 33
Rainbow Cone, 182
Rainbow Motel, 234
Rat Lady, 245
Raven Sky
  Hang-Gliding, 6
Raven's Grin Inn, 266
Ray's Evergreen
  Tavern, 34
Redmoon Theater, 96
Replogle Globes, 165
Revolutionary War
  Reenactors, 80
Ricobene's Classic Car
  Museum, 136
Riverbend Benders
  Watercross, 33
Rockabilly Night, 83
Rockefeller Chapel
  Carillon, 102
Rodizios Restaurant at
  Meyer's Castle, 178
Rolle Bolle, 34
Rope Warrior David
  Fisher, 53
Rosehill Cemetery and
  Mausoleum, 150

Rosenblum's World of
  Judaica, 216
ROTC, Righteously
  Outrageous
  Twirling Corp, 102

S

Salvage One, 216
Samba Bamba!, 102
Sarkis' Café, 178
Sausage Man Joe
  Perl, 235
Schmidt, Mike, 220
Scholl Feet First
  Museum, 137
Schramek, Jeffrey, 122
Scrub Your Pup, 256
Scuba Diving, 7
Seen On Screen, 207
Segami, Amy Lee, 112
Serpent Safari, 252
Shake, Rattle and
  Read, 208
"Shortest Butt, Biggest
  Ash" Contest, 35
Showman Milt Trenier, 97
Siebel Institute of
  Technology, 54
Sinderson, Dale, 113
Singer Pat McCurdy, 97
Singing Cab Driver Ray
  St. Ray, 236
Single Gourmet, 73
Skora, Ben, 65
Sky Soaring Gliders, 9
Skydive Chicago, 8
Skydive Illinois, 11
Skyview Photography, 241
Sled Hockey and Beep
  Baseball, 36
Smell and Taste Research
  Center, 236
Smith, Charles, 114

Society for Creative Anachronism, 73

Sock Puppet Theater, 87

Something Old, Something New, 208

South Shore Drill Team, 98

Southport Lanes, 151

SpaceTime Tanks Flotation Center, 237

Special Music by Special People, 56

Spinning Top Museum, 267

Sports Exchange, 216

Squirrel Lover's Club, 74

St. Luke's Bottle Band, 99

St. Ray, Ray, 236

Stanton Hobby Shop, 129

Stars Our Destination Books, 216

Stereo Exchange, 238

Stewarts Private Blend Coffee, 162

Stitch 'n' Bitch, 75

Stoner Connection, 210

Strictly Men, 211

Summer Ski Jumping, 37

Sutton Dog Photography, 252

Swedish Bakery, 179

T

Tattoo Removal, 238

Tekky Toys, 163

Ten Thousand Villages, 211

Test and Tune, 37

Textile Discount Outlet, 212

Think Small by Rosebud Dollhouses, 76

34 Drive-In, 267

Those Darn Accordions, 102

Thrift Store Art, 115

Toby Jug Musuem, 140

Tony Spavone's Ristorante, 180

Tour de Donut, 37

Transformations, 213

Trapeze Classes, 56

Trenier, Milt, 97

Trikes, 3

Turtle Races, 38

Tuszynski, Chester, 80

Two-Story Outhouse, 268

Typewriter Repair, 239

U

"UFO Guy" Chester Tuszynski, 80

Ultimate Frisbee, 39

Uncle Fun Toys and Nostalgia, 216

Underwater Hockey, 40

Unshackled, 151

U-Pull-It Auto Parts, 214

Urban Adventure Race, 11

V

Vahle's Bird and Pet Shop, 253

Valhalla Pet Cemetery, 254

Valley of the Kings Sanctuary and Retreat, 255

Valley View Model Railroad, 76

Van Barriger, John, 68

Vienna Beef Factory and Store, 165

Vintage Base Ball Association, 40

Volo Auto Museum, 138

W

Water Cross Snowmobile Racing, 33

Water Riders, 138

Watson's Wild West Museum, 269

We Fix Bikes, 240

Weeds, 99

Wheaton Community Radio Amateurs, 77

Wheels Rallye, 42

White Fence Farm, 181

Whizzers Club, 78

Wild Chicago Revue, 102

William Harris Lee Violins, 163

Willowbrook Ballroom, 152

Will-U-Canoe, 9

Wilmot Mountain, 11

Windy City Balloon Port, 10

Windy City Pro Wrestling, 54

Wm. Darke Psychocircus and Freak Show Spectacular, 102

Wolf, Steve, 115

Women's Rugby, 31

Worm Farmer, 248

Y

Yasukunai Bonsai Garden, 78

Yesterday Store, 214

WILL CLINGER is currently the host and segment producer of *Wild Chicago*, and his work on it has earned him fourteen Midwest Emmys. Will has appeared as an actor on film, television, and stage and bears a startling resemblance to Willie B. Famous of the bluegrass-comedy group the Famous Brothers.

MINDY BELL is an actor who has appeared at Chicago's Second City Theater as a writer and performer. She is currently a correspondent on *Wild Chicago*.

HARVEY MOSHMAN has been the series producer of *Wild Chicago* since 1992 and was the editor of the show at its inception in 1988. He actually has more Emmys than Will but refuses to say how many. Harvey enjoys scuba diving, travel, and writing about himself in the third person.